Lend Me an Ear

———

The Temperament, Selection, and Training of the Hearing Dog

By

Martha Hoffman

Doral Publishing, Inc.
Wilsonville, Oregon

PUBLISHED BY DORAL PUBLISHING
8560 SW SALISH LANE
WILSONVILLE, OREGON 97070
1-800-633-5385
HTTP://WWW.DORALPUB.COM

PRINTED IN THE UNITED STATES OF AMERICA

EDITED BY MARK ANDERSON
COVER DESIGN BY RANDY CONGER
INTERIOR LAYOUT BY MARK ANDERSON

LIBRARY OF CONGRESS CARD NUMBER: 99-60289

THE PROGRAMS ENUMERATED IN THIS TEXT HAVE BEEN DESIGNED TO TEACH THE CONCEPTS OF TESTING AND TRAINING THE PROSPECTIVE HEARING DOG AND IN NO WAY IS THE AUTHOR RESPONSIBLE FOR ERRORS AND OMISSIONS WHICH COULD CAUSE HARM TO THE INSTRUCTOR OR THE DOG.
THESE PROGRAMS WERE DEVELOPED THROUGH LONG EXPERIENCE TO TEACH TRAINERS AND PEOPLE TRAINING THEIR OWN DOG SO THAT THEY CAN LEARN BY EXPERIENCE.

Hoffman, Martha
   Lend me an Ear : the temperament, selection
and training of the hearing dog / Martha
Hoffman ; editor Mark Anderson — 1st ed.
   p. cm.
   Includes bibliographical references.
   LCCN: 99-60289
   ISBN: 0-944875-56-4

   1. Hearing ear dogs—Selection. 2. Hearing ear
dogs—Training. I. Title.

HV2509.H64 1999   636.7'088
                  QBI99-784

Contents

Acknowledgments

The San Francisco SPCA Hearing Dog Program has been in existence since 1978. Director Ralph Dennard was recruited to start it by SPCA president Richard Avanzino, who saw something innovative and exciting in this concept. The only other program at the time, the American Humane Association Hearing Dog Program, was in Denver, Colorado. Ralph researched the Denver program and then started to build a program for adopting, training, and placing Hearing Dogs in California. Through much experimentation over the years, he, together with other trainers like Mel Robles and Becky Woodruff, developed selection and training systems.

In 1989 Kathy O'Brien, Shelley Monson, and I joined the staff. Kathy has been training and breeding dogs and trailing with them since she was a child. Her extensive experience with sighthounds allowed her to train the most difficult Hearing Dog adoptees. Shelley's experience was in training and handling wolves and other wild animals; she often joked that Hearing Dogs were just another kind of wild critter. I had trained my own two dogs in AKC obedience, tracking, and tricks. We were all "dog crazy" and spent all our spare time at training classes, seminars, and trials. We've had many good times over the years, and the hundreds of joyful, exuberant, and sometimes difficult and frustrating Hearing Dogs that passed through the program kept us from growing complacent about our skills.

Ralph, Kathy, Shelley, and I spent countless hours debating what traits made up Hearing Dog temperament and whether it even existed. If it did, what factors were important? How could we predict which dogs would succeed? Gradually, we began to sort out the mysterious qualities that interacted to produce Hearing Dog temperament. Such a blueprint, we reasoned, would help us in the selection and training of individual dogs.

This book, then, is grounded in our

Martha Hoffman with some San Francisco dogs. (Photo by Glassner, SF-SPCA)

joint work and history. In addition to those mentioned above, I would also like to thank trainers Patricia Cook, Ivan Balabanov, and Dean Calderon. Ruth Zultner, a fellow dog enthusiast and writer, contributed conceptual editing and encouragement. Mark Anderson, my editor, showed remarkable skill at making brilliant condensations of difficult concepts. My parents, Lynn and Ted Hoffman, always made writing books seem easy when I was a child, and whenever I've complained about how hard writing really is, they helped with organizing and editing. The most important clues were supplied by those who know Hearing Dogs best, their human partners. It was they who shared the many examples of Hearing Dog perspicacity that enliven the text.

— Martha Hoffman
San Francisco, California

Introduction

Compared to dogs, all humans are hearing-impaired. Over the long course of their domestication, dogs have been valued for their ability to hear sounds that humans cannot. Their ability to alert their canine or human pack members to sounds relevant to hunting or survival opportunities has been preserved or intensified in many breeds. Deaf and hard-of-hearing people have, of course, appreciated these abilities even more, and have a long history of training their own dogs. However, it is only in the last twenty years that any organized effort has been made to systematically train or breed dogs for this purpose. Because the breeding effort has been limited to attempts to create suitable strains within a few breeds, there is no new breed or mix developed specifically for use as a Hearing Dog.

Many breeds of dog possess some of the traits necessary for sound alerting work, but no single breed displays all of them consistently. In addition, many breeds that are partially suitable also show undesirable traits that negate their potential. Part of the reason that mixed breeds have proven to be so successful as Hearing Dogs is that they may accidentally inherit the optimum combination of qualities needed. Although the effects of random mixing of breeds and hybrid vigor might seem sufficient to explain why so many training programs use more mixed breeds than purebreds, there are other factors at work as well; crossing dogs from certain functional breed groups can produce individuals that seem as if they were born to become Hearing Dogs.

"What is a Hearing Dog?" Because most people have not yet heard of this type of assistance dog, I probably answer this question at least twice a day. I'm happy to explain that it's a dog that alerts its hearing impaired partner to sounds that they would want to know about. But my confident answer always amuses me, because I don't really know what a Hearing Dog is. For ten years, I've been trying to figure this out. Every dog adds some little clue to the puzzle, and every dog also puts doubt into the new theories I come up with. But Hearing Dogs are very real and are everywhere you look—when you know what you're looking for!

We all may have met a potential Hearing Dog, but not recognized it as such. We might have encountered it on a walk and, amused by its exuberant friendliness and love of life, asked its owner what kind of dog it is. "Oh, I got her from the shelter," the owner might reply. "I don't know what she is. They said she's just a little Benji mutt. But she's the most wonderful dog I've ever had. Do you know, whenever my baby cries, she jumps right up and pesters me until I go make sure he's okay?"

When I first started to train Hearing Dogs, I was humbled to discover that some of the dogs appeared to have already been trained to alert people to sounds. But if previous owners had gone to all the effort to teach these dogs sound alerting, then why hadn't they also housebroken them or taught them to sit? Most were so untrained in every other way that their sound alerting abilities were as unexpected as finding a Rembrandt at a yard sale.

The dogs that appeared to be "naturals" would react to a phone ring or other sound with an intensely startled movement that was not fearful but fascinated. This reaction was never a methodical investigation, but almost reflexive, and the dog would either focus intently on the sound or rush towards it as fast as possible. Although these dogs had high food drive, they would sometimes prefer to go to sounds even when being offered food. It seemed as though the training I was doing was simply reinforcing existing behaviors, focusing the dogs on specific sounds and proofing them to ensure that they would work in real life. They also were already interested in interacting with me, so they tended to learn to alert (go back and forth from sound to trainer) far faster than would seem possible for even a super-intelligent dog. While it was enough to make a person question their stand on reincarnation, I felt sure that had these same dogs been adopted by a deaf or hard-of-hearing person, even without any formal training, they still would have functioned proficiently enough to alert their owner to sounds.

And that wasn't all. The dogs that learned sound alerting so effortlessly usually performed well after they were placed, regardless of their partner's level of training ability. They showed unexpected abilities, often alerting to sounds that they had never been trained for: abandoned baby birds, lost kittens, unusual mechanical noises, and even a choking baby. And, incredibly, they sometimes alerted to unusual situations that were not sounds, such as an unconscious neighbor in the next yard, a gasoline leak in a car, smoke from fires, and impending earthquakes. Although Hearing Dogs need regular practice in sound alerting to keep their skills up, partners of these special dogs would sometimes confide to me that they rarely practiced because their dog didn't seem to need it.

Cisco's expression reflects his busy personality. Without a job to do, he'd be very mischievous. Partner Amy Wooten says he keeps himself very busy, alerting her to intruding spiders in the house and to hummingbirds outside. (Photo by Wooten)

Adding to the mystery, the dogs that seemed to have a natural talent for sound alerting also had unusual personalities and shared many problematic characteristics. They were active, easily awakened from sleep, and showed extreme curiosity about everything around them. They tended to bark a lot. Veterinarians had trouble with them because they would often become hysterical when restrained; although selected for low tendency to bite, they would struggle and work themselves into a state from which it was difficult to calm them down from, and their temperatures would rise to 103 or 104 degrees. Their lightning-fast reaction times made obedience training difficult, and the "stay" exercises never seemed perfected. They didn't tremble nervously, but I could perceive a kind of intense vibration in them similar to that of a mouse or bird. Busy or noisy environments could either overwhelm them or overexcite them. They rarely ever walked anywhere, but always trotted, busily getting into all kinds of trouble. It was easy to see why they had been dumped at animal shelters.

But I loved these unusual dogs for their intense "aliveness." They were like little Geiger counters ticking away constantly; it was impossible to ignore the world when they were around. Their constant desire for interaction with humans made them fun to be around, and the tasks of obedience and sound alerting focused their scattered energies. Other types of dogs began to seem dull and lifeless to me by comparison.

When I first began training Hearing Dogs, I was under the impression that if I discovered the right training methods, I would become more successful in producing Hearing Dogs. It soon became apparent, however, that although bad training would certainly hinder a dog's progress, good training alone would not guarantee a dog's success. Only dogs with a specific temperament type had the aptitude for this work. Although successful Hearing Dogs are usually mixed breeds from diverse genetic backgrounds, they show amazing similarities. Romping in a pack, they give the impression at a distance of being as close in behavior as a school of fish. They could not be more unlike in appearance, but their eyes all sparkle with the same eager question: "What's going to happen *next??!!*" I now think of these dogs not as fortuitous accidents of breeding or the result of special training, but as a functional breed of dog, and I evaluate them in my mind on their degree of "Hearing Dog-ness." These talented dogs resemble each other in behavior just as members of a pure breed do, and anyone who has worked with them soon begins to be able to recognize them by their behavior alone. For the trainer, understanding Hearing Dog temperament and being able to select talented dogs for training is far more important than the training itself. These dogs are unique, they are rare, and they are capable of bringing the dry word "partnership" to life; many Hearing Dog owners define their dog not as a partner, but as "a part of me."

Chihuahua mix, Ren, convinced me that he had big goals in life. I took this photo even before I tested him because his personality and attitude stood out in a shelter of 150 dogs. Of course, he passed!

Many hearing-impaired people have told me about remarkable dogs they have owned who alerted them faithfully to sounds with no training. Although their owners sometimes believed that their dog had a conscious knowledge that they were hearing impaired and acted out of a desire to help, the actual truth is just as amazing—that the unusual temperament found in these dogs just *happened* to fulfill a need. I always marvel that this especially talented dog and this loving person found each other and formed such a wonderful partnership.

But I also think of all the dogs and people who never met, who could have done so much together. I would hope that by learning to recognize potential Hearing Dogs, we could all work towards making more of these partnerships happen by design and not just by luck. Our shelters are full of dogs with undiscovered talents, unappreciated for their qualities, and thrown away like trash. How many great Hearing Dogs are euthanized each year?

I am grateful to have been allowed to save some of them, and feel privileged to have worked with them. They have taught me so much about potential, both human and canine. I hope that this book will help others to have a second chance.

Lend Me an Ear

PART ONE:

HEARING DOG BASICS

Chapter One
What is a Hearing Dog?

Hearing Dogs alert Deaf and hard-of-hearing people to sounds they might otherwise miss. They may work in the home, or alert to sounds outdoors as well. Because barking might not be audible to their owners, most are taught to use physical contact to alert to sounds. They are legally entitled to public access to places where pet dogs are not allowed, being covered under the same laws that apply to guide dogs for the blind.

Dogs that prefer interacting with people over all other activities form the close partnership with their owner that is needed to make a bonded working team. This relationship provides emotional support as well as the motivation for the interactive component of sound alerting behavior. Therefore, they must have a temperament that allows them to enjoy these situations without stress or fear.

An innate responsiveness to sounds and a desire to interact with its partner give a Hearing Dog potential in the sound-alerting role. The more natural talent a dog has, the

The first class I helped train in 1989. Of these, Blackjack became our demo dog, and Jackie, Patches, Pepper, Fresno, and Star enjoyed long lives with devoted partners. Star, the Toy Poodle, alerted to both a burglary in an adjoining apartment and to a fire far away in a laundry room.

better it will withstand all the daily influences that lower its motivation to alert.

A Hearing Dog is not simply a dog with specialized training. Most breeds that are developed for some kind of work fill one primary role, such as guarding, herding, or retrieving. Hearing Dogs, however, need to fill three important roles, each requiring certain temperament traits. In the home, they function as a close, interactive companion; in public as a safe member of the community who can also educate the public about the limitless value and potential of animals; and in their sound alerting role, as a closely tuned-in link to the auditory world. While the companion and public access roles are easily understood, the sound alerting role is complex and mysterious. The temperament traits that help the dog fulfill each role interplay in countless ways, and are especially contradictory when sound alerting talents are weighed against talents for the other two roles.

Having talked to Hearing Dog trainers from programs across the country, I've found that every program uses different training methods. These vary in regards to factors such as food versus toy rewards, importance of praise, amount of compulsion (if any), amount of training time, what behaviors are taught for sound alerting, shaping versus physical guiding of the dog, number of commands taught, sequence in which commands are taught, and so on. Strangely, all of these trainers feel that they have hit upon an excellent method that works well, and are not desperate to find a better way. Naturally, different trainers will always find many ways to achieve the same goal, but the fact that so many training philosophies all produce good working Hearing Dogs indicates to me that the training method used is less important than the dog's temperament and its aptitude for the work. Everyone does agree, however, that the three roles are necessary for success in a Hearing Dog.

Companion Role

A Hearing Dog fills this role in much the same way as any other pet dog, providing friendship, a sense of security, and a social icebreaker. Each of these functions is even more important in a Hearing Dog, because without a real partnership, there is no motivation for the dog to alert its owner to sounds. The dog must *want* to alert its partner.

People who lose their hearing late in life or were isolated from full communication early in life sometimes feel socially isolated, and may appreciate a dog's companion qualities even more than most people. Sometimes, hearing impaired people even feel isolated from their own families. When one woman wanted a Hearing Dog, her family gave her no support. They were in denial of the extent of her hearing loss, and preferred to think of her as hearing. She got the dog anyway, and developed a wonderful relationship with it, but was then faced with rejection from her family, who didn't want the dog visiting or accompanying her to work at the family business. After the dog alerted her to a violent intruder, an ex-boyfriend breaking a restraining order, their attitude changed. The family made the dog welcome, and even got their own pet dog for the first time.

To be a true companion, a Hearing Dog should be intensely interested in interacting with its partner, both for emotional reasons and because this is a vital component of sound alerting behavior. Independent, asocial dogs do not show enough interaction for sound alerting roles.

I used to be very concerned about a dog's level of sound alerting ability, but in the last few years I have realized that the relationship and compatibility of dog and partner are equally important. One Hearing Dog partner, Lisa Rogers, recently expressed this important aspect of Hearing Dogs very clearly. Lisa and her Hearing Dog Brandy, an Australian Shepherd mix, had only a few years together before Brandy's early death. Lisa later received Hearing Dog Tawny, a Golden Retriever, and in adjusting to a different dog, has been thinking a lot about Brandy and their partnership together.

I was in law school when I experienced a hearing loss. Suddenly I was cut off from the other students, who didn't know how to react to me. I didn't know how to communicate with them, and I was also faced with a school situation with no accommodations set up for people like me. I had to study twice as hard as before, and I didn't think I was going to make it.

When I received Brandy, I discovered that she solved so many problems for me. I felt like I had emotional support when I could play Frisbee with her after a bad day. Other students made an effort to relate to me because of her presence. With her companionship, I could get my studying done. My mother and stepdad later told me that I really changed after my hearing loss, and that when I got Brandy, I was suddenly back to my old self. I had had pet dogs growing up, but my relationship with Brandy was totally different. She was my shadow, and through her I knew everything that was happening. Sometimes she would just listen to something and look at me, and from her expression I would know exactly which kind of sound she was hearing.

People think that Hearing Dogs are important because they alert to sounds, but that ability pales in comparison with how important it is just having them there with you and depending on their presence so you can relax.

Another quality that Hearing Dogs need is a desire for physical contact. Although some dogs successfully alert by making eye contact, most people prefer some physical contact for alerting, since they may miss a visual signal if not watching the dog. Although almost any dog could be taught to perform a nose nudge or pawing motion, some dogs enjoy contact as a part of their affectionate interaction with their partner, and take very naturally to this part of alerting. Training helps to mold a good companion; all dogs must learn house manners, accept restraint for grooming, and respect their owner's leadership, but having a dog with the right temperament allows the companion relationship to develop more easily.

A dog that is a real companion can literally be a lifesaver. When Jimmy and Lara (not their real names) were matched, we knew that Lara was a gentle person with some depression and anxiety problems which meant that she needed an equally gentle, easy to manage dog. Jimmy, a small Poodle-Terrier mix, was cheerful and empathetic. Soon after they went home together, we began to get calls and letters from Lara's friends and her doc-

Lois Palma-Brown with her first Hearing Dog, Buttons. These two are in perfect harmony. (Photo by Glassner, SF-SPCA)

tor. We hadn't known that Lara had formerly been very suicidal, and her friends told us about a dramatic change. She no longer stayed home, but went out on long walks with Jimmy every day, talking to new acquaintances that Jimmy had helped her to meet. She at first had trouble with store owners refusing to admit Jimmy, so she arranged for the local newspaper to write about the town's new Hearing Dog resident, and eventually educated all of the restaurants and stores in town about the public access rights of Hearing Dogs. Jimmy loved his very public life, and was even welcome at the discount store where he had once been apprehended leaving the store with a pair of stolen socks in his mouth. Lara told everyone who was interested about Hearing Dogs and the work they do, and encouraged donations to our program. She started to do educational demos with Jimmy to show people how he alerted her to sounds, and visited hospitals with him. Lara, who herself had many health problems, died after eight years with Jimmy, but everyone who knew her feels that due to Jimmy's companionship her last years were happy ones.

Much is written about the unconditional love that dogs give people, but I don't think it is as widespread as we think. In reality, most dogs only love conditionally; it is we who would like to believe it is unconditional. But some dogs really do love people unconditionally and absolutely, and of course these are the best companions, the ones that people always remember over all their other pets. Testing dogs in shelters makes it clear that very few dogs have this quality, and fewer still expand it to include most of the human race, a necessary trait for public access. Having been around this kind of dog for the last ten years, sometimes surrounded by ten or twenty at a time, makes me wonder why anyone would settle for less, when these incredible dogs have so much more to give.

Public Access Role

Because Hearing Dogs are by law allowed public access almost anywhere their partner wishes to go, they come into close contact with many people. They are expected to behave in very un-dog like ways. Instinctive, normal canine behaviors need to be inhibited by training down to compliant, "stuffed dog" level. Far easier to train is the dog that lacks many of these behaviors in the first place, such as fear of strangers.

To be suitable for public access situations, a dog should accept strangers as potential pack members rather than potential threats. These dogs are more trustworthy in public, although they are also more likely to be overly friendly. They can often be seen pestering strangers by staring, panting, and excitedly jumping up, reacting to any friendly glance or word with wild abandon. They certainly do not fit the "guide dog image" of a sedate, unobtrusive companion who blends into the background. All one can say in their defense is that at least the small ones can't knock anyone down! Jumping up on people may be a minor offense compared to the worst behavior problems that reactive dogs can exhibit, but people do find it annoying, and it gives the image of an untrained, out-of-control dog. The best dogs in public are those that show a slight disinterest in strangers, but without suspicion, and are ready to make friends with a small amount of encouragement.

The dog must be safe for the public to encounter, and have a temperament that enjoys this lifestyle, which can require a unique dog. A simple excursion to a mall by bus exposes a dog to many potentially stressful events. On a noisy, rocking bus, the driver may shout angrily at the dog's partner to "Get that animal off the bus!" until convinced that the dog is a legal passenger. The partner may quite rightly be upset by this encounter, and the dog will be distressed too. Once it avoids the maze of human feet and finds a place to lie down, it's off the bus and into the mall, another crowded noisy environment. It's quite possible that children may run screaming toward the dog, skid to a halt, and hug it before the owner has noticed their approach. For some dogs, this day would be a traumatic nightmare. For those with the right temperament it would be a thrilling adventure.

Because Hearing Dogs perform most of their work at home, as opposed to guide dogs for the blind, which are primarily "on duty" in public, people often wonder why a Hearing Dog should need to be in public places. Aside from the fact that the law covers all service dogs equally, Hearing Dogs perform some valuable favors for their partner when they accompany them in public. Some are trained to alert to sirens and other warning sounds when their partner is out walking or driving, and some will alert to a person calling their partners by name. Even for sounds that the dog is not trained for, it may still alert to them because of its natural abilities and/or because it can generalize its trained responses to include new sounds.

T-Bone, a Boxer mix, is calm and confident at at a mall food court with partner Jackie Close. (Photo by Dennard)

In addition, and just as important, keeping an eye on the dog's body language can tell the partner about many things that are happening nearby. A friendly glance backward and a wagging tail is sufficient alert that a person is approaching from behind, as is apprehensive body language that indicates Rollerbladers on suicide missions. Several people I know have reported that their lives were saved when their Hearing Dog pulled them back as a car was about to hit them. Such behavior might be natural to any dog with a sense of self-preservation, but dogs with Hearing Dog temperament tend to be especially alert and responsive to their environment, and thus are good barometers of events.

The public access role of a Hearing Dog can overlap with its companion role. Hearing Dogs can be helpful friends in public by making communication between hearing and Deaf people easier. Many hearing-impaired people express frustration over the difficulty of dealing with strangers in public. Some strangers are insensitive to hearing impairments ("You're not deaf! You turned around when I yelled at you!"). And some well-meaning strangers are intimidated by communication challenges. Curiosity about a Hearing Dog often motivates people to make an effort to communicate, and many partners of Hearing Dogs find that having the dog gives them more confidence, as well as a social opening that leads to more conversations and friendships. My personal experience is that the benefits of having my Hearing Dogs accompany me in public outweigh the inevitable negatives of rude security guards denying the dog public access, although this can be so stressful that some people choose not to exercise their public access rights with their dog.

The benefit of public access rights should not be all on the partner's side. The dog also needs to be comfortable in public. Trying to take a fearful, unsocialized, or aggressive dog into public situations is stressful for the dog, no fun for the partner, and potentially dangerous for the public. Being hard-of-hearing, I often am not aware of situations happening behind me, and I miss low growling noises as well! I need to be confident that my dog will react positively to situations that some dogs would interpret as negative. All of the following actually happened to me: a singing man playfully smacked my dog on the head with a rolled-up newspaper; a woman grabbed up my Yorkie and hugged him tightly, weeping and saying that she was sure I was going into the SPCA to put him to sleep; and a toddler got very close and then had a panic attack of screaming and hitting. The list could go on and on, and could be added to by anyone else with a Hearing Dog. In all of the above situations, my dogs had the temperament to be puzzled or amused, not to be emotionally traumatized or to involve me in a lawsuit. It's important to be able to trust the behavior of the dog, because one certainly can't trust the behavior of the public!

The Americans with Disabilities Act

A major step forward in human rights, this law has opened many complicated questions about the rights of Hearing Dogs and other service animals. It can be read on the internet at www.usdoj.gov/crt/ada/adahom1.htm, or perform a search for the Americans with Disabilities Act. A condensed form is available at the site for the Justice Department, www.usdoj.gov. Its main relevance to the partner of a Hearing Dog are:

1. Partners of Hearing Dogs may train them themselves and do not need documentation from any trainer or training program "certifying" them as Hearing Dogs in order to have public access rights. On the plus side, this gives people freedom to select and train their own dog. On the minus side, there is no system to screen out dogs that are unsafe to be around the general public.

2. Partners do not need to prove or discuss their disabilities with anyone in order to use their public access rights for their Hearing Dogs. On the plus side, this prevents harassment of people with less visible disabilities, such as those who are hard of hearing. On the minus side, people with no hearing impairment who wish for whatever reason to pretend that their dog is a Hearing Dog cannot be challenged to prove their need for the animal.

Although the Americans With Disabilities Act states that partners of Hearing Dogs may train them themselves and do not need documentation from any trainer or training program, in real life, the situation is different. Many people, even some law enforcement officials, are not familiar with these aspects of the ADA. While taking a Hearing Dog into stores and restaurants is usually easy, attempting to rent apartments or to take them into hotels, airplanes, hospitals, and on public transportation often presents problems. In particular, low-paid security guards are unlikely to be familiar with the ADA. I once was refused entrance onto a bus because my dog, wearing a vest and with an ID card, lacked a harness with handle similar to the ones guide dogs for the blind use. This was the only symbol the bus driver knew that signified public access rights. These rights should not be abused; dogs must be trained to behave safely in public and should not be taken into public places until they are. Hearing Dog programs that are members of Assistance Dogs International voluntarily agree to train their dogs to a certain standard of performance; this set of criteria can be viewed on the ADI website. The following websites give an incredible amount of information on aspects of all types of assistance dogs:

- Assistance Dogs International – www.assistance-dogs-intl.org
- International Association of Assistance Dog Partners – www.ismi.net/iaadp
- The Delta Society (which also promotes educational programs for potential trainers of all types of assistance dogs) – www.deltasociety.org

Sound Alerting Role

Although alerting humans to sounds seems simple from a human point of view, the work is complex, and were it not that some dogs are so incredibly gifted, it might seem too complex to expect from a dog, or even from a more intelligent animal.

Hearing Dogs have none of the advantages enjoyed by other trained dogs. Most other forms of dog training involve teaching a dog to respond to cues from humans with predictable positive and negative consequences and in more or less consistent situations. Instead, the Hearing Dog cues its human partner to act instead of waiting for a command from the partner. Additionally, because the partner probably will not hear the alertable sounds that cue the dog, the partner is unable to assist or motivate the dog to initiate the alert, so it must have the initiative to act on its own. The conditions are not predictable; sounds that it alerts to may happen at any time during the day or night, and the dog and partner will not be waiting expectantly for sounds to occur, but will be involved in some other activity. Therefore, the dog needs to be able to generalize its responses to constantly varying situations. It will never be able to alert if it can only perform a rigid behavior sequence by rote. (Many dogs' rote behavior makes them slow to adjust when a telephone or other sound is moved to a new place; they continue for a while to go to the old location, confused.) The dog is likely to be sleeping when many sounds happen, and must be reactive enough to wake up instantly. This initiative is aided by lots of cheerleading on the owner's part; instead of being trained to inhibit instinctive canine behaviors, as in the other two roles, the dog must be helped to feel energized, uninhibited, and free to make decisions.

Upon hearing a cue, which could be either a sound the dog is trained to alert to or any other sound the dog perceives as noteworthy or "alertable," a Hearing Dog must both interact with its partner as well as somehow indicate the location or type of the sound. Most training programs teach the dog to lead its partner to sounds such as doorbells, telephones, timers, or people calling the partner's name. In the case of smoke alarms, it is safer to train the dog to stay with its partner rather than approach a possible fire.

To be most effective in alerting its human partner to sounds, a Hearing Dog ideally should have a very strong orienting or investigative response to sounds, and a low tendency to habituate to familiar sounds. Such a dog will train rapidly, as well as show consistent alerting behavior in real-life situations.

Sound alerting involves both mental and physical effort on the part of the dog. The mental effort includes locating the sound, deciding whether to respond, searching for the partner, observing the partner's body language and position, determining how to make contact, and then retracing its way to the sound. If the sound is novel—such as a crying kitten, a different brand of telephone, or a stranger's unfamiliar knocking style— the dog must make still more decisions. Physical effort is required, because the dog should alert quickly, before visitors leave or callers hang up. The dog may need to search throughout a house to find its partner, and might make several trips back and forth between partner and sound.

Penny, the Hearing Dog Program's demo dog for seventeen years, alerts owner Ralph Dennard to an alarm clock. (Photo by SF-SPCA)

Hearing Dogs often perform sound alerting for inconsistent and poorly timed rewards, due to the variable nature of sound alerting situations. Once the dog initiates the alert, it might have to work a long time before it is rewarded. For instance, the partner may be several rooms away, may not realize right away that the dog is attempting to alert, may forget to praise in the hurry to answer the phone, and so on. Delayed reward is commonly accepted to be detrimental to an animal's performance in a training situation, and long behavior chains can break down easily.

Unlike other training programs, should the dog choose not to respond to the sound, there are no adverse consequences: Its partner may never be aware that the dog failed to alert. Some forms of mild corrections can be used successfully during sound alerting training, but are difficult to apply in real life situations. In any case, if the dog's only motivation for alerting was to avoid something negative, then in real life—with constant opportunities to discover that ignoring sounds has no negative consequences—the dog may stop alerting. In any case, dogs that are talented and easily motivated in sound alerting do not require aversive training to perform it, and will alert happily for infrequent rewards. Their behavior is easily maintained.

When one considers how difficult it is to teach a dog to perform well even under controlled, consistent conditions, it would seem unrealistic to expect a dog to overcome all the obstacles that interfere with a Hearing Dog's alerting. Well, it *is* unrealistic. After hundreds and hundreds of hours trying to train dogs that were unsuitable for the work, I can safely say that I learned a lot, but I can't say that those dogs did. After my experiences with the dogs that were so gifted for sound alerting work that they only seemed to need a little reminding to realize that this was their mission in life, I lost interest in finding new ways to work a miracle with dogs that had low potential. Instead, I've realized that the "real" Hearing Dogs themselves are the miracle, and that they are worth every effort to find them.

Taz, who looks like a small black Springer Spaniel, is a good example of a "real" Hearing Dog. He effortlessly fills all three roles. Sonja Wilson, his partner, keeps up his training for standard sounds, but finds that Taz's abilities often surprise her.

Taz is my partner; we're always together. One night at three a.m., he woke me up, and he was so freaked out, barking and upset. I was a little surprised, because he never does that normally. I didn't have my hearing aids in, so I couldn't figure out what it was. He was looking at the door, and I realized someone was trying to get in by breaking the door. Normally Taz is happy when visitors knock, but this time I could tell the difference. I was really scared. After awhile, Taz happily alerted me to a normal knocking on the door. I looked through the peephole and it was the police—the neighbors had called 911 when they heard the intruder.

Taz goes with me on camping trips. Our first trip was a week and a half, and at first he was so scared, but then he loved it and enjoyed checking out everything. Then the only problem was he was scared to cross streams. I had to carry him as well as my pack. After a few times I told him, "You're just going to have to cross yourself, I can't carry you every time." The next stream we came to, he crossed by himself.

One night, there was a group of us hiking, and Taz woke me up. Everyone was trying to sleep, but Taz was waking them up whimpering and growling. I told him "Quiet, quiet," but he kept on. I peeked outside the tent, and there was a huge brown bear! "Shhh! Nobody move!" I said. There was no food around, and we waited until the bear left. I think Taz's presence might have scared him away. Taz always tells me if he senses animals when we're hiking. He caught a scent once, and I could tell it was something unusual, but I couldn't see anything. I looked all around with my binoculars, and about 100 yards away there was a gorgeous mountain lion. Luckily, it didn't want to come closer.

Sometimes at home Taz alerts me, and I check everything out, but it's not a phone call, or the door, and I ask him what it is, and he won't show me, he just keeps alerting. Then we have an earthquake! He knows it about five minutes before it happens. This year we're going to climb Mount Whitney and next year I'm running in the L.A. Marathon. My friend will bring Taz to run with me for the last few miles so we can cross the finish line together.

Chapter Two
The Naturals:
Reactivity and Its Impact on Temperament

Reactivity affects how Hearing Dogs function in all three roles they play. It has a neu-rological basis, and sets the threshold for the expression of temperament traits, making them seem exaggerated and intense, or slow-paced and mild. A dog with low reactivity requires greater stimulation from the environment before it shows a reaction. A dog with high reactivity requires only a small amount of stimulation to show the same reaction. Reactivity to sounds is a subset of overall reactivity, and derives from the interplay of sev-eral temperament traits. Dogs that are sound reactive can "teach themselves" to alert to sounds if they have the right balance of temperament traits and the right relationship with their owner.

Reactivity

The dogs that seem born Hearing Dogs display different facets of reactivity. Webster defines reactivity as "the ability to respond to a stimulus." Dogs that are reactive have a nervous system that is easily excited by any stimulus. These reactions are automatic, not conscious, and these dogs cannot easily inhibit their behavior. I've observed that these reactive dogs also do not easily habituate to familiar stimuli. Reactivity, therefore, is the key factor that gives dogs potential in sound alerting.

A dog's level of reactivity seems to be hardwired into its nervous system. Reactivity causes all of its other temperament traits to be more easily triggered, but does not influ-ence the actual level of these (such as fearfulness, territoriality, or sociability).

For example, let's say that two dogs possess exactly the same level of being highly sociable with strangers. A non-reactive dog might calmly approach the stranger to be pet-ted. If the person starts behaving excitedly, the dog might temporarily become excited, but would then calm down. The highly reactive dog, on the other hand, would become extremely excited at the stranger's mere approach; jumping up, licking, and possibly knocking the stranger down. If the person then behaved in an excited manner, this dog would escalate its behavior dramatically. Both of these dogs show the same level of trust and desire to make contact, but they are perceived by the casual onlooker as having total-ly different personalities. The first dog would be considered suitable for a family pet. The second might be abandoned at an animal shelter and, if lucky, adopted by a Hearing Dog program. In fact, the highly reactive dog I just described is my friend, Digby, who finally learned to sit for treats instead of leaping up and clawing me.

Because reactivity simply exposes what already exists in the dog's temperament, it is neither "good" nor "bad." Desirable qualities, such as friendly social interaction, are as exposed as much as undesirable ones such as fearfulness or aggression. If reactive dogs were alarm systems, they would be permanently set at the most easily triggered level. Such an alarm system would be appropriate for the Hope Diamond in a quiet museum, but inappropriate for a car on a busy street. In the same way, the dog that instantly wakes up at night to alert frantically to a smoke alarm is the same dog that will seem overstimulated and out of control at a shopping mall.

Highly reactive dogs are often described as "sensitive." This loaded term is very misleading, and implies that the dog is emotionally vulnerable, easily inhibited, and even that it might have the potential to become fearful. On the plus side, "sensitive" implies that the dog is empathetic and aware of its surroundings. Although a reactive dog may have any of these qualities, it also might not. It might just as well happen to be independent, uninhibited, fearless, and aggressive.

One could characterize highly reactive dogs as "excitable," but I also have problems with this term. It is too emotionally loaded, and connotes the positive side of reactivity, such as alertness, without the negative side, such as panic reactions. In addition, most of the research and general writing on dog behavior that is currently in print confuses excitability with high activity levels. In dogs at least, activity levels and reactivity levels are not linked, and can be observed in different proportions in each dog.

Non-Reactive Dogs

In contrast to dogs like Digby, who often were highly talented in sound alerting, another type of dog that I frequently adopted seemed to have non-reactive temperaments. Although dogs like this had passed temperament tests easily, they usually showed only a mild interest in sounds rather than an obsessive searching response. They were adaptable and easygoing, and it seemed as if they would make excellent companions, especially for the people who requested a calmer, easier-to-handle partner than the usual fireball Hearing Dog. These dogs were easy to train in obedience, and it seemed logical that such trainable, interactive dogs should easily be trained to alert to sounds. Unfortunately, even with many extra training sessions and intensive use of motivational and "drive-building" methods, most of them never achieved the ability to alert in anything resembling a real-life scenario. Two problems appeared: first, their alerting behavior would be slow to start; and second, once alerting got

Julie Francis with her Hearing Dog Chevy, a Yellow Lab. (Photo by Dennard)

started, it never became intense.

The slow-start problem appeared to be caused by the dogs' need to receive some cue to start working—but why was the sound itself not acting as a cue, as it did for the more naturally talented dogs? These slowpoke non-reactive dogs appeared only to use cues related to the training scenario to determine when to alert, rather than responding to the sounds themselves. When the scenarios changed, such as a new room or a new trainer, the dogs did not generalize, and required re-training for each new situation. Because they had no natural reaction to sounds, they were just as likely to focus on cues such as the trainer's position as the sound. When they did focus on the sound as a cue, the association was later easily weakened.

The lack of intensity was associated with an inability to adjust to lowered reinforcement schedules. In real-life alerting, food cannot be delivered consistently and frequently (at the SF-SPCA Hearing Dog Program, the dog is never completely "weaned off" food treats; instead, the new partner is instructed in how to continue the maintenance training using food). Unless they were very highly food-motivated, these dogs did not find it worthwhile to alert for minimal reinforcement. They had no natural response to sounds in the first place, so when their trained behavior disintegrated, their behavior was even less helpful than that of a sound-reactive dog that had received no training at all. Dogs that lacked interest in sounds, but were very highly motivated by food, could achieve apparently reliable alerting behavior at real-life reinforcement levels. However, their high food motivation sometimes actually distracted them from alerting—if they were hunting for crumbs under a toddler's chair, for instance. Without a strong natural response to sounds, they considered sound alerting just one of many ways to obtain food.

Even at their best, these dogs did not always have an immediate response to sounds if sleeping, playing, or being petted otherwise occupied them. They sometimes responded eventually, but the long lag time between the sound and the dog's response meant that the alert came too late: Visitors left, or callers hung up phones. Their lack of response when they were sleeping was scary; fires are more dangerous at night, when sleeping people do not see or smell smoke, and Hearing Dogs *must* wake up instantly when a smoke alarm goes off. Their behavior easily became that of a sweet, non-working pal, excelling as a family pet or therapy dog.

If non-reactive dogs are not strongly motivated by primary reinforcers—food, toys, or social rewards—it is impossible to achieve any strong conditioned reinforcer effects with the sounds. If they are highly motivated by primary reinforcers and receive expert training and maintenance, their responses to sounds can be quite good, but may never approach the intensity and reliability of the reactive dogs.

The failure of non-reactive dogs is especially frustrating when their behavior is contrasted with the progress of the "natural" workers, who start ignoring food rewards on their own as they become more and more intense in their alerting behavior, eventually finding alerting to sounds rewarding in itself. Food and social rewards at a very low level are enough to keep the natural worker highly motivated.

Reactivity proved to be a two-edged sword, and a painful one for the Hearing Dog trainer. The highly reactive dogs were easily trained to do incredible "soundwork," alerting to everything, but they sometimes also showed temperament problems that prevented them from graduating. Fearfulness, aggression, territoriality, and dominance were as exaggerated and as easily stimulated as all their desirable traits, and precluded them from succeeding in companion or public access roles. Dogs with low reactivity often had beautiful temperaments, eminently suitable for companion or public access roles, but failed in their sound-alerting role, calmly ignoring important sounds. Once both of these groups had been dropped out of the training program, the remaining dogs either showed acceptable compromises between temperament and working ability, or were the rare superstars, excelling in all roles. Watching such a high dropout rate was frustrating. How I longed to do temperament transplants! But why agonize over the failures, when the superstars proved that some dogs could do it all? Finding out even more about what made these dogs so specially gifted, and figuring out how to find them, became a primary goal.

Sound Reactivity

One quality showed by the dogs with a natural ability in sound alerting is not just high reactivity but high *sound reactivity*—an intense response to any sound. Dogs can also be especially reactive to any of their other senses, as in the visual reactivity of sighthounds, which intensely watch moving objects. Most dogs with high overall reactivity show equal reactivity to all sensory input, sounds included. Their talent for sound alerting is high, but so is their potential to be distracted by other sensory input. In some dogs, sound-reactivity is the dominant sense, and their reactions to sounds may instead overshadow all other input. These dogs are not easily distracted when sounds are occurring.

Ideally, a Hearing Dog should have low overall reactivity, coupled with high sound reactivity, but I have never seen this combination; it just doesn't seem to "fit" with the way reactivity works. The average dog with low overall reactivity shows an equally low sound reactivity. The closest I have seen to perfection are dogs with moderate overall reactivity and high sound reactivity, and these rare dogs are very suitable for all three Hearing Dog roles.

Sound reactivity has two components: an orienting reflex, and an investigative approach to the sound.

Orienting Reflex

Dogs that show a strong response to sounds are exhibiting a natural reflex that is common to all animals. This is called the orienting response, and it refers to the animal's behavior when any of its senses are stimulated. This helps the animal to focus on the stimulus in order to evaluate its relevance to survival. In dogs, the orienting response to sound is to align the head to so that the ears can identify the sound and determine its location. The dog tilts its head and moves its ears until targeted exactly on the sound.

Investigation

Although a dog that merely orients toward sounds without approaching them is showing very good potential, a dog that also investigates sounds is the ideal training prospect. The ideal dog will not creep forward cautiously, ready to escape, but will boldly and quickly run toward the sound, and continue to examine it even after the first sniff establishes that it is not edible or interesting in any other way. This highly sound-reactive, investigative dog might whine, scratch at the noise source, sniff, dig, spin around, or run in excitement. It might also show playful interaction with a nearby person as a displacement activity. This dog will interrupt most other activities when it notices a sound, even waking up or stopping play. Its reaction often appears completely involuntary.

Habituation and Sensitization

If a stimulus is found to be irrelevant, an animal "habituates" and learns to ignore it, to avoid wasting energy on irrelevant stimuli and allow it to concentrate on relevant stimuli. "Sensitization" is the opposite of habituation. If the stimulus is perceived as relevant to survival, the animal takes appropriate action depending on whether the stimulus is beneficial or dangerous, and learns to react appropriately in the future. Eventually, an animal becomes completely habituated to meaningless stimuli, ignoring them no matter how strongly it reacted to them at first. It will also be sensitized to meaningful stimuli, reacting intensely, even if these stimuli were hardly noticeable at first. For example, when a dog goes to a new home, it may at first be startled by the regular screech of bus brakes outside the window, but not notice the faint click of a downstairs lock when its new owner comes home. Within a few days the dog ignores the buses, but the click is a world-shaking event. Habituation and sensitization have helped it to prioritize its perceptions of the world.

Habituation can be a problem in sound alerting. If the sounds the dog responds to lose their relevance, the dog ceases to alert to them. Typically, this happens because the dog is either no longer receiving sufficient reward for alerting, or is receiving more reward from some other activity, such as playing with kids or chasing squirrels. Events in the life of a Hearing Dog are constantly eroding trained responses in this way, unless habituation is actively prevented by maintenance training.

Some dogs habituate more rapidly than others. On the plus side, one could describe these dogs as "adaptable," since they quickly adjust to changes in their environment. Adaptability is a plus for companion and public access roles, but can cause problems in sound alerting, such as habituating rapidly to all the sounds their partner needs to be alerted to. By contrast, a dog that does not habituate easily will continue to respond even to irrelevant sounds. This seems contradictory; after all, habituation is learning, and any dog will eventually learn not to waste energy on investigating irrelevant sounds. But because

My dog Jinx shows an orienting response to the human voice- the word "pine cone."
(Photo by Susan Schelling)

reactivity to sounds is a *basic* characteristic of the dogs' nervous system, it is less affect-ed by the learning process than the response of a dog simply *trained* to react to a sound. Truly sound-reactive dogs respond to sounds without thinking first; they appear to be operating by instinct, and instantly approach or intensely orient, only then pausing to determine relevance.

It would seem that life could be stressful for such a dog, but sound-reactive dogs that are not fearful of sounds are self-rewarded by reacting. All dogs find it difficult to inhib-it their natural instinctive behaviors, but reactive dogs, being less inhibitable anyway, find this even harder. They take longer to learn to filter out extraneous stimuli, and tend to take longer to become controllable in public places.

Some dogs are easily sensitized. This phenomenon is well known when it involves fear-fulness and phobias, but the same process can be very positive when it helps dogs alert to sounds. By learning which sounds are highly relevant to them, they become intensely aware of them, yet without fearfulness.

Darla is a Jack Russell mix, partnered with Rosemary Blanchard, who has become highly sensitized to car sounds.

I live in an apartment complex, and there are cars and people constantly coming and going. I have several friends who visit a lot, and Darla knows long before they arrive. She gets restless in my lap, listening, and finally gets down, and waits at the door, but they still haven't arrived. She has learned their cars' sounds, and can hear them from so far away, I almost have enough time to bake a cake for them! Anybody who visits several times gets their car memorized. The strangest thing is that she alerts to visitors coming to see me that have never been here before. I can tell the difference, because this alert is a little more hesitant, not always accurate, and it's not so far in advance. She seems to know by the time they are in the parking lot. I thought she must be psychic, because there are always at least fifteen cars in the parking lot, which is pretty far from my place. Finally I figured out that she was alerting to any strange car parking in the lot, since those sometimes mean a visitor is coming. She doesn't alert to the other tenant's cars. So not only does she remember all my friends' car sounds, but also knows to ignore all the tenants' car sounds, and alerts to all the strange cars!

While Darla learned to generalize her response to strangers' cars to include all unknown cars, Mamie Williams' Dachshund/Cocker mix, Chia, learned to generalize one alert to include other relevant sounds:

Every morning, I would put a teapot of water on the stove to boil water for drip coffee while I wander around the house doing various early morning things. The teapot used to have a bird whistle, which has since disappeared. Chia *hated* the whistle and would run to me to take it off the stove. Well, now the whistle is gone, but Chia, daily, will leave her breakfast if necessary to come find me when the water starts to boil without the whistle. This has carried over to my cooking dinner as well. If I leave a pot on the stove for any reason and it begins to bub-ble, she will come and find me.

Mamie also writes about an interesting experience with Chia that illustrates the concept of sensitization:

Over the almost five years since I have returned to Charleston, Chia has become very fond of my parents. When we go to my parents' house, she literally cries with joy as we drive up their driveway and hops out of the car to run to their door. Once inside, she is very content to play with her toy, steal my mother's chair and scrounge for crumbs around my father's chair. She has never shown any sign of discomfort or impatience being in their home until recently. A couple of weeks ago she was with me on the brief afternoon drop-by. She flew inside as usual but within two minutes she was sitting at the front door staring at me. She came up to me and went back to the door. The three of us watched with some amazement, having no idea what the problem could be. I took her for a walk, thinking she needed to go out. When we returned, she did the same thing. I apologized and we left. The next couple of visits she did the same thing. We were baffled. One day I was helping my Dad with something so I couldn't walk her. I let her out (my parents have a huge yard) and went out a few minutes later. She was sitting like a sentinel at the end of the walk, staring. I put her in the car and off we went. A few days later my mother tells me that she thinks she hears a smoke alarm making its occasional chirps that indicate a dying battery. The folks asked a handyman to come look, and sure enough, a smoke alarm, 20 feet up in the attic was beeping. This made Chia's behavior immediately understandable to me! She had been telling us for weeks!! Stupid people! Once the battery was replaced, Chia returned to her usual loving enthusiastic self!

Chia showed intense sensitization to the sound of the smoke alarm, almost to the point of fearfulness. She has been trained that this sound is an important event, and hearing its brief "low-battery" beep at irregular intervals was stressful to her, especially when she did not get Mamie's usual enthusiastically grateful response. Over the weeks, she never habituated to it.

Inhibition

Reactive dogs, by the very nature of their reactivity, are less able to inhibit their responses to stimuli. Their nervous systems react instantly, giving the impression of a dog that "acts before it thinks." Needless to say, this lack of inhibition leads to better sound alerting, but in all other roles, it leads to trouble. A dog at the mercy of its reactive nervous system doesn't really have much choice about reacting to stimuli, and often faces "unfair" consequences from the environment or from humans. These dogs often leap and hit themselves on objects or walls, get their feet caught in things, and in general get themselves into situations that other dogs would have avoided. Socially, they get into trouble easily with other dogs. Normally, dogs learn to inhibit many behaviors or face threats and punishment from dominant dogs, which quickly react to uninhibited behavior. Such behavior is interpreted as "uppity" because it has the effect of getting the pack in tune with that dog's mood. Leading pack behavior in such a brash way is an affront, whereas socially sensitive dogs will change the pack's mood tactfully in a way that doesn't annoy the leader. Dogs that cannot learn this do not fit in well in dog or human packs, since their reactivity causes them to become stressed by attempts to inhibit them. After all, their nervous system itself is being asked to change, and it cannot.

The average person wants a dog that behaves, and thinks of most instinctive dog behavior as "misbehavior." The ideal pet dog's temperament is inhibited to the point of showing almost no dog behaviors at all and moves slowly enough for even the most clumsy human to easily keep up with it mentally and physically. Obedience training is usually designed to inhibit natural behaviors and to teach new behaviors that can be used to replace unwanted behaviors. Dogs with naturally inhibited temperaments respond better to this basic control training. It is only in advanced training for functional working dogs of any type that this inhibited dog is at a disadvantage, unable to make decisions or follow its instincts freely. Uninhibited dogs show good aptitude for fast, action-oriented behaviors such as retrieving, jumping, and, of course, sound alerting, but require lengthy and patient training to learn inhibiting behaviors such as staying in place for long periods.

Most people are in over their heads when dealing with reactive dogs. I am sure this is why many of these dogs end up in shelters. When faced with a dog that yields to almost every impulse, most people interpret the dog's behavior as unruly, stupid, and disobedient. Understanding these dogs means accepting that such a dog has trouble controlling its behavior, even if it is strongly motivated to do so.

A high activity level might seem to facilitate approach to sounds. Dogs that are active are certainly better at alerting, if only because the moving dog is more likely to be noticed by its partner. High activity level without sound reactivity, however, produces a dog that merely moves about without reacting to sounds.

Why Dogs Approach and Investigate Sounds

Dogs may approach sounds for several different reasons, bringing into play the complex behaviors of predation, territoriality, social communication, and curiosity.

Predation

A dog uses all of its senses when hunting for food. When prey is hidden from sight or scent, hearing becomes vital. Wild canines can scent small rodents concealed by thick grass, but cannot locate them precisely. Many small rodents communicate using high-frequency squeaks that canines have evolved to hear easily. Using their binaural hearing to sense squeaks or rustling noises, canines can pinpoint the spot where a hard pounce with the forefeet will pin down the hidden creature. This quick, intense orienting response ensures that crucial seconds are not lost, and the pounce follows at lightning speed.

Most behavior researchers agree that the act of predation should not be labeled "aggression." Killing and gobbling up a rat is merely feeding behavior, and any continued biting of larger prey is only done to weaken it enough to finally kill it safely and then eat it. These behaviors are totally different than those seen in social aggression to members of the same species. In this book, for practical purposes, the somewhat imprecise term "predatory aggression" refers to dogs that attempt to seriously bite or kill other animals—or those that seem to "hunt" other dogs as prey. The aspects of predation that involve the earlier parts of the sequence up to chasing behavior, discussed below, are generally accepted to be harmless, or easily controlled in dogs.

The screaming of wounded prey animals (or humans) often triggers killing behavior in dogs with high predatory aggression, or extreme excitement in dogs with lower predatory aggression. Our emergency warning devices—smoke alarms, sirens, etc.—often sound similar to these high-pitched sounds of prey animals. In fact, these warning devices are designed this way, because human beings also have an automatic intense rescuing or aggressive response to sounds with the same frequencies as the screaming of animals, babies, or adult humans. Unfortunately, most hearing losses involve the higher frequencies, and many people who can hear speech tones cannot hear smoke alarms. Many dogs, especially those of the predatory breeds, have an intense response to these high-pitched alarm sounds, and will investigate them.

The intensity of a predatory response to sounds depends upon which aspects of predatory behavior the dog is showing. Predatory behavior in wild canines is a complex sequence of many behaviors that all link together. Orienting, scenting, tracking, chasing, attacking, killing, and eating behaviors result in productive hunting. In domestic dogs, these behaviors have often been individually isolated and intensified, or the original sequence has been halted at some point. A Bloodhound, which is primarily interested in tracking, has no impulse to chase, attack, or eat the "prey" it has been tracking. Its hunting behavior has been truncated at the tracking segment. Herding behavior consists of all the actions that prevent the escape of the prey animal by either driving it towards pack members, or blocking its forward motion, but without the attacking and killing behavior that would naturally follow. This last part of the sequence is genetically inhibited, and usually expressed in nipping rather than biting to kill. Many people think that Border Collies herd out of a nurturing, caring impulse to "tend" their flock. Watching their intense, driven focus when working will reveal the same single-mindedness shown by wolves hunting large game.

When any form of hunting behavior is seen with lowered aggression, the resulting behavior appears to be playful rather than survival-oriented. This makes perfect sense, since play is usually defined by behavior researchers as the expression of natural behaviors, but without aggression, and often out of sequence. In watching dogs respond to sounds, a distinct difference is seen depending on the dog's predatory aggression level. Dogs that are more aggressive will show very high intensity as they rush up to a sound, scratching or perhaps biting at the source. If they realize that the sound is not edible or interesting to chew, they may show displacement behavior such as barking, running, or biting other objects (or people, in the case of some working-bred terriers). These dogs appear serious and focused, not playful. Dogs that are less aggressive but still predatory toward sounds, do appear playful. They show looser body language and less displacement behavior. They may run toward and pounce on a kitchen timer, but rather than biting it or mangling it they are more likely to gently pick it up and carry it.

Both types of reactions show a potential to alert to sounds, but of course the dog with the more aggressive, intense reaction will show more intense, focused alerting although a dog with a more playful alert is more likely to succeed as a Hearing Dog.

Territoriality

Some dogs appear to react to unusual sounds in a territorial way. They investigate with a suspicious response, possibly barking. This behavior is less intense when the dog is off its territory, and thus is harder to detect if a dog is in an unfamiliar place such as a shelter. If the dog is territorial, but lacks sound reactivity, it responds only to unusual sounds and to sounds that the dog has learned to associate with territorial invasion. Some guard breeds show this type of reaction, and might guard the house intensely, yet be very difficult to train to alert to an "irrelevant" sound such as a telephone. Dogs that are both sound reactive and territorial show responses to a wide variety of sounds, and are easier to train in sound alerting.

Dogs that are territorial vary in aggression levels. While those that have higher aggression show major problems both in public and as companions, other dogs are territorial yet without any apparent aggression. Their response is excited and overly friendly, alerting to visitors with barking and frantic behavior that evaporates into greeting behavior when guests are admitted to the house. Although harmless, their behavior is interpreted as aggressive if they show it in public places. If they show this noisy territoriality only at home, they can still function well in their public access role.

Hearing Dog "Dinkum" is a small black Scottie mix whose favorite activity at home is to sit at the front window and monitor the street for potential troublemakers. She is friendly to visitors, but makes quite a fuss barking at harmless people walking down the street. She's also very good at her sound alerting, but I felt that all this window watching would make her more territorial and distract her from her alerting. I recommended that her partner, Rae Sammons, put up some curtains or paper so that Dinkum couldn't see outside, but he felt that she was enjoying herself so much that he just couldn't deprive her of this fun activity. A neighbor who had just gotten out of the hospital visited one day, and shortly after he had left, Dinkum ran to the back of the house, searching for Rae. She ran back and forth frantically, and he finally followed her to the front window. Dinkum was looking into the next yard, where the neighbor was lying unconscious on the ground. Still weak from recent surgery, he had fainted. Dinkum's territoriality made her interested in things that happened outside, but it was not so strong that she could not leave her post to alert her partner that something unusual had happened. Why Dinkum felt that someone lying quietly on the ground was reason to alert, we will never know, but she showed true natural Hearing Dog abilities, alerting to a situation that was unrelated to her experience or training.

Social Behavior

When dogs respond to certain sounds that resemble distress cries of puppies, or whining or howling by adult dogs, their responses may vary from maternal caregiving to aggression. Some breeds have a reputation for insufficient maternal instincts, and some mothers in these breeds will not rescue a puppy crying because it is lost or is being accidentally crushed by her. Some breeders feel that these dams are hearing-impaired for the frequency of a puppy cry, and some feel that the instinct to respond is missing. Dogs with strong maternal (or paternal) instincts might also be ones that test well for sound reactivity.

Curiosity

Investigation, whether of sounds or of other stimuli, can benefit an animal by helping it to hunt, maintain a territory, or facilitate social communication. Some investigation seems random and purposeless, and could be labeled "curiosity." But what purpose can curiosity serve? David McFarland (*The Oxford Companion to Animal Behavior*)

Springer, PJ, investigates a feather, ready to bolt away if it proves dangerous. He pokes at it with a paw, and eventually picked it up and played with it.

defines curiosity as "a voluntary form of exploratory behavior." This is different from a startle response, which is more like an orienting reflex, in which the startled animal orients towards the stimulus, then investigates. When "curious," the animal investigates cautiously, discovering whether the stimulus is edible or dangerous. McFarland speculates that curiosity is simply a normal part of feeding behavior, helping animals to learn more about food sources.

Nosy Niji provides amusement for an elderly neighbor.

Sometimes curiosity is linked with fear; many prey animals, including gazelles and ducks, actually approach when they perceive a potential predator, or a novel item in their environment. This would seem to be detrimental to their survival, but it is thought that there must be some value in learning about dangerous or novel things in this way. Certainly it sometimes is detrimental, as when foxes cavort and romp on shore, luring fascinated ducks within reach. Curiosity balances another strong trait in wild animals, called neophobia. Meaning "fear of the new," neophobia keeps animals cautious and helps them avoid danger. After brief periods of adaptability when they are young, during which they imprint the familiar aspects of their world, neophobia often takes over. The urge to investigate the unfamiliar is equally necessary, however. Survival involves much more than just avoiding danger. Searching for food sources, mates, and new territory would not be possible for a completely neophobic animal. When confronted with some novel stimulus, animals can be seen advancing cautiously, then bolting back to safety, then advancing a bit closer, until finally the new stimulus is integrated into the animal's world-view as beneficial, neutral, or dangerous.

It is hard to evaluate a dog's level of curiosity, since most investigative behavior can also be attributed to other motivations such as hunger. But the same dogs that are very reactive to sounds are usually very interested in investigating any type of novel item or situation as well. Good Hearing Dogs are often inquisitive busybodies who gain much apparent satisfaction from their behavior. Fox (*Behaviour of Wolves, Dogs, and Related Canines*, 1987) describes variations in curiosity:

> ...Wolves are extremely inquisitive, and are constantly active in the home, exploring, manipulating, chewing, pulling, and carrying all interesting objects, and they will attempt to dig holes in all soft surfaces—carpets, chairs, and sofas. Contrast this hyper-exploratory behavior with that of the average pet dog that is content to sleep and eat most of the day and never seek to learn what is under or inside the sofa, or what lies out of sight on top of the sideboard. The motivation to explore is a prerequisite to learning, and I believe that the wild canid is an extremely alert and intelligent animal compared to the average dog.

Curious behavior gives Hearing Dogs sound alerting potential, but I am sure that many of the dogs I have adopted ended up in a shelter partly due to the problem behaviors a curious dog can display.

Fear of Sounds

Some dogs tread a fine line between fear and fascination with sounds. They may appear confidently inquisitive about some sounds, but very fearful of other sounds. Often a dog can learn to feel secure about the sounds it is trained to alert to, yet be terrified of strange ones. These dogs can function well in a stable, supportive household, but might find public access situations terrifying.

Reactivity is not always correlated with a fear of sounds. Some dogs that seem nonreactive can show a learned or inherited fear of sounds. Some very reactive dogs are fearless even with noise levels that stress normal dogs. "Sound-shyness" is considered by most dog breeders to be genetic. I've encountered many dogs that were fearless and confident except for being fearful of sounds, and an equal number who were fearful of people, strange places, and anything new, except for sounds.

Some dog owners report that their dog's fear of certain sounds is a helpful alert. It would be unfair, however, to deliberately expose a dog to sounds it is afraid of for the purpose of training. I once received a phone call from a trainer who was trying to train a Hearing Dog for a client. I offered some advice on the smoke alarm, but she said she didn't need it. "He's all trained on it already. He's terrified of the smoke alarm, and he comes to hide behind me every time!" That may well have been, but from a practical standpoint, aside from the stress involved, the dog will probably develop some sound phobias eventually, and its alert would not be so helpful if it decided that hiding under the bed would be safer than approaching its partner.

Stubby: The Ultimate Sound-Reactive Dog

Stubby is a shaggy, wire-haired, bobtailed dog that might have Schnauzer and Australian Shepherd in her ancestry—or, then again, maybe not. She learned sound alerting quickly, but was hypersensitive to the mood of whoever was training her, and would be hesitant in her alerting if she sensed any negative feelings from her trainer. On the other hand, she was empathetic and very responsive to positive feelings. Once out of the kennel environment and placed with an older woman with a calm lifestyle, her confidence grew, and she became an active, playful dog.

However, Stubby adjusted a little too well. Her partner, Jill, soon had an unusual complaint; Stubby was alerting her to all her household sounds, but also to everything happening in the whole apartment complex. It seemed as if every other minute Stubby was alerting Jill to things she didn't need to know about—but of course, she didn't know if Stubby's alerts were relevant until she got up and investigated each time. On the off chance that a visitor had arrived, Jill would open her door, only to see a visitor at the neighbor's apartment. She felt embarrassed, because this made the neighbors view her as a nosy snoop! She loved Stubby, but wondered if there was a way to tone down her workaholic Hearing Dog. At my suggestion, Jill stopped rewarding Stubby for alerting, but this made no difference. Stubby continued alerting Jill to everything she needed to know about, plus anything else that Stubby felt was of note. On one visit, I mentioned to Jill that Stubby still needed to practice with the smoke alarm and get rewards, because that was such an important sound. Jill replied that she hadn't practiced the smoke alarm in two years, but that Stubby had alerted her to a burning pan on the stove just the other week!

Stubby's alerting did lessen a bit, until one morning when she began alerting persistently although there was nothing happening.

Stubby acted worried and frantic, and would not leave Jill alone. She continued this behavior for eight hours straight, and Jill admitted she was getting frantic herself, wondering about her pet's strange behavior. At 5:04 p.m., the October '89 earthquake hit the Bay Area, and Stubby's actions were explained. Now, her partner, who promises to call the Hearing Dog Program if Stubby reports any other impending Big Ones, carefully watches Stubby's behavior!

Stubby is one of those fascinating dogs that I believe was simply born to be a Hearing Dog. Even without her earthquake-detecting talent, she would still be unusual, even compared to other Hearing Dogs. Her close bond with her partner, together with her natural reactivity to sounds, enabled her to put more effort and enthusiasm into her "job" than any dog that was merely following a trained routine.

Dogs that Alert to Sounds without Training

Hearing Dog training programs teach dogs to alert to sounds by a wide variety of methods, usually involving step-by-step teaching of the alerting behavior by the use of food, toys, or social rewards. This process takes months of intensive training. But every Hearing Dog trainer has heard many stories about amazing dogs that alert their owners to sounds without any formal training at all. I am often told by people, both hearing and deaf, that their dog runs back and forth between them and sounds, coming "to get them." The hearing owners are either amused or annoyed, but hearing-impaired owners marvel at how their dog could have trained itself. Although the excitement and interest shown by the owner are major factors in developing and reinforcing a dog's "self-trained" behavior, there are actually a number of instincts at work that help motivate such a dog and get the behavior started in the first place.

Hunting with the Pack

Dogs tend to mimic the behavior of their pack, synchronizing their activities. A major part of pack life is hunting, which involves running and exploring together. When the human pack members get up suddenly and rush toward sounds, dogs naturally join in "the hunt." I believe that when dogs run with people, they feel that they are hunting together in a pack, an activity that would fill many hours a day in the life of a wild canine, but is lacking in the life of most pets. This can be satisfying in itself, even if the dog has no desire to hunt telephones specifically. The dog will soon learn that certain sounds precede activity, and anticipate this, running to the sounds before the owner has reacted to them. When the owner inevitably ignores or doesn't hear a sound, the dog may feel frustrated, then approaches the owner to initiate the fun running activity. If the person then notices the sound and accompanies the excited dog to it, the dog is then being rewarded for its inadvertent alert, and the behavior will become a learned one. Some Hearing Dogs from herding breeds perceive the owner's movements as compliance with their herding efforts, and begin to herd their "sheep" obsessively to the phone or door—sometimes discovering that nipping will hasten the livestock's movements!

I first experienced the ability of dogs to learn to alert to sounds when, knowing only vaguely that there was a new thing called a "Hearing Dog," I taught my Yorkie, Niji, through this pack mentality to bark and run with me to the phone. Every time I could hear the phone, I ran to it wildly and encouraged him to chase me and bark. Since he was more motivated to chase and bark at me than by toys or food, this worked well, as I could hear his barking from a greater distance than I could hear the phone. (I also spent the next 13 years trying to untrain the barking!) His alert was of limited value when I couldn't see or hear him, but one day, as I was operating some loud machinery while making jewelry, I realized Niji was jumping on me and barking. As I turned to look at him, he dashed towards the phone, barking while looking back at me. I was really thrilled that he had thought to come and find me. I built a darkroom when I became interested in photography, and was amazed to find that Niji would scratch and jump against the door when the phone rang. Living alone in a loft in New York City, I often joined Niji in crouching and peering under my triple-barred door to see who was sneaking around the open building testing the locks, and this encouraged Niji to alert me more to the door. I taught Niji lots of tricks, but I could tell that his sound alerting abilities were far beyond tricks; there was really something special about him.

Many dogs learn to alert to sounds in this way. Dogs that are not sound reactive might only alert when feeling playful or when they have nothing more interesting to do, but they can certainly learn to alert to one or two sounds. Dogs that already were sound reactive will of course take to this inadvertent training quickly, and begin generalizing their behavior to other sounds that excite them or their owners. While hearing owners may discourage or ignore this behavior, hearing impaired owners will show thrilled appreciation to their amazing pet, reinforcing the behavior strongly. (Deaf people can be aware of sounds in many ways; through vibrations, flashing light devices, or associated visual cues; in addition, many Deaf people can hear at least some types of sounds. Therefore, this training can happen regardless of an owner's hearing ability.)

Defending Territory

Territorial dogs usually stay at the outer perimeters of their area when investigating sounds, and are reluctant to return to their owner, but territorial dogs that are also fearful may feel overwhelmed when facing an intrusion (such as a visitor) alone. This threat may cause them to retreat to find security from their owner or to recruit pack support against the danger. Since the owner is probably already on the way to the door, the dog's approach will inadvertently be rewarded by the chance to defend the territory with full pack support. Returning to the owner may then become an established behavior pattern. Such dogs may be useful to alert to doorbells and suspicious noises, but may or may not have the temperament to also alert to sounds like the telephone, smoke alarm, and timer, which are without relevance to territorial intrusion and therefore not interesting to the dog.

Quartering Behavior

Some dogs may exhibit quartering behavior (searching back and forth across an area) if they are of certain hunting breeds like spaniels. This behavior, if triggered by excitement, can lead to the dog's accidental approach to the owner, who may reward it for alerting to the sounds that triggered the excitement. Such dogs may display more circling or random rushing about than directed alerting, but their behavior can be just as useful in alerting to sounds.

Social Interaction

Dogs that are both sound reactive and highly socially interactive can learn to alert for slightly different reasons. If they are excited by sounds and investigate them, they will then find themselves separated from their owner, and their desire to interact will motivate them to return to the owner. The dog will continue to be in an excited state for as long as the sound continues to interest it. The owner's approval of the dog's alert will reward the dog with interaction, which it craves anyway, and the dog, still more excited, may then feel a need to approach the sound once again. If encouraged, this back-and-forth alerting behavior can become consistent and the dog will work reliably, learning to generalize its alert to many other sounds.

Dogs that do not show both sound reactivity and a high desire for social interaction are difficult to train. If they show only sound reactivity, they may orient or approach towards sounds, but they will not be motivated to approach their owner. The owner might notice this behavior, but dogs that are not socially interactive are less likely to be in visual range. A less interactive dog is also less suitable as a close companion. Equally difficult are dogs that show no sound reactivity but thrive on social rewards and would "do anything" for positive interaction. They would indeed do anything for their partner—except to leave their beloved owner's side in order to approach a sound.

I'm reminded of "Itty-Bitty." This seven-pound Chihuahua mix had the short legs and cuddly body shape of a hamster. She showed none of the typical Chihuahua suspicion of strangers, but loved everyone, especially the trainers. Her adoring gaze never wavered, whether she was sitting on my lap, or on the floor near the ringing phone. I thought that perhaps she could alert to sounds in a less energetic way than most Hearing Dogs, because there were several very elderly applicants for Hearing Dogs who all needed an "Itty-Bitty" rather than a bouncy young thing like the other dogs that were in training. Unfortunately, Itty-Bitty wouldn't even turn her head for sounds, because she went into a happy trance whenever she was touched, and if she wasn't being touched, she was making desperate eye contact in order to be picked up. Of course, there were people waiting in line for her to drop out of the program! Itty-Bitty found a home with people who appreciated her special breed, the "Lapland Lingerlonger."

Hearing Dogs that Alert to Sounds They Weren't Trained For

When a dog with the right temperament is by accident or design placed in the right environment with a partner who is tuned in to the dog, some kind of communication that leads to sound alerting is bound to grow. The possibilities are infinite. It would be easy to attribute this phenomenon of alerting to sounds they weren't trained for to generalization of training, in which a dog broadens its category of "alertable" sounds. But I have noticed that the less-talented dogs I've worked with rarely generalized their trained responses to include other sounds and were difficult even to train at all. I feel that the following dogs really were doing something special.

Kimba, a Cocker Spaniel, alerted his sleepy and reluctant partner, Sheila Ravenscroft, to wake up during a fire. Hours after the firemen had left and the fire put out, he alerted her again. Thinking he was still upset from all the commotion, she kept telling him to go back to sleep, until she realized he meant business. She got up and discovered that the fire had been smoldering in the attic and had flared up. The smoke alarm had been damaged in the first fire and removed, so how did Kimba know that the fire itself should be alerted to, despite the lack of beeping? While alerting her to the first fire, he also ran to the door of a room where the cat was shut in, and Sheila realized the cat was inside and rescued it. Nobody had trained Kimba to alert to the cat. Kimba's actions derived more from his personality and close relationship with Sheila than from the training he had received.

On a lighter note, Chloe, a Pekingese mix, alerts every time the cat wants to come in. Her partner, Ruth Jensen, hustles to the door expecting to find visitors, only to find her cat. Ruth says she is not really sure where she fits into this animal hierarchy, but she suspects it's near the bottom.

Scotty, a Terrier mix, wouldn't let Nancy Cummins, his partner, in the car. She was mystified until she realized it had a bad gasoline leak.

Trixie led her partner, Caroline, over and over again to a window where Caroline was sure nothing was happening—until she discovered there was an abandoned baby bird on the ground below. Trixie and Caroline raised the bird until it could fly.

Ruth Jensen and Chloe, who alerts Ruth when the cat wants in! (Photo by Dennard)

Jack Byers really appreciates his Hearing Dog, Clover, who alerts to an important sound he never trained her for—the radar detector in his car.

None of these were situations in which anyone would have expected alerting, yet the dogs were somehow motivated to communicate with their partners.

I'm sure that there are many more ways than I have described for dogs to "teach themselves" to alert to sounds. A high degree of sound-reactivity is not necessary for the dog to learn some alerting behavior, but the bottom line is that the dogs which *are* sound-reactive have limitless potential that can be developed simply by a close relationship between dog and owner, with no formal training or expertise needed.

Designing the Sound-Reactive Dog

If we could design a dog that was both sound reactive and suitable for the other Hearing Dog roles, we would need to start with an imaginary reactive dog. We would like to tailor this overall reactivity to our needs. Because we only desire sound-reactivity, we can specify that the dog be more reactive to sounds than to anything else. We then have a dog that, while reactive, shows fewer competing responses that distract it from its sound alerting work or hinder it in other roles. A moderate reactivity level would work better for the other two roles, as long as sound reactivity was high. Could selective breeding produce dogs that show high reactivity to sounds coupled with a low overall reactivity level? Only a breeding program could provide the answer to this question, but I feel that it would be possible.

One bit of evidence that convinces me is the temperament of sighthounds and scenthounds. It has always seemed paradoxical that the "lazy" hound dog on the porch could also hunt raccoons all night without quitting. But perhaps the dog's reactivity is expressed mainly when stimulated by scent. It would then appear non-reactive except when hunting. Sighthounds also seem calm, except when they explode in a chase after prey. It might be possible to selectively breed a Hearing Dog with a similarly fine-tuned reaction to sounds. Such a dog would be easy to live with and take in public places, filling all three roles effortlessly.

Chapter Three
How Reactivity Affects Hearing Dog Potential

Reactivity is an integral requirement for the sound-alerting role in Hearing Dogs, but its intense effects can be confusing when trying to understand temperament. Both desirable and undesirable traits are far more easily stimulated in reactive dogs, so their importance is also magnified. Many traits are harmless when exaggerated by reactivity, but when a reactive dog shows potentially dangerous behavior, it should be taken seriously, not lightly discounted with, "Oh, he's just overly reactive."

The optimum levels of all the traits depend on the skill of the partner; some traits that are undesirable can be controlled with good handling, but emerge strongly with inexperienced handling. In fact, many training and handling techniques can actually cause very undesirable behavior in reactive dogs. The ideal Hearing Dog has a specific sound-reactive temperament free of fearfulness in which submissiveness and social interactivity are foremost.

Reactivity and a dog's activity level are very different traits and shouldn't be confused. Activity levels are internally generated and not as influenced by external factors, whereas reactivity is more influenced by external factors. Distinguishing the two can be difficult. Activity levels and reactivity interact to influence how well dogs can perform the sound alerting role. In the companion and public access roles, highly active dogs can be harder to manage.

On the surface, active dogs appear to be good training candidates. After all, Hearing Dogs need to be active in order to enjoy sound alerting. Active dogs are also more likely to be awake and alert when sounds happen. But high activity alone, without sound reactivity, will cause a dog to be extremely difficult to train. Obedience training and sound alerting both depend upon cues that interrupt ongoing behaviors, but active dogs are not easily distracted from their program of activity. Constant refocusing may be necessary just to get the dog to remain aware of the training situation. Stays are difficult for these dogs, because their internal impulse to move around overcomes their weak awareness of commands. Reactive dogs also have trouble with stays, but for a different reason altogether; their strong impulse to react to all stimuli in their environment can overpower their trained responses to commands.

Dogs with both high levels of activity and reactivity can be incredible workers, never missing a sound, perhaps working well for the lifetime of the dog, with minimal maintenance training. But spending a lifetime with such a dog might make its partner long to live in a soundless, dog-free world. They are not easy to live with!

The ideal combination for good working ability depends on the human partner's lifestyle, energy level, and sound alerting needs. My Hearing Dog, Snap, is an example of good balance for me. Snap is a highly reactive American Eskimo. She is friendly and sociable, and her activity level is moderate. She is easily stimulated by any sound, but never acts restless. She is wildly active when stimulated by games or toys, and loves to run when outside, but calm when I am not interacting with her. She reacts as strongly to my moods as she does to sounds, and her behavior mimics mine; she is very empathic, and synchronized with everything I do. When I am active or hyper, she is interactive to the point of being pesky. When I am quietly occupied, she rests. Still, even when sleeping, she will awaken to alert to sounds.

Many people use the term "hyperactive" in a casual way to describe a highly active dog. True hyperactivity is different. These dogs seem to have a neurological abnormality. They cannot be focused for long enough for learning to occur, and their activity appears undirected toward any particular goal. This should not be confused with the quartering behavior of some hunting dogs, which can seem like purposeless wandering until they are seen in a field with game birds. Attempts to train hyperactive dogs often result in frustrated trainers who resort to escalating corrections. Unlike normal dogs, these corrections do not influence the dog to change its behavior; instead, the hyperactive dog becomes confused due to its learning disability. It tries to escape the situation, becoming more and more upset and still learning nothing.

Stress

Stress is defined by Roger Abrantes in *Dog Language: An Encyclopedia of Canine Behavior* as "a physiological reaction to external factors which prepares an animal for dealing with extreme situations. When a dog senses danger, stress prepares it for fight or flight...Stress is a healthy reaction from the organism and serves self-preservation." Dogs that have less fearfulness also have less perception of danger, and thus less stress.

Reactive dogs respond to stress as they do to anything else—with exaggerated, hair-trigger reactions, which brings out unexpected behaviors, caused by the dredging up of normally hidden layers of buried traits. It is important to teach reactive dogs cues that promote calming, such as a word like "settle" associated with massage, or use the many fascinating natural calming signals Turid Rugaas describes in her book, *On Talking Terms With Dogs: Calming Signals*.

Age and Reactivity

A younger animal has more potential to be socialized than an older one, but it is also harder to evaluate temperaments in younger pups. Many temperament traits like fear and aggression only appear or intensify after the first few months of life. Dogs show more reactivity as puppies, less at maturity. Many dogs are dumped in shelters at around seven to nine months, once the owner realizes that their untrained puppy is growing into its behavior problems, not out of them. Dogs of this age are very trainable, though immature. For Hearing Dogs, age one to one and a half years old is preferable, particularly if there is no time to intensively socialize a puppy. But if the dog has the right temperament, not much else seems to matter. I've adopted many dogs whose history was known to be totally inadequate for the social needs of a potential Hearing Dog, and they have been happily adaptable to any situation. Age also doesn't seem to matter as far as sound-alerting training goes. Older dogs learn more slowly, and get confused when asked to change long-established behavior patterns, but given the right temperament, even dogs five to seven years old have trained quickly.

Size and Reactivity

Most Hearing Dogs that I've worked with have been in the size range of ten to forty pounds. This has to do both with owner preference and with how temperament and size interact. Smaller dogs fit in better with smaller living places, older people with age-related hearing losses, and public access situations. This is a fortunate coincidence, because it is actually easier to find small dogs that show Hearing Dog temperament. Smaller breeds are more fre-

Can a Hearing Dog be too tiny? Four-pound Tribble looks for a treat as the phone rings. Partner Betty Lou Asch reports that Tribble always wakes up even from a sound sleep to alert.

quently designed to be companion-oriented, and are more often reactive and active. Larger breeds more often fulfill guard roles and tend to be less reactive and more aggressive. Mixes derived from large or small breeds reflect their heritage. When large dogs with correct temperament are found, they are proportionately more difficult to control, exercise, and handle, due to their intensity and initiative. A ten-pound dog energetically ricocheting around the house is amusing, but a sixty-pounder doing the same thing would be, well, a "problem dog." However, a Hearing Dog's size is really irrelevant. If a dog can wake us up in the event of a fire (even a teeny dog can leap on the bed via a footstool and lick our face till we wake up), then it's the right size.

Social Interactivity

Hearing dogs should show a preference for interacting with people over most other activities—except, of course, for investigating sounds. Otherwise, they may prefer to stay in laps rather than alert. Such dogs are cooperative in performing many behaviors for social rewards—except for leaving their beloved owner to go to sounds! An interactive dog continues to find the relationship with its partner the most interesting thing in its life, more interesting than exploring, urine marking, playing with other dogs, hunting, and other normal dog behaviors. Temperament testing in this book is primarily designed to find this type of dog; no amount of training is going to turn an independent explorer into a devoted, interactive companion.

Mamie Williams describes her Hearing Dog Chia's attitude to visitors: "Chia loves it when visitors come to stay at the house, especially family. Over time, I have learned that Chia gets a little wired the first few days of visitors and she sleeps restlessly, moving to sounds that are unfamiliar. What I didn't know, until my sister and several other guests told me, was that Chia was going into their rooms at night to check on them. She doesn't hop on the bed, or bark, she just walks up to the bed near their head as if to see if they are breathing. She will make the rounds from room to room if there is more than one person here at a time. I didn't know, because she wasn't waking me up to tell me anything was wrong!"

Dogs that are very reactive and interactive can be perceived as either annoying pests and intrusive, or as marvelously intuitive and empathetic, depending on the person's viewpoint. People who enjoy the intense relationships that these dogs thrive on find that their companion has a limitless potential to make emotional connections. Many people actually become anxious and upset when around this type of dog, and find they are happier with a more independent pet dog and an arsenal of sound-alerting gadgets.

Children and Reactive Dogs

Selecting a dog with the right temperament for living with children presents some challenges. Most parents seek a dog with a companion temperament (see Chapter 5), although dogs of many different temperaments can be successful if properly raised from a young age with children. Brian Kilcommon's book, *Childproofing Your Dog*, offers excellent practical advice, including how to dog-proof your child! I often read very scary statements about certain breeds, claiming that they are "good family dogs," simply because the dog, with proper raising and training, can become accustomed to the family's own children. Then comes the

Golden Retriever mix Mitzi only has eyes for partner James Reeves. James' left eye is still swollen from a mugging attack in which Mitzi grabbed the mugger's sleeve and frightened him away. Mitzi is normally calm and trusting with strangers but reacted instantly to real danger. (Photo by Dennard)

inevitable qualification—that the dog may react negatively to strange children. To me, a "family dog" is one that fits in with a family's activities, which include unpredictable strange children visiting. A Hearing Dog should also be tolerant of the often-inappropriate behavior of the children it encounters in public places.

From a dog's perspective on humans, women are the least frightening, men more frightening, and children completely terrifying. Dogs that are fearful of people in general will be very sensitive to the inadvertent violation by children of every canine social rule. Staring, threatening gestures, sexual harassment (many dogs interpret hugging as mounting attempts), loud weird vocalizations, predator- or prey-mimicking movements, and disrespect of all physical boundaries make it a miracle that any dogs like children at all. The dogs that do are often companion-temperament dogs that show very low levels of any survival instincts.

Cisco, a Cocker mix, that is partnered with Amy Wooten, a kindergarten teacher, seems incapable of perceiving any threat or danger from children's behavior, even a large group of them. He seemed to love children, but Amy was cautioned to keep him from getting stressed by groups of kids when she began taking him to school with her. Amy reported back that Cisco was indeed stressed, but only when she tried to separate him from the children. Unless he could be with them every minute, he trembled anxiously and stared longingly at them during class activities that didn't include him. Amy takes him to school every Friday as a reward for the children; she says that if she brought him every day, both the kids and Cisco would be too excited for her to get any teaching done.

It's too bad that all children cannot handle dogs as well as these young Deaf and hard-of-hearing volunteers. Experienced with their teacher's dog, they were experts at teaching new Hearing Dogs to enjoy handling by kids. Summer is inhibited and fearful, but these girls touch her so delicately that she stays rather than escapes.

Selecting a Hearing Dog becomes tricky when trying to find a dog that can both perform sound alerting and get along with children. The primary challenge is reactivity. Because children are so stimulating, reactive dogs with any undesirable temperament traits will be easily triggered to display them. The conflicting requirements of a highly reactive, active dog for sound alerting and a calm, non-reactive companion for a family means that compromises may have to be made.

After some disillusionment, several mothers have told me that prospective Hearing Dog partners who have kids should be forewarned that getting a new Hearing Dog is more like having an additional young child around than the four-legged babysitter they had hoped for. They had confused the behavior of a dog trained to alert to a baby's cry with the ability to make Lassie-like judgments about child safety issues. I sometimes suggest to very busy, overburdened families that a calm pet dog, together with some sophisticated flashing light and vibration systems, might be a good alternative to a Hearing Dog. Other families feel that the rewards of having a Hearing Dog are well worth the extra effort.

Since the previous experiences of most shelter dogs are unknown, for safety reasons they should be considered "not good with children" until proven otherwise. I know of one shelter that flat-out refuses to adopt any dog to families with children under four years old, no matter how well the dog seems to behave around kids. Their very responsible attitude is that they cannot predict the dog's behavior if they do not know its history. I know I have trained many dogs that I felt were great with children and often been proven wrong, although luckily no bites beyond a scratch have occurred. Very few dogs have both the right temperament and have received the socialization and training required for living around children. The dog I would pick for children would have a very passive response to handling, the type of dog that "melts" when touched.

Quite often, dogs are surrendered at shelters for problems with children that are unrelated to aggression. Missy, a tiny Japanese Chin, was almost passed over at a shelter by Ralph Dennard due to a report from the former owner stating that Missy had problems with children. Luckily, the report specified "knocks kids down." This ludicrous charge was indeed true; Missy likes kissing people on the nose, and has an incredible ability to leap. I have no doubt that many toddlers bit the dust when Missy flew through the air. Luckily, her partner can easily control Missy's kissing mania.

Character Traits and Reactivity: Dominance and Submissiveness

Evaluating the dominance and submissiveness levels of dogs is essential in matching a Hearing Dog with a potential partner, and, of course, these levels will be much more on display with a reactive dog. The terms "dominant" and "submissive" both have negative connotations. They bring to mind images of a dictatorial, bullying sadist and a subservient, masochistic brown-noser. More accurate terms for "dominant" in human terms would be: "assertive, secure, leader, charismatic, controlling." More accurate ones for "submissive" might be: "cooperative, acquiescent, follower, respectful, insecure." I would prefer to substitute the terms "assertive" and "acquiescent," but find it easier to stick with the common usage of "dominant" and "submissive."

Dominant dogs impact their world,

SF-SPCA employee Joanne McGarry and shelter dog Sam. This Springer shows the level of trust, interactivity, and enjoyment of physical contact that make a great Hearing Dog. When I test a dog that "melts" into me like this, I know I have a good one. (Photo by Glassner, SF-SPCA)

rather than let their world impact them. Challenges are perceived as enjoyable; the act of overcoming obstacles is self-rewarding. Obstacles may be environmental, such as fences or agility equipment, or mental, such as social status.

The following description of wolf behavior is derived from Roger Abrantes' book, *Evolution of Canine Social Behavior*.

As aggressive social predators, wolves gain several advantages from pack life. Pack life allows them to hunt larger prey, increases the survival rate of puppies, and protects them from strange wolves. However, competition between all of the pack members for the resources of food and breeding partners exists in a fragile balance within this cooperative strategy. The goal is to pass on genes, and food and mates are the ultimate key to survival. Abrantes defines aggression as the drive to eliminate competition in order to survive. Since pack members are each other's main competitors, they are the triggers for aggression. Fear is defined as the drive to react to any threat to survival, by escaping, freezing, or the use of aggressive behavior if the other two strategies do not work. Fear and aggression led to the evolution of ritualized social behavior that allows competition without destroying the pack structure. Dominance is a ritualized behavior motivated by competition, and submission is a ritualized behavior motivated by threat. Dominant strategies work by controlling the resources that make reproduction possible, whereas submissive strategies avoid conflict with more powerful pack mates, getting the benefits of safe pack life while waiting for conditions to change. For instance, a young pack member could at first only function within the pack by adopting a submissive strategy, but as it matures and builds alliances, and others decline through age or injury, it may be able to adopt the dominant strategy it needs to reproduce. Although any wolf might choose either strategy at any time depending on the circumstances, there are individual variations in tendency toward dominance and submission. .

The effect of domestication on dogs causes imbalances and the dilution of basic wolf behavior, but dogs have also been selected for compatibility with human packs. Dogs that tend to use submissive strategies to get through life are more desirable as companions; they avoid conflict, surrender resources, and are less likely to use aggressive behavior. Dogs that prefer dominant strategies require constant management if they are to fit in a human pack. Either type can be a superb companion; it simply depends on the owner's tendency to be dominant or submissive, their ability to receive and transmit canine communication signals, and their commitment to making the relationship work.

But far better for a companion is a dog that shows *neither* intense dominant nor submissive behavior. How can this be? The answer is that by lowering the levels of both fearfulness and aggression in some domesticated dogs, the basic motivations for dominance and submission are removed. Lowered aggression means less awareness of competition from pack members so the dog does not show dominant behavior even in situations where survival issues would dictate its use. Lowered fearfulness means less motivation to show submissive behavior, since threat cannot be perceived. The dog with both low aggression and fearfulness coexists with its canine or human pack members in a rather mild-mannered, simplistic way, and has no strong awareness or reaction to threat from strange dogs or people. It certainly could not survive in the wild, but its companion traits are now the ones that lead to reproductive success in its new environment. Compared to wolves and primeval dogs, its behavior is incredibly diluted.

Problems arise when a dog has very high aggression and very low fearfulness, making it unable to cooperate within a pack, or high fearfulness and low aggression, making it constantly stressed and unable to function socially. Variations of these imbalances occur frequently when dogs are bred together without regard to the desired temperament of the offspring.

As far as I can tell, displaying aggression is a very rewarding emotion for dogs. Because aggression is such a problem in human behavior, we think of it as bad and all cultures have developed ways to control and properly direct its expression. Cultural standards prevent us from realizing that aggression is an intensely rewarding feeling of power and control over our own survival. Henry Kissinger confused the issue when he said, "Power is the ultimate aphrodisiac." Because both sexuality and aggression lead to our survival and of our species we are all wired to feel intense reward from both.

Proper training and socializing techniques used in puppyhood can shape canine behavior in the same way. There are many remedial and control methods that have been developed for adult dogs, but there is no substitute for early conditioning. When testing shelter dogs, one must assume that proper raising has not happened, and be prepared to discover that the dog may be in the shelter for reasons of aggression. Testing for this requires an investigative attitude on the part of the tester. While " looking for the best" in each dog, for safety reasons it is also essential to look for the worst.

Although non-reactive dogs that are dominant may be controlling in a calmly manipulative way, reactive dogs that are also dominant seem to have "a chip on their shoulder." They march around looking for trouble, and if they are aggressive as well, may use preemptive strikes if they perceive insolence brewing in their canine or human pack.

Most dog trainers would label as "dominant" a dog that begs or physically pushes its owner for food, who attempts to control all activities of its human pack, bullies them into playing or petting, and is always first on the scene of any event. Interestingly, these are the very behaviors that people appreciate and encourage when training dogs to alert to sounds. A Hearing Dog needs to be strongly motivated to interact with its partner, demanding interaction, not waiting passively for cues. It feels rewarded when its partner follows its lead, whether playing or alerting to sounds. It is first to alert when visitors arrive, and is gratified when the human pack follows it to the door. When the phone or smoke alarm rings, the dog is able to get the pack up and moving, possibly dispensing toys or treats. Pushing people physically to get them moving is fun for this dog, and perhaps viewed by the dog as a playful way of testing dominance.

Obviously, a dog that is dominant and bossy is going to take very well to a career of sound alerting, being self-motivated and enjoying its role immensely. When it alerts to sounds it will be rewarded for its bossy behavior; however, when it attempts to be bossy in other ways, its partner may attempt to correct or control it. Obviously, there could be difficulty in managing a dog that is getting so many mixed messages about its role in the household. Dominant dogs need partners who can give them proper leadership if their sound-alerting talents are to be useful. Otherwise, they will fail in companion and possibly public access roles.

Bartie, ten-pound Yorkingese, lives with his partner and her two grandkids, one of whom is autistic. In addition to the usual sounds, he runs to alert his partner if the girls are arguing. He also knows all the behaviors that get the girls in trouble with their grandmother, and any time they break house rules he runs to her. He is not consciously being a "tattletale"; he has simply learned what events cause his partner to run to the kids. Like many dogs, he also enjoys joining the pack leader in disciplining other pack members. (My Yorkie made my cat's life difficult by barking at her whenever she did anything "not allowed," even if I was not present.) Bartie's interest in controlling pack interactions is useful to his partner, who can feel comfortable not having to supervise her grandchildren constantly.

Submissiveness

Dominant dogs do not show leadership only by continually enforcing their role. Research on wolf behavior shows that dominant wolves are also supported by pack members who continually demonstrate their own submissive roles. Called "active submission," these rituals result in mutual cooperation that helps things flow smoothly and avoids fighting. Submission is often confused with fear, but submissive behavior is a specific appeasement ritual that lessens aggressive behavior by pack members and strengthens social bonds. Dogs with a tendency to behave submissively avoid social conflict, and they are easier for humans to control. They accept leadership easily, and find comfort and securi-

ty in letting their owner make decisions. If they are forced into a leadership role, they will fill it, but also
sometimes show stressed and bizarre
behavior as well.

Some people are also uncomfortable with leadership roles, and find
comfort and security in having other
people, or dogs, make decisions for
them. They feel less stressed when
they do not have to constantly make
decisions, but can encounter problems when their dog takes advantage
of its dominant position to enforce its
decisions by biting. People who own
dominant dogs need to make an effort
to give at least the impression of
being a decision-maker, and this is a
lot of work for people who are not
naturally bossy. Such people, by
selecting submissive dogs, can save
themselves a lot of trouble. Even
when submissive dogs get bossy due
to a lack of leadership, they rarely
show problems as severe as really
dominant ones do.

*Tasha submissively approaches a tolerant Jekyll.
When matched with humans, both these attitudes
make for good companion suitability.*

Many dog trainers, being dominant types of people (or else they wouldn't have found
controlling and changing the behavior of dogs and owners to be an interesting activity),
do not understand submissive types of people, and are constantly directing these dog owners to behave in assertive ways that are contrary to their personality style. Luckily, there
are many training methods available that are more enjoyable to non-dominant people.
Quite a few dog trainers would deny that they are "control freaks," obsessed by dominating dogs. Interestingly, these same trainers often make it their life's work to control and
change the behavior of other dog trainers who follow training philosophies they disagree
with!

Dogs that behave too submissively with a bossy dog trainer rarely show this when
paired with a submissive owner. Many problems like submissive urination can magically
disappear, although other problems can magically appear as well. "The Worm" was our
nickname for a very meek little German Shepherd mix. She spent most of her time with
us crawling and leaking submissively. She was good at sound alerting if every effort was
made to avoid accidentally intimidating her, which took a huge effort by the trainers. The
Worm was nervous outside on leash, and tended to creep down the street timidly, lagging
behind the trainers. She was also a very empathic and relational dog, and it seemed she
would be perfect for a gentle, shy woman who had made it very clear that she would never
"abuse" a dog by correcting it in any way. After a few days with her new partner, a miraculous change occurred, and I was shocked by the sight of The Worm confidently march-

ing ahead of her partner, who complained that she was being dragged down the street by this uncontrollable dog! The Worm was as sweet as ever, but no longer submissively urinated. Although her partner always did have trouble making The Worm behave properly, the dog never showed any aggressive or really difficult behavior.

Submissive dogs behave differently than do dominant ones in sound alerting. They are more easily inhibited by their partner's body language or by tense social situations like family quarrels. Still, they enjoy alerting intensely, becoming excited by the chance to interact. They may even get a big ego boost by being allowed to act a little dominantly, and as a result, gain in confidence. Submissive dogs will often work hard to gain social rewards, and are empathic to their owner's moods.

Care must be taken not to inhibit reactive submissive dogs in their sound alerting work. Copper, a spaniel mix, suddenly stopped alerting to the phone. He had always been reliable, and Ann Nally, his partner, couldn't understand it. He now even seemed fearful of the phone ring. On thinking about it, she realized that she had been having problems with an insurance company, having tense discussions on the phone with them, and had even begun to get upset when expecting these phone calls. Her dog interpreted Ann's emotional state as intimidating, and correctly associated it with the phone ring, since his behavior to her otherwise was as trusting as usual. When she made a determined effort to act cheerful when the phone rang, and put Copper in the yard when expecting a difficult call so he would not hear her talking, he soon returned to his former happy alerting behavior.

Handling Reactive Dogs Physically

Many people mistakenly assume that a dog that is eager to be petted and loves to be massaged and scratched also should be easy to handle. They are often surprised when the dog snaps if touched in the "wrong" place or by the "wrong" person. They wonder why they can pet the dog's muzzle with their hand, but are not allowed to open its mouth to check out its teeth. This dog has a specific set of conditions that must be met to fit its category of "pleasurable handling." What people often overlook is that a dog who actively seeks out petting, scratching, or massage may perceive tight hugging or holding for grooming as totally negative experiences. These are perceived as restraining, a very different category in the dog's perception. Restraint prevents freedom and is often associated with unpleasant experiences. Dogs may groom other dogs, but they never restrain them unless they are dominating, disciplining, or fighting them, and restraint by environmental influences (entangling bushes, collapsing burrows, predators) is always a severe threat to survival. A physically restrained dog might struggle or bite in out of panic, or confidently attempt to get free by threatening or biting; either reac-

Ren is very reactive, but enjoys any contact. He trusts this stranger totally.

tion rules it out for the companion or public access roles of a Hearing Dog.

Dogs can learn to accept restraint and even perceive it as enjoyable. Teaching a dog to enjoy being hugged is essential if it is to live with small children, and many dogs do learn that it's just another of those silly things humans like to do. Restraint might make a dog uncomfortable, but dogs that enjoy social interaction and physical contact find any interaction so rewarding that minor discomfort triggers no fear or resentment. Dogs that prefer contact do not demand the usual canine personal space around them. Their trust and acceptance give them great potential as companions. They also find the physical contact in sound alerting very self-motivating.

Reactive dogs respond to physical contact in complicated ways. They may be hypersensitive to it, either by struggling to avoid it, or licking, jumping, and pawing to receive it. How they are handled makes a big difference in their behavior, so care should be taken in interpreting their reactions too hastily. If they do not desire handling, they may unfairly be labeled hysterical or overly aggressive, and if they do desire it, they may be categorized as demanding pests. Although difficult, it's important to learn to read their actual feelings and deal appropriately with their behavior.

Handling Reactive Dogs Mentally

Reactive dogs require different handling and obedience training approaches than do other dogs. They can be confusing creatures. Although they are quick to notice cues, they are equally quick to notice and react to everything else that is going on. Typically, a quick response to a learned command may cause the trainer to believe that the dog is now reliably trained, but the dog is so easily distracted that the trainer interprets the dog's subsequent failure to obey as willful disobedience. The dog then reacts intensely to the negative reactions from the trainer. Trainer and dog may escalate their miscommunication increasingly, ending up far from the goal, in what is known to some of us as the "Train Wreck." It might then seem as if the dog hasn't learned anything, but it actually has: it's learned to associate the training situation with feelings of conflict and frustration. This will be obvious upon beginning the next training session, when the dog will behave even more reactively than usual. The trainer may complicate things by also being prepared to feel conflict and frustration in working with this "difficult" dog. The escalation of mutual reactions and stress causes the dog to show unexpected behaviors so that submissive urination, freezing, panic, biting, escape attempts, over-excited playfulness, or aggression may appear "out of the blue."

These behaviors may be due to temperament problems, but often are side effects of insensitive handling. A good trainer will distinguish this difference. Reactive dogs need trainers with good reflexes who understand dog behavior. If the dog exhibits negative behavior during training, the method being used should be evaluated to see whether it is actually causing or even intensifying the problem. The trainer needs to stay calm and focused, and to help the dog stay calm and focused as well.

The lightning-fast reaction time and exaggerated responses of reactive dogs can make training them similar to playing a video game that's always at a level a little too high for your skill level—but it's thrilling when just for a few seconds everything's in synch. The ability to exist in the exact moment and deal continuously with reality, not fantasy, is essential in all good training, but especially with reactive dogs. Likewise, training plans need to be thought out ahead of time, with contingencies predicted and backup systems in place. All training methods have "side effects." These are the results of either unintended or shortsighted training, which then conflict with later training goals. Foresight in planning determines whether these side effects will be stumbling blocks to be later overcome, or building blocks for later progress.

Anyone who wants a Hearing Dog should be prepared to make efforts to understand that although a reactive dog may not fit their perception of an easygoing companion, there are many compensations for the extra effort and dedication required. Acute awareness, emotional intensity, and joy in every moment of living are some of the unique qualities that they possess and are willing to share.

Distractibility, the trait that is so annoying in obedience training, is actually the valuable attribute that causes the dog to interrupt its normal behavior to alert to an unexpected telephone ring or smoke alarm. In everyday life, the dog appears to have a short attention span. It does not. If no other stimulus intruded, the dog would stay focused on one activity as long as any other dog. But because it reacts to everything that happens, it can give the impression of a dog that lacks concentration due to a learning disability.

Initiative

A dog with initiative will *initiate* behavior, and in sound alerting, this is our goal. Initiative is easy to see in a bossy dog who constantly attempts to maneuver humans into behaving for the dog's benefit, but it can be equally strong in a submissive dog who has the same goals, yet uses more subtle means to achieve them. Many very "wimpy" Hearing Dogs have shown amazing initiative in unusual situations in which one would have never expected a dog to respond at all.

In many other forms of dog training, the dog responds to cues from humans. In sound alerting, the Hearing Dog is responding to unpredictable cues from the environment and then cueing humans. Only dogs with initiative will continue to alert under the distracting and confusing conditions every Hearing Dog faces. Sometimes the dog is even corrected for trying to alert, because in real life we are always occupied with some activity, and the dog must interrupt us. I'm reminded of a mom with a new baby, whose gentle, inhibited Hearing Dog (chosen for his suitability with children) stopped alerting her. She interpreted his behavior as jealousy towards the baby, but it turned out that she had discouraged the dog if he alerted when she was holding the baby. Naturally, he had to learn not to scratch or bump the baby, but her worried behavior had discouraged the dog to the point where he ceased alerting at all. A dog with more initiative might have solved the problem on its own.

Dogs that appear to lack enough initiative should not be faulted too much during testing. Stress and fear inhibit overall display of *any* behavior, and a dog might not show initiative until it has a good relationship with a partner. While an overtly dominant human will certainly inhibit the dog, any stranger, even a submissive one, might have the same inhibiting effect on a dog, since the dog has not yet evaluated the stranger's social status or potential threat. Until it does, its safest route is to inhibit itself and wait. Dogs with inhibited temperaments often are in a constant state of inhibition unless released, whereas most other dogs are uninhibited at all times unless inhibited by a specific command.

Observing groups of dogs makes it clear that showing initiative is a punishable offense, perceived as a challenge by more dominant dogs. A lower ranking dog may initiate behavior in a submissive way, testing the waters, and the dominant dog may then accept the invitation to hunt or play, but any brash, decisive initiation of activity often stimulates the dominant dog to act aggressively.

Initiative is seen most clearly when dogs respond to alerts they have never been trained to alert to. Jill is a Border Collie that I had a lot of doubts about. She was submissive and easily inhibited, and her sound work showed lack of initiative. On the other hand, she was affectionate with kids, learned quickly, and liked everyone. She was placed with a Deaf man who had a hearing wife and toddler son. They were expecting a baby as well, so a dog that liked kids was really important. Jill fit in well and was good with the toddler, but she was hesitant to alert the husband to sounds when he was sleeping. He was a deep sleeper and didn't wake up easily. Jill would instead alert the wife, who could hear perfectly well. The night the mom came home with their new son, she was exhausted, and fell into a deep sleep. She realized that Jill was alerting her; she didn't hear anything, and tried to go back to sleep. Jill continued to wake her, going back and forth from the crib, and she finally woke up enough to follow her. The baby was blue and not breathing. Luckily, his mother was able to clear his airway and he began breathing again.

Jill had received no training to alert to a baby's crying. In any case, this baby was not crying, but perhaps gasping a little. The baby had only come home that day, so I wonder how Jill would have known which baby sounds were unusual and which were normal. Did the baby sound like a puppy in trouble? I'm always telling mothers who want a Hearing Dog that Lassie is fictitious and that a Hearing Dog is not going to save their kids from danger or know to get mom when they are in trouble, but Jill's behavior gave me second thoughts. What made Jill decide to alert will always be a mystery, but the other important part of the story to me is that she tried so hard to alert her sleepy owner. From her timid behavior during training, I would never have predicted this. Perhaps her new family had built up her confidence and security so that she could act with true initiative on what she thought was important.

Resiliency

The ability to bounce back from negative experiences is important for any dog that will experience more than the quietest of lifestyles. It's one of the traits most valued by dog trainers. "Hard" and "soft" are used to refer to a dog's level of resiliency, but also describe other traits such as dominance and submissiveness. Resiliency is more than just habituation; truly resilient dogs seem to gain confidence with every new experience.

Lack of resilience, on the other hand, means that a dog builds negative impressions rather than growing in confidence. If a dog doesn't bounce back every time it is upset, it is instead registering yet another situation that it will try to avoid in the future. In trying to find the best techniques to teach a dog, the trainer sometimes first discovers what doesn't work, then tries other methods. Non-resilient dogs stop enjoying the training situation after one or two false starts by the trainer. By the time the trainer discovers the best way to teach the dog, its attitude to the trainer and the training situation may be very negative.

The term "forgiveness" specifically describes resiliency and applies to social interactions. I've often tested dogs that trusted me until I did something they didn't enjoy, such as handling their feet, restraining them, or tugging on their leash. Their attitude then changed dramatically. They would give me a hard, suspicious look, pull out their mental "little black book," look up my name, and cross it out. From then on, I might as well stop testing; no forgiveness was imminent. These dogs showed no resilience to slight stress.

On the other hand, dogs that are too resilient may have a problem in that they avoid only the most severe of negative experiences. This makes it hard for them to avoid danger, and training them can be difficult. Here, too, dogs with too much resilience do well in sound alerting, but are difficult in companion or public access roles.

Resiliency is important in sound alerting. One Hearing Dog was frightened when a wobbly table made a phone fall to the floor. She took months to recover, and would never again approach a phone on a low table like the one that wobbled. The phone was placed on the floor, and lots of rehabilitation was necessary to solve her new fear of the ringing phone. Sound-alerting training is sometimes full of inadvertent negatives; a practice smoke alarm held too close to the dog's ear when it suddenly blares out, timers slip out of the trainers hands and hits the dog on the head, people thrash about when the dog tries to wake them up, and so on. To continue to find sound alerting fun, dogs really need to trust their partner's good intentions and bounce back from accidents.

I often see dogs with a known history of neglect or abuse that recover quickly when placed in a good environment. These dogs show incredible resilience. Shaggy is a good example. Matted, thin, and fearful of restraint, his first reactions to being on leash were extreme panic and thrashing if the collar tightened, and he would shoot backwards or forwards to avoid enclosed places he felt were scary. These are responses that usually mean a failing grade, but because Shaggy responded so well to jollying, and would snap out of his fearful state if given enthusiastic cheerleading, I adopted him myself. I kept working with him, although I was often discouraged by setbacks, and exhausted by having to be so maniacally happy whenever I was training him. After a few months, he became a different dog, almost too enthusiastic to control, and so eager to get his chain collar and leash on that he needed extra training to put his head through on his own instead of bouncing up and down. His former pawing behavior at the hated leash became transformed into a manipulatively cute handshake and pawing for attention. His original behavior was similar to hundreds of shelter dogs I had had to leave behind, but his resiliency gave an important clue to his ultimate potential.

Stability

Stable dogs are enjoyable companions both at home and in public. The term refers to predictable, positive behavior, which allows the dog's partner to easily anticipate the dog's reactions, knowing when to relax and when extra control may be needed.

Reactive dogs are often unfairly labeled as "unstable." I believe there is a big difference between the two. "Unstable" implies that the dog is unpredictable in behavior. For example, dogs that bite when fearful are often classified as unstable, even if their biting behavior is all too predictable! Reactive dogs are not necessarily unpredictable, it's just that their reactions happen quickly, and only expert trainers can accurately analyze their motivations and predict their reactions to stimuli.

I prefer to use "unstable" for dogs whose behavior results from some neurological or abuse problem. I have encountered quite a few dogs that display bizarre and contradictory behaviors in short spaces of time, or whose behavior seems unconnected to reality. These dogs may have a medical problem and need to be treated by a veterinary behavior specialist, or possibly euthanized. In addition, dogs that have been abused may display learned reactions that mimic very unstable behavior. One may never find out what stimulus has triggered such a reaction, so in these cases it seems appropriate to classify the dog as unstable.

Some dogs are both reactive and unstable. This is one of the worst combinations that can be seen in a dog, and such dogs can be very dangerous. When unusual behavior is seen in reactive dogs, the cause often turns out to be an unstable temperament made more obvious by severe stress.

Fearfulness

Fear is an important survival trait in wild animals. Many wild animals exhibit a general fear of anything novel, termed "neophobia." This useful trait ensures that the animal can avoid many dangers without having to risk its life through a trial-and-error process every time it encounters something new (Fox). After all, anything unfamiliar is potentially more dangerous than the familiar things which it already knows how to safely deal with.

Domestication can result in either high or low levels of fearfulness, because of selective breeding for different functions that dogs perform. A very tiny, almost invisible, amount of fearfulness is necessary in herding, hunting, alarm function dogs. We simply label it differently, calling it caution, wariness, or suspicion.

This very unpredictable dog literally does not know what it is going to do next. It shows a mixture of fearful and aggressive signals, and was evaluated by several trainers as being truly unstable.

Without this, herding and hunting dogs might be injured by large livestock or prey, and alarm dogs would be incapable of perceiving danger. Fearfulness also varies from breed to breed and individually within breeds. It appears more during the stages of growth in the puppy in which, if it were a wild canine, it would be out of the den and encountering predators and other dangers. Some dogs never show these stages during their development, and some remain consistently fearful throughout their life.

Dogs that can fulfill the companion and public access roles of a Hearing Dog have almost no fearfulness at all. Very few dog breeds are selectively bred for these low levels, which are seen mostly in some retriever and companion breeds. Wild animals that showed such complete lack of fear could not survive long, but humans can protect dogs from danger.

Dogs who are fearful in any way do not make good prospects for Hearing Dog work. Most growling and barking at strangers is caused by fearfulness, and the stress of going into crowded public places can intensify the reactions of a dog that is already fearful of strangers. A Masters thesis by Steve Grunow shows that fearfulness is the major cause of

Dogs feel more secure with their pack, whether human or canine. Facing an unfamiliar area, these young explorers find security in close contact.

This puppy shows extreme fear in its expression and posture. It is probably unsocialized or abused. If not genetically fearful, it possibly could be rehabilitated, but shows low potential for Hearing Dog roles. (Photo by SF-SPCA)

Longhaired dogs are harder to read, but Niji shows avoidance of the tormenting cat by pressing into the chair and looking away from her. He keeps one ear focused on her instead. He had been told to stay for a photo, so he is in conflict with his desire to escape. In a more stressful situation, this kind of mental cornering could lead to aggression.

failure to graduate Service Dog, Hearing Dog, and Guide Dog programs.

Fearfulness is a problem for programs that use shelter dogs of unknown genetics and upbringing as well as for those that have carefully designed breeding and socializing systems. Determining the reason for fearful behavior in shelter dogs is very difficult, since it could stem from inherited shyness, lack of socialization, or learning. When working with these dogs, I hope for very rapid improvement, and if I don't see it, I have to realize that the rehabilitation or socialization process may be long-term and labor-intensive, with microscopic gains.

Many people have devoted years to a beloved dog's rehabilitation, and would do it all over again. But if the goal is a companion that will be not be stressed by public access, professional advice should be sought before attempting the impossible. The amount of rehabilitation necessary to make a dog comfortable in a predictable, stable environment can be a worthwhile project, but it might be unfair and unrealistic to ever expect the same dog to handle public access situations.

Predictably, dogs that are reactive as well as fearful can become hysterical easily, exhibiting panic reactions, and they can also easily develop phobias that escalate with each negative experience. They are hard to handle, since humans have a hard time keeping up with their lightning-fast perceptions and predicting what they will react to. But predict them the trainer must, as well as having a plan that will defuse fear before it starts its downward spiral.

Fearful dogs attempt to escape danger by submission or escape. Normal social behavior includes using aggression when submissive behavior is not working. If the dog cannot flee, and life-threatening challenges to survival continue when it submits, its only option is to attack. However, a good companion does not misinterpret normal bumbling human behavior as life threatening. Dogs can quickly learn that threatening behavior causes scary-appearing people or animals to retreat, and that escalating these "counterattacks" will bring safety even faster. (Children often teach fearfully aggressive dogs to lunge out and snap simply by being themselves. Intentional teasing and abuse are not necessary to produce biting. The child may simply approach the dog cautiously, then jump back or run away if the dog growls or barks.)

A dog may still feel trapped in a large space, if it perceives no exit. Even dogs that are outside and off leash may feel mentally trapped by the pressure of commands they cannot understand combined with the threat of punishment they cannot avoid. Many so-called "unpredictable" attacks stem from this type of mental cornering. Such attacks are very serious; dogs that bite out of fear are in a panic state, convinced that they are fighting for their lives, and they bite very hard. A dog that is fearful and reactive is totally unsuitable for any of the Hearing Dog roles.

Just because a training method is *helpful* with fearful dogs does not mean it will cure a fearfulness problem. It is quite a feat to simply get a dog used to one new place or person at a time, and the dog may never generalize its confidence to future unfamiliar places or people. After all, merely enlarging the category of "familiar" in the dog's mind may never affect its attitude toward "unfamiliar." I personally know of no more frustrating task than trying to work with fearful dogs. Every minor success only builds me up for a big disappointment when the dog's fears resurface in some unexpected way. For these dogs, being taken into public places is like a trip through a house of horrors where some new and hideous surprise awaits around every corner.

Aggression

Aggression in dogs is associated with many different instincts and motivations, which can be endlessly discussed and debated. The bottom line is that any type of aggression impairs the ability of a dog to fulfill the public access and companion roles of a Hearing Dog.

Because aggression problems such as biting people or other dogs can often be controlled by proper handling and training, it is always tempting to fantasize that such a dog could be taught to be a good companion or public access dog. Many aggression problems can easily be masked by confident, capable trainers, but they often re-emerge the minute the dog is transferred to a less confident or capable person. Controlling a dog like this in public places is a difficult, full-time job, because both the dog's and the public's behavior must be monitored. For a Hearing Dog partner, this means that their dog is a worrisome burden rather than a helpful companion.

Biting

The public role of a Hearing Dog (or the lifestyle of any dog that lives with children) presents daily situations that might lead to biting. Since reactive dogs are less able to inhibit their reactions to stimuli, one would expect that they would be more likely to bite. This is only true for reactive dogs with temperaments that would lead to biting anyway. Many dogs are strongly inhibited from biting, and refuse to, even under circumstances in which most people would agree that a bite was justified. Amazingly, even with intense encouragement or provocation, many dogs absolutely refuse to bite, which surprises some owners of protection breeds when they discover that their expensive purebred "Manglemuncher" is a pacifist.

Dogs that refuse to bite can be very reactive as well, but their reactivity takes the form of screaming, escaping, or turning their heads quickly away, or mouthing in an inhibited way. A dog that inhibits itself from biting will also refuse to defend itself, so its owner must protect it.

When a dog does show biting behavior, people need to face reality and not excuse it. Biting is biting. Dogs have reflexes fast enough to choose and control whether they will snap and miss, bump with closed mouth, pinch, pierce skin, or do severe damage. Puppies are inexperienced in using social signals correctly and have teeth sharp enough to break skin even if used in an inhibited fashion, but adult dogs are different. If an adult dog chooses to bite severely enough to pinch or break skin in a social confrontation (for instance, snapping at a hand while chewing a bone), this is always deliberate. When dogs interact with each other, they very consciously control their bite pressure. I have seen countless "fights" that looked as if gallons of blood should be flowing, but no injuries occurred; the dogs were simply negotiating the rules of their relationship.

Most of what appears to be biting behavior in dogs is a variety of signals that gradually escalate in intensity. When dogs fight and even a small injury occurs, it is always due to another, higher level of aggression; the dog is now determined to actually bite hard.

Bite style is strongly genetic, and hard to influence even with early training. Certain breeds and mixes show hard, uninhibited bites. Even when playing, their style is evident. Teaching dogs to take food treats gently can be difficult when their instincts tell them to grab hard. I've trained many Australian Cattle Dog mixes who would try with every fiber of their body to reach gently toward my treat, and in the last millimeter, suddenly grab as

Interpreting dog behavior can be very tricky. Anyone would think that the next moment will be the last for some of these fingers, but Shordy is actually playing. He mock-defends his blanket from owner Gail Gaffney or anyone else who reaches for it—but he has never snapped or bitten. It is always safer to assume that a strange dog is not playing when it shows any threatening behavior.

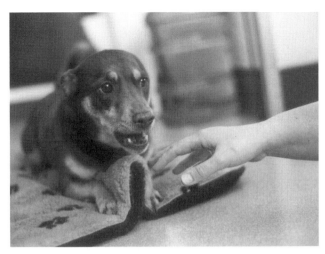

Spaniel mix snarls slightly and stares at the hand touching his bone. He then snapped when his threat was ignored. This photo was taken to illustrate behavior, and does not show safe testing procedure.

After training to surrender the bone, this dog shows pacifying signals when approached, lifting a hind leg, licking, and, most importantly, looking away from the hand. He then rolled over all the way and allowed the bone to be removed. The effect of this training is mostly limited to his relationship with the person who did the training; other people will need to establish a dominant relationship as well or the snapping behavior will recur with them. This photo was taken to illustrate behavior and does not show safe testing procedure.

hard as they would a cow's heel.

Dogs that grab hard for treats or toys should not be placed with children, even if adults can inhibit the behavior. It's too hard on children to be nipped while feeding treats to a dog, to have their cookies roughly stolen, or to give up their dog because of this problem.

Dog trainers need to realize how their behavior affects a dog's tendency to bite. Dogs are often inhibited from biting by either the dominance of the trainer or by expert handling that prevents the dog from getting stressed to the point of biting. Trainers may easily fool themselves into thinking that such a dog has no tendency to bite. If a dog shows any biting behavior at all when working with a good trainer, the probability is high that with a bad trainer or a non-trainer the behavior will be intensified. I've met many people who were abused as children, and will not or cannot express anger or aggression. Some dogs may become nasty bullies with these people. People who have difficulty asserting themselves, or have ever been bitten and are fearful of dogs, need a gentle, empathic dog that will not show aggression.

Other-Dog Aggression

Fear or aggression towards strange dogs is unfortunately normal behavior for many breeds. Assistance dog partners find this to be one of the most worrisome problems they encounter, especially when exhibited by their own dog. In some very domesticated breeds with low fearfulness and aggression, this tendency has been reduced, probably by selecting for neoteny (retention of puppy-like traits). Instead of maturing to the very socially restricted behavior of the adult wolf, some dogs forever retain a flexible, puppylike perception of "pack," keeping the potential to enlarge their circle of social relationships even after reaching adulthood.

It is important to distinguish between other-dog aggression that which is the result of insufficient socialization with other dogs, and that which is inherited or learned. Naive dogs with little experience may show hysterical, intense-appearing aggression based on fear, which may disappear after the dog learns to communicate properly. Unsocialized older dogs take several weeks or more of daily play with compatible dogs to learn to read the same signals that they can give out instinctively. Learned or inherited aggression toward other dogs is often self-rewarding and can only be controlled, not changed. An important point is that learning to accept a widening circle of familiar dogs does not usually change the behavior of a dog that shows problems with strange dogs.

Fearfulness plays a large part in most other-dog aggression, especially when dogs are restrained on leash and feel their only escape route is to attack forward. Turid Rugaas (*On Talking*

A snarl warns two Malinois, Dyna and Jekyll, away from Jinx's toy. Both thieves acknowledge her message by submissively squinting their eyes and averting their heads.

Terms with Dogs) points out that dogs never normally approach each other directly if free, moving in wide arcs towards each other, unless they have aggressive intentions. Therefore, straight city sidewalks can be blamed for many problems! But this is a situation that urban dogs and those with public access often face, and dogs that overreact aggressively or fearfully to other dogs are not suitable for Hearing Dog roles. A Hearing Dog is always under intense scrutiny by people who are curious about the presence of a dog in a non-doggy place.

Dyna ignored the threat by approaching and is punished with a lunge and snap. Jekyll reaps the benefits of his more submissive strategy and prepares to steal the toy.

Much dog-to-dog aggression is easily controlled by good training and handling, but dogs that sense nervousness or ineptitude on the part of the handler tend to react both to lack of leadership and inadvertent reinforcement of their bad behavior. I once was helping a woman whose Hearing Dog was showing terrible behavior when he saw strange dogs; lunging, snapping, barking, and being totally uncontrollable. He didn't show it when *I* was walking him, so I decided to set up a little situation to judge it for myself. I explained to his partner that I would walk around the corner with my Belgian Malinois, Jekyll. I also explained that Jek, who the Hearing Dog didn't know, was very friendly to people and dogs, and would not hurt the other dog even if they got too close. As Jek and I walked around the corner, the Hearing Dog looked a little surprised. Before he could react further, his partner threw up her hands, screamed, and leapt back, dragging him with her. After that, I had no trouble understanding the problem: a reactive human!

Reactive dogs often have difficulties in communicating with other dogs. Their quick, intense behavior and strong reactions to social signals are often interpreted as aggressive or annoying. They rarely approach other dogs calmly, instead showing frantic eagerness to interact. The other dog may react negatively to this, whereupon the reactive dog may show fearful, excited, or aggressive behavior, escalating the problem. The reactive dog's signals can also be interpreted as pushy and challenging by dominant dogs, who would react better to calm behavior that would allow both dogs to establish status slowly. The screaming of a reactive, panicked dog that has gotten itself into social trouble can cause other dogs to react aggressively, as do the quick, scurrying movements of small reactive dogs who trigger predatory responses. When two or more reactive dogs meet, anything can happen!

Territoriality

Territorial guarding is derived from wolf behavior; it protects the resources within an area from competitors of the same species, and many domestic dogs show a specialized intensification of this behavior. Most of us value territoriality in our dogs. We need to know about potential intruders or danger, whether or not we are hard of hearing. Moderate territoriality that is expressed by barking rather than biting is sufficient for most people. Alarm barking and growling may be acceptable at home to the partner of a Hearing Dog, but the same behavior in public is both annoying and frightening to members of the public. Many dogs only behave this way at home, but some dogs will build a weak sense of territory after being in a new place for only fifteen to thirty minutes, and will then be suspicious of strangers approaching. This typically happens when a Hearing Dog accompanies its

Two dogs showing different responses to territorial invasion: Golden mix, Alsina, watches her owner (at right) for cues as to how to react, but Rottweiler, Bogie, stares and sniffs with head upraised to check out the photographer.

partner to a meeting or classroom, then sounds the alarm at latecomers (who had probably hoped to enter unobtrusively). Dogs that are highly territorial carry a portable sense of territory around with them, and may claim any space their body happens to land on.

Territorial behavior can vary in aggression levels. Aggressive dogs will both threaten and possibly attack intruders. Less aggressive dogs are less territorial, simply because they have less motivation to guard resources. Dogs can also be territorial without aggression, merely becoming noisily excited at any intrusion and behaving in a friendly way to visitors.

Reactive dogs that are territorial alert rapidly when any threat is perceived. Such a dog is hard to control in public, because it alerts to very minor situations that are hard for its partner to notice (or hear). They often have extreme sensitivity to any sound that may indicate invasion, and also often have overall reactivity to all sounds, making them easy to train in sound alerting. However, they tend to remain at doors and windows, barking, rather than return to their partner.

The following is a letter from Rhonda Geer about Tessa, her small Shepherd mix.

One night during the first spring after I got Tessa, I was home alone with my son, who had just turned three years old. My husband was at work. It was early evening about six or seven o'clock. I was watching TV and all of a sudden Tessa started barking and running from the front door to the back of the house and jumping on me in between. At first I thought she was playing a game because she kept running to my bedroom and jumping at the window then she would nearly knock me over then run to the front door then back to me. She was really moving fast. Boy, was I shocked when I looked out the window on the front door and there stood a man with a "Rambo" knife (a long blade on one side and a serrated edge on the other side) on my front porch. I didn't know it at the time but there was another man in the back of the house by my bedroom window. I hid my son behind a chair in the corner and called 911. Three police cars were at my house in three minutes and fortunately they were able to apprehend the two men. I am not sure what would have happened if Tessa had not alerted me to the men being there, but I am really glad I did not have to find out!

Tessa's behavior was perfect for this life-threatening situation precisely because she was *not* overly territorial. Instead of remaining at the front door or the back bedroom and barking there—perhaps unheard and unseen by her partner—she ran to both locations in turn, touching her. The men obviously had not been frightened away by the presence of the dog, and if Tessa had stayed at one location, the other intruder might have been able to enter the house unnoticed. Perhaps this was even their plan, foiled by this very wonderful dog.

Predatory Behavior

Predatory behavior can be problematic, depending on how much of the original complete sequence of hunting behavior is present. Some dogs have the desire to chase moving objects without attacking them, whether animals, humans, or tennis balls. They may attempt to stop the movement, but do not bite hard, and when the movement stops, they are no longer stimulated. This type of behavior may be easy to control when the dog is leashed in public, but difficult at home when loose, resulting in chasing and perhaps accidentally injuring children and pets. More complete predatory behavior involves chasing,

biting, and killing. Many herding breeds are bred for a certain level of bite strength when herding, and bite in order to force livestock to go in the direction desired by the dog.

Reactivity can easily stimulate a predatory dog to show behavior ranging from chasing to killing. A dog that is both reactive and predatorily aggressive may have fast and fatal responses to mov-

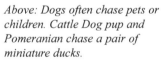

Above: Dogs often chase pets or children. Cattle Dog pup and Pomeranian chase a pair of miniature ducks.

Left: Stalking behavior using "eye": An Australian Cattle Dog pup eyes Border Collie pup, Brink, who in turn eyes a frightened gosling.

ing or screaming children or animals.

The ideal level of predatory aggression for companion and public access roles is zero.

Food and Object Aggression (Resource Guarding)

It is always a surprise when a dog seems to tolerate everything under the sun except when someone tries to take away their food or other possessions. Dogs who are protecting their food freeze and stop eating or chewing as the thief approaches. If the person does not take this signal seriously and continues to approach, he or she may trigger the next level of guarding behavior that ranges from eye contact to sudden lunging. Behavior from dog to dog is so variable that it is hard to predict. The point at which I find a dog's behavior unacceptable and potentially dangerous is when it freezes and stops eating, or growls while gobbling. The key issue here is the fact that the dog believes the object or food belongs to it. Dogs that have been trained to believe that their human pack members own everything, including dog food, do not guard it. They walk away from it when approached by a person.

From a dog's point of view, any direct attempt by humans to force a dog to drop an item is completely insensitive to dog social systems. Unfortunately, this rude and tactless behavior is normal for humans, and if dogs are to live with humans, they need to respond nonviolently to human attempts to steal possessions. For their own safety, dangerous items must be taken away quickly from dogs, and for the safety of people around them, they must not threaten or bite to keep possessions or food.

Fearful people who are already afraid to take away an item will often jerk back at the slightest movement from the dog. Such people can easily train even a very submissive dog to guard food or toys confidently. This type of person needs a dog that absolutely shows no guarding behavior at all. Even a very gentle nose nudge towards an intruding hand is a statement of possession; nonviolent and perhaps even polite, but still communicating a wish to keep the object. The most desirable dog is the one that never really felt that it owned the food or toy in the first place.

Intelligence

Intelligence has little to do with the working ability of Hearing Dogs. Intelligent dogs, though, have the advantage of learning faster, remembering better, and generalizing their experiences to new situations faster. It's the *desire* to do the sound alerting work that is far more important than intelligence in the long run, because even a less intelligent dog will get it eventually if it really wants to learn.

I value intelligence in dogs highly and find smart dogs fascinating, and I dread the tedious process of step-by-tiny-step training of dull dogs. They make take longer to train, but in terms of the working lifetime of a Hearing Dog, this really is irrelevant. Dogs with learning disabilities or low intelligence can find training stressful if not done sensitively to their needs, and appear stubborn or bored when the trainer expects progress beyond the dog's abilities and confuses the dog. I often suspect that breeds that are supposed to be "too intelligent to do the same thing over and over" are actually quite dumb. Smart dogs are eager to learn and have long attention spans when properly motivated. Generalizing in particular will be slow to occur in less intelligent dogs, and they function best in stable, unchanging environments. Radical changes such as a different telephone ring or a new placement of a familiar sound will require more assistance for the dull dog to adjust to.

One positive comment often made by trainers about less intelligent dogs is that they do not usually discover loopholes in human rules as easily as intelligent ones, and in sound alerting they tend to notice inconsistencies in reward frequency less—making them actually more reliable than some intelligent ones. Dogs with both intelligence and Hearing Dog temperament are of course capable of amazing things if matched with a partner who appreciates their intellect and keeps their minds busy. Naturally, smart dogs can learn bad habits faster!

Freckles was an Australian Shepherd mix who was often bullied by the larger dogs. She loved the small dogs, and was always put in with them during the day for playtime. In the individual kennels at night, she learned how to slide her kennel latch and escape into the hallway. It wasn't until after a few days of upturned trash and chewed hoses I discovered that it was not human error that left the door unlatched. One morning I entered the hallway to again find Freckles loose, but this time she was accompanied by four or five other dogs. Had they watched Freckles? It was unlikely, since dogs don't mimic very well. Besides, I realized that these dogs were all too small to have reached the latches. Freckles had let them out! Not only that, but she had only let out her little friends, not the big bullies. I was curious as to how she opened the latches, and watched her let herself out of her kennel by using her paw to reach through the wire and raise and then slide the bolt. I tried to watch her let out other dogs, but she was too interested in me if I was present. Leaving Freckles in the aisle, I locked myself into a kennel and whined pitifully. Freckles became agitated and this time used her teeth to raise and slide the bolt and set me free. She had figured out an entirely different technique to open kennel doors from the outside! I wish that Freckle's intelligence had helped her in other ways, but she was fearful of strangers and of new places, and was placed as a pet.

Conclusions on Reactivity and Temperament

Once the effect of reactivity has been analyzed, it becomes obvious that it always gives a dog potential in sound alerting, even though the specific quality of sound reactivity is more desirable than overall reactivity. Reactivity also presents problems in both companion and public roles, and once the dogs that are unsuitable are weeded out, we are left with very few that can perform them all. Only reactive dogs that are both submissive and socially interactive have good potential.

Can all of the needed traits really be found in one dog? Not often. Are all these traits really needed in one dog? Not always. Every potential partner of a Hearing Dog has different needs. People rarely require a dog that excels in all three roles. Some people value companionship more than sound alerting, some

Jinx enjoys my jokes—or at least, being a part of the group! Here, we wait to compete in agility.

value sound alerting more than public access. Many do not even want public access and prefer to take the dog only to places a pet would go. Dogs that are a little uneven in their ability to fill the different roles merely need a good match with the right partner.

Is any Hearing Dog really perfect? Absolutely not. The factors that make a dog very talented in one role can be detrimental to its aptitude for another role, and it is up to the partner to see that the dog receives extra maintenance training in the areas that they are lacking. A good match will ensure that success will be attainable by both.

PART TWO:

BEHIND THE HEARING DOG TEMPERAMENT

Chapter Four
Classifying Dogs by Function

The unique Hearing Dog temperament, most often found in mixed breed dogs, is actually a serendipitous blend of basic traits that long ago were carefully isolated and developed in their purebred ancestors. To successfully select potential Hearing Dogs from shelters, it is helpful to understand these purebred temperament components.

The specific temperament required to fill the three roles Hearing Dogs play is complex, and few dogs possess it. We take for granted the unique temperaments of the hundreds of dog breeds, each finely tuned for one or more specific purposes. Some of these purposes require a very tricky balance of different instincts in one dog. Hearing Dog temperament is just as tricky, but seems perhaps more challenging just because there is no ready-made breed for this function.

Rather than look at specific breeds, I find it more useful to look at the different basic functions that dogs have evolved to perform, such as retrieving or herding. Once we know the temperament required for each function, we can compare each of those temperaments with the ideal Hearing Dog temperament. Once we know the individual temperament traits that make each function possible, we can see how these traits could interact when purebred or mixed breed dogs are produced. A "shopping list" of desirable traits can be made with the aim of searching for, or breeding, the perfect Hearing Dog.

Certain types of mixed breeds are more successful Hearing Dogs than others. Because so many mixed-breed dogs are found suitable for Hearing Dogs suggests that they must get the desirable traits from somewhere in their heritage, and 83% of mixed breeds that I've seen in shelters have some easily identified purebred heritage, it is worthwhile to examine the temperaments of these purebred ancestors. Therefore, we need to understand purebred temperaments in relation to Hearing Dog temperament whether we are seeking to find dogs with Hearing Dog temperament in shelters, to breed them, or to decide whether to use purebreds or mixed breeds.

Evolution of Functional Groups

While most animals have evolved through a process of natural selection, dogs are somewhat unique in that they developed over the last 10,000 years by an unnatural selection method. Most of the selection process has been related to their ability to help humans with basic survival needs. Hunting, herding, guard, alarm functions, and even companionship are all aspects of dog behavior that can be separated out and discarded or intensified to create types of dogs that can be helpful to humans. This creation of many functional types of dogs eventually became specialized into what we now call "breeds." Hearing Dogs can be viewed in the same way as any other functional dog. They help their

partners with three basic survival needs:
1. communicating with other people – by assisting with door and telephone
2. personal safety issues – by alerting to smoke alarms and other danger signals
3. social needs – both by canine friendship as well as being a social facilitator for interaction with other people

The Purebred Concept

Our concept of "purebred" is probably less than 200 years old. Prior to this, function as well as appearance defined dogs, and the dog's genetic ancestry was less important.

Modern dog breeds have changed greatly over the last couple of centuries, as they were bred less and less to perform their original functions. Fragile, specialized behaviors were quickly lost through neglect or selection for new functions such as "show dog," leaving sometimes only a "flavoring" of the original temperament. The difference between a dog that can just barely pass a herding instinct test and a dog that can perform complicated herding work with little training is like the difference between a toddler who can sing a song learned from a kiddie show on television and a musically gifted toddler who can sing perfectly every song he has ever heard once.

In looking for Hearing Dogs among the purebreds, one needs to keep an open mind. It would be a tragedy if a dog were overlooked simply because it came from an "unsuitable" breed. Every dog groomer or trainer enjoys telling endless horror stories about "Breed X, those awful biters, they're impossible to groom and handle...see this scar on my arm? Except Mrs. Phillips' tan one, he's so sweet. He would *never* bite, we can even cut his nails!" On the other hand, we should not be swayed by the illogical thinking that just because "Breed Y" is made up of such gentle companions then this dog will automatically be one too.

Few breeds were designed to perform one function and one function only. Many tasks are not needed constantly, and some are seasonal in nature. For instance, herding needs vary according to time of year or breeding patterns of livestock, and many herding breeds have several secondary functions such as guarding or hunting.

Blueprints for Functional Groups

My definition of a "blueprint" is similar to a breed standard but instead describes the temperament needed to perform a function. Because purebreds have changed so much in the last 200 years, both in appearance and temperament, I find it helpful to forget what they are like now, and focus on what they were like when they were first bred. Examining the original functions that dogs were evolved to fill allows us to design a "blueprint" for the appropriate temperament for each function.

The most basic classifications are: primeval, sled, scenthound/sighthound, guard, setter/pointer, herding, retriever, terrier, alarm, companion, and spaniel. These do not correlate to any one kennel club classification system, but are helpful in understanding dog temperaments in general.

Blueprint for a Primeval Dog

Ray Coppinger's work is the source for much of my information on primeval dogs. His research and theories should be read by anyone interested in dog behavior and evolution.

Few dogs actually possess a completely primeval temperament; most show one or more specialized functions as well, yet retain many characteristics that helped them to reproduce and forage in harsh environments. The Dingo and Israeli Canaan Dog are classically primeval, able to survive easily on their own, and the Basenji is a good example of a primeval dog that is starting to change in temperament to become more domesticated, now that it has been bred for many generations in the West. The function of the primeval dog is to be a useful scavenger that

A prehistoric dog at the dawn of time? Actually, Australian Cattle Dog OTCH Scotswood INXS, "Brock."

clears bones, food scraps, and human feces from campsites or settlements. It provides food in the form of edible puppies, and wearable skins for clothing. It is not usually necessary to train it to hunt; its natural hunting behavior gives dogs and humans mutual benefit by joining together on hunting trips. Alarm and flock guard functions arise naturally from its territoriality, fearfulness, and pack instincts.

Reactivity: high. Hunting for prey animals and escaping from predators makes reactivity essential.

Sound reactivity: moderate. Survival instincts dictate that all senses should be balanced according to relevance to survival. Other senses may therefore overshadow sound reactivity.

Activity: high. May be lower in those semi-specialized for guard functions.

Interactivity: low. These dogs live in loose association with human groups. Typically, they avoid contact with strangers. Although sociable with their owners, by our standards they would be classified as very independent, living lives that run parallel to their human companions rather than closely interconnected as companion dogs would be.

Territoriality: high.

Predatory instinct: high, since it often must hunt for itself. Dingoes kept as pets show a motivation to hunt constantly for food (from insects to cats) to the exclusion of many pet-like activities.

Biting: high; possibly inhibited with its owners, but most potential biting situations are kept in check because people in societies that have these dogs know better than to touch strange dogs, and the dogs' natural fearfulness prevents them from getting close enough to strangers to bite.

Initiative: high.

Fearfulness: high. Although alarm functions are valued in most primeval function dogs, their fearfulness has evolved mostly for self-preservation rather than selectively bred for it. Extreme neophobia and xenophobia are desirable, as well as all the other traits that enable dogs to survive without active human assistance.

Dominance/submission: variable, within a canine pack structure. Breeding and feeding both depend on gaining high rank as well as cooperation within a pack.

Other-dog aggression: usually high, especially to strange dogs, which by their presence threaten the pack and its resources.

Primeval traits are antithetical to those needed for Hearing Dog temperament, so this group offers few possibilities. I'm always hopeful about finding an atypical individual, because some of these breeds are becoming more domesticated over recent generations as a result of breeders selecting towards a companion temperament.

Hearing Dog suitability:
- For sound alerting role: moderate
- For companion role: low
- For public access role: low

Blueprint for a Sled Dog

Sled dogs need enough primeval traits to survive under hard conditions, and not just in winter; many sled dog breeds in the Arctic were, or perhaps still are, required to survive on their own during the summers. Some have dual functions as hunting dogs. Those that have a dual function as herding dogs (e.g., the Samoyed) show a slightly different temperament profile.

Reactivity: moderate but variable. A dog with moderate reactivity is more easily handled while harnessing or if injured, and might be less distractible while pulling. Higher reactivity is needed to survive on its own.

Sound reactivity: moderate. This dog might have some sound reactivity, but its other senses will also be important to it, due to the primeval traits it possesses. It shows little potential for making the actual physical alert to its partner because its main motivation is not to make social contact, but to leave people in order to explore. This would be called "running away" if it were not attached to a sled.

Activity: high. Should be able to pull for many miles a day.

Interactivity: low. The dogs need to be handled and harnessed, and are usually kept tied up when not working. The dog's function calls for it to not be interactive; a dog that turns back from its sled-pulling to get social contact with people would be quickly eliminated from both the gene pool and the sled team.

Territoriality: low. Protecting territory is irrelevant to sled pulling. Once tied out at a destination, the dogs may alert to anything unusual. Due to their primeval nature and use for game hunting, they would alert to animal intruders in any case. Sled dogs may travel with nomadic peoples, which requires that the dog not cling to its own territory but eagerly travel through strange areas.

Predatory instinct: high. The dual function for hunting game combined with the dog's own survival instincts result in high predatory aggression.

Biting: moderate to high. Dogs tied out near a village or camp must be reasonably safe around people, but the hunting and primeval functions of sled dogs suggest a high biting potential.

Initiative: moderate to high. Survival requires initiative, and while pulling a sled the dog is constantly showing the initiative to explore and investigate. It does need to respond to commands.

Fearfulness: variable. Survival demands caution to prevent injury while hunting. The sled dog function demands that the dog intrepidly explore new environments, yet show strong caution and awareness of dangerous conditions such as thin ice.

Dominance/submission: variable. Sled function requires a dog that is somewhat submissive to people for control and handling.

Other-dog aggression: variable. Primeval pack survival instincts affect relationships with other dogs. Most sled dogs are kept tied to kennels, not allowed to run free to form their own pack structure (and never come back). They need to coexist to work in harness together, but most sled dog books emphasize that the owner must be able to control aggression within the team or to strange teams.

Hearing Dog suitability:
- For sound alerting: low
- For companion role: low
- For public access role: low

Blueprint for a Scenthound

Hounds need high scent reactivity and a desire to hunt that is stronger than their moderate social interactivity with people.

Reactivity: moderate. Hound function demands that the dog not be overly distracted from hunting and be easily handled when injured, yet react to prey movements quickly to avoid injury.

Sound reactivity: extremely low. Scenthounds should have an intense reactivity to scent; high enough to screen out any other sensory input that might distract it from following a trail.

Activity: high. It should be active enough to hunt for miles, but conserve its energy when not hunting. This is achieved by creating a dog that is highly active when stimulated by predatory instinct, but inactive otherwise.

Interactivity: moderate. Too much desire for social interaction might interfere with its ability to hunt independently at several miles distance from the hunter, yet it needs to be easily handled when not hunting. Its social interactivity with strangers is variable, which is irrelevant to hunting function, although dogs sometimes hunt around strangers, especially at trials. Dual functions as alarm or guard dogs may also affect this trait.

Territoriality: low. Hounds must range widely when hunting, and not feel inhibited when off their own territory. Dual functions as guard or alarm dogs may heighten territoriality.

Predatory instinct: high. This is vital for scenthound function, although predatory aggression levels vary depending on whether the prey must be killed or just held at bay until the arrival of a hunter or specialized killing dog.

Biting: variable.

Initiative: high. The nature of this type of hunting demands extreme initiative, to follow the scent wherever it takes the hound.

Fearfulness: Slight fearfulness may help it avoid getting killed by large game, but it should have no fear of strange environments.

Dominance/submission: variable. Submission to humans aids in handling injured dogs. Although scenthounds hunt independently, they must follow some commands while hunting, and overcoming strong instinctive behaviors is easier with submissive dogs.

Other-dog aggression: low. Many scenthounds live together and hunt in packs that cooperate rather than compete.

Two breeds within the hound grouping are of interest to Hearing Dog trainers, and both are atypical. Beagles, although good hunting dogs, also possess more companion traits than the others, and figure strongly in the heritage of many mixed-breed Hearing Dogs. Dachshunds, although usually classified as hounds, are actually more like a dual terrier/companion/alarm function dog than a hound. The Hearing Dog Program does not usually adopt purebred Dachshunds, due to prevalence of back problems in the breed. Dachshund mixes, however, often show great potential as Hearing Dogs, as well as fewer back problems. Scenthound mixes derived from these breeds graduated from the HDP at a 37% rate.

Hearing Dog suitability:
- For sound alerting: very low (Dachshund: high)
- For companion role: low (Beagle: moderate, Dachshund: moderate)
- For public access role: moderate (Dachshund: low to moderate)

Blueprint for a Sighthound

The profile for sighthound function is nearly identical to scenthound, with the obvious exception of the dog keying in on visual activity rather than scent. This visual reactivity overshadows other senses, resulting in predatory chasing of moving objects. Sighthounds are usually expected to show killing behavior when they catch up with their prey, which ranges in size from rabbits to wolves and antelopes. They often show a more fearful temperament than do the Scenthounds, which makes them closer to primeval function dogs. Many show other dual functions such as guard.

Blueprint for a Guarding Dog

I define the guarding function as a territory or flock guard rather than a police K9 guard dog, which has a more complex role requiring predatory instincts not needed or wanted in the traditional guarding dog. Guarding dogs are required not simply to alert to danger, but also to eliminate it if necessary. The focus of their aggression can be animal predators but also humans. They are often expected to remain alone to guard property. In this they are unlike most other dogs, which typically are courageous and confident only when in a pack.

Reactivity: low. To defend against humans and predators, a guarding dog needs to be large, but it needs to have very low reactivity. This provides a safety catch and ensures that aggression is only seen when the dog is strongly stimulated. Since it often lives with the people it is intended to protect, low reactivity also helps the dog to ignore the behavior of children, who might stimulate aggression in a reactive dog. The desirable response is for the dog to first evaluate the situation instead of reflexively biting when startled, or chasing off predators it sees on the next hill and thereby leaving the flock unguarded.

Sound reactivity: low to moderate. Guarding dogs need some sound reactivity, but only to unusual noises, and they should habituate very quickly to all irrelevant sounds to ensure that the dog does not behave aggressively in normal situations. Even when aroused by unusual sounds, or familiar ones that it relates to intrusion, (i.e. clicking of the garden gate), it should react slowly, evaluating the potential danger of the situation first, then giving warning, then attacking only when strongly threatened.

Activity: low. Low activity levels can provide another safety catch. This large and powerful dog is less likely to injure people accidentally if it is inactive. The main job of the guard dog is to wait for danger to approach the territory, so only enough energy to calmly stay at a good vantage point or occasionally patrol boundaries is needed. An inactive large dog requires less food as well.

Interactivity: moderate. Although it is definitely a part of its human pack, dependency and clinging behavior interferes with the independent decision-making needed in this dog. Its interest in guarding should be more apparent than its need for constant interaction. If hiring a bodyguard, most of us would prefer a reserved, serious person to an intensely sociable person who might get distracted from his or her duties. Social interactivity also interferes with the dog's ability to confidently guard when alone. Social interactivity with strangers is low. Just as in law enforcement security situations, all unfamiliar people must be considered suspect until proven to be harmless.

Territoriality: high. Aggression is part of the desired type of territoriality. Not only should the dog strongly perceive territory as an area to be protected, it should perceive the outlying areas as irrelevant, and be motivated to remain on its own property. Once off its territory, it may show a totally different attitude, being calmly accepting and neutral to stimuli that would trigger aggression at home.

Predatory instinct: low. Predatory instinct is undesirable as it may mean injury for the children or livestock it is supposed to protect. It can also motivate the dog to chase intruders or predators until it ranges far away, leaving its territory unguarded.

Biting: high. This dog must defend itself as well as its territory and family. Its opponents, mainly large predators or human beings, are capable of killing it.

Initiative: high. The dog must be able to evaluate situations independently and make its own decisions when it is left alone.

Fearfulness: low but present. A tiny amount of fearfulness enables guard function dogs to sense the difference between the familiar and the abnormal, and to give them caution when dealing with dangerous opponents. This fearfulness is invisible to the observer, and is only evident when the dog shows a watchful suspicion of unfamiliar people or situations. If fearfulness can be observed at all, then the dog is unsuitable for guard function. Too much fearfulness can result in a lethal temperament; panicking in fear can result in attacks on the feared object, which is often a child. Poor breeding creates many individuals within the guard breeds with high fearfulness and aggression, made even more dangerous by lacking the safety catches of low reactivity and low activity levels.

Dominance/submission: dominant. A dog designed to attack intruders must be dominant with strangers and with other dogs that approach the territory. It may also tend to be dominant within its own human pack, but its low activity and low reactivity makes this less problematic. Intense awareness of pack social structure and communication gives a guard dog the ability to notice potential threats easily. Most guidebooks to dog breeds emphasize very early control and consistent training to manage guardian breeds safely. Without this control, these dogs are capable of becoming very dangerous.

Other-dog aggression: high. Predators that endanger livestock or people include stray dogs, coyotes, and wolves. Aggression directed at other canids is therefore vital to guarding.

As far as Hearing Dog potential goes, we don't have much to work with here, and most of the traits shown are actually detrimental to the roles that Hearing Dogs play. Slow reactions to sounds, low reactivity and activity levels, and low need for social interaction work against us in the sound alerting role. Even strong reactions to the sounds of visitors or intruders can be useless if the dog is reluctant to abandon its defending position at the door in order to alert its partner.

Perhaps the greatest barrier to their success is the expert early handling and training during puppyhood that is required to make these dogs suitable as companions and in public. If these conditions are met, the result is a trustworthy companion that behaves acceptably in public places. Unfortunately, the average person is neither qualified to manage these dogs nor willing to invest in extensive training time, and the average guard group purebred does not have good guard temperament.

In addition, guard breeds are very difficult to breed correctly, and their popularity means that most are badly bred. The calm, tolerant, and confident Rottweiler bred by good breeders is almost a different species altogether from the fearfully aggressive Rottweiler seen attacking the bars at so many shelters. When the dog with bad temperament and the unqualified owner meet, the result is doubly disastrous. Anyone thinking of testing guard breeds for adoption should contact a trainer experienced with aggressive dogs to do the testing in order to avoid adopting a dog with severe behavior problems caused by genetics or a previous owner.

Hearing Dog suitability:
- For sound alerting: low except for intruder sounds.
- For companion role: moderate.
- For public access role: low to moderate.

Blueprint for Setters and Pointers

A dog that will range independently and point to birds when it locates them is desired. It should have no aggression towards humans and have an inhibited bite. Many setters and pointers are dual-function dogs, showing some alarm or scenthound functions. Some are specialized for one type of hunting or prey, and others are adapted for more all-around use.

Reactivity: moderate.

Sound reactivity: moderate. The dog must also be reactive to olfactory and visual sensory input, which may overshadow any sound reactivity it has. Breeding stock selection for lack of fearfulness of gunshots may actually produce dogs that have little sound reactivity at all. The tendency to freeze (point) when sensing prey is counter to sound alerting suitability, which requires a dog that is *activated* by stimuli and approaches them in an in an uninhibited way.

Activity: high. This dog must enjoy running for hours. The high desire to be active and somewhat independent may interfere with sound alerting.

Interactivity: moderate. The dog should be interactive enough to follow commands and work in partnership with the hunter, but overly interactive dogs might not range out far enough to be efficient hunters. Since these dogs are sometimes loaned to other hunters, they should also be interactive and friendly with strangers.

Territoriality: low. As with any hunting dog, this dog must be able to leave its home.

Predatory instinct: high. This is coupled with an inhibited bite and low aggression, since this function may include retrieving. Some setters and pointer function dogs have a dual purpose of hound function, and show more predatory aggression. Strong reactions to seeing, hearing, or scenting birds may make this dog difficult to focus in public.

Biting: An inhibited bite is necessary for retrieving, but dual functions may affect this.

Initiative: moderate to high. Dog must have enough initiative to go after game, but still be responsive to commands.

Fearfulness: low. As with retrievers, it should have no fear of strangers, gunshots, or new environments.

Dominance/submission: variable but often submissive. The dog must be submissive enough for the hunter to be able to sometimes inhibit its strong hunting instincts at a distance. The instinct to point is an inhibition of predatory behavior, exaggerated from stalking and preparing to rush forward towards prey. Easily inhibited dogs have problems in sound alerting.

Other-dog aggression: low. Its hunting ability demands that dogs work around other hunting dogs and ignore them.

Hearing Dog suitability:
- For sound alerting role: low.
- For companion role: moderate.
- For public access role: moderate.

Blueprint for a Herding Dog

Farms have many jobs a dog can do, and a versatile dog is appreciated. Herding dogs are also often selected for either alarm or guard functions. Dual functions confuse the analysis of herding traits, so this discussion is intended to deal only with herding traits. Probably the dog with the most pure herding traits and the least alarm/guard function is the trial-bred Border Collie, whose breeders are focused almost entirely on creating a dog that has the ability to both herd and to adapt to unfamiliar trial locations.

Most herding dogs are tied or otherwise confined when not herding, for the reason that unsupervised herding on the dog's own can lead to stress, abortion, or accidental death of livestock, or the development of the killing behavior that lies just around the corner from the herding behavior sequence. When kept as free-running pets, herding function dogs often get into trouble when allowed to fulfill their instincts on intruding cars, joggers, and bicyclists.

Reactivity: high. Quick response to stock movements is essential.

Sound reactivity: moderate. Visual reactivity helps the dog respond to stock movements, but herding dogs also need sound reactivity in order to be keenly responsive to the shepherd's verbal or whistled commands. Unfortunately, this sound reactivity is often more fearful than confident.

Bishop George Reid with his Hearing Dog, Bingo. Bingo is unusual for a Border Collie in that he can attend church services without being fazed by the thunderous church organ. (Photo by SF-SPCA)

Commands must be able to inhibit the dog's strong predatory behavior and focus it in the direction needed by the handler. An excited response to sounds would be undesirable, causing the dog to get out of control. As a result, slight to severe "sound-shyness" is often seen in herding breeds. A dog that is overly inhibited or fearful of loud sounds close up will still react strongly to them when far away from the shepherd, showing the right level of quick inhibition and obedience. Sound shyness is not much of a problem on a farm, compared to life in a city. I have read many accounts of fearful Border Collies who, when busy working sheep, don't show fear of the things they are normally afraid of. And it is the dog's working behavior that is valued and selected for, not whether it enjoys going to town or hides when guns are fired when it is off-duty. Fearfulness of sounds is strongly genetic; it is interesting to note the differences between the three Belgian Shepherd breeds. Belgian Malinois from European working lines are generally accepted to be the least fearful of sounds of the three. These Malinois come from generations of dogs that have had all sound-shy individuals culled. I have seen many working-bred Malinois puppies that don't merely ignore loud sounds, but become intensely excited and playfully aggressive.

Activity: high. To have staying power, very high activity levels are required. Working Border Collies have been measured to run more than 50 miles a day when herding.

Interactivity: high. Because the dog is intended to work closely with a shepherd, it needs a high desire for interaction. It must be able to form a cooperative partnership, not simply follow commands by rote. Its social interaction with strangers is low, because this is not needed for the herding dog's work, and may actually be undesirable if the dog has a dual purpose of both herding and guard or alarm function.

Territoriality: moderate. For the function of herding, some awareness of territory may be useful, to keep the dog close to home base. The high territoriality seen in many herding function dogs is a result of fulfilling additional functions of alarm and guard.

Predatory instinct: high. A herding dog needs predatory behavior with enough aggression to control livestock without overly stressing or damaging it.

Biting: high. Biting is an integral part of much herding behavior. Even if rarely used, there are times that the dog must be able to back up its control over livestock with a bite or the convincing threat of one. However, the desired bite is the predatory bite used to stop prey or change its direction of escape, not that used to kill it. This inhibited bite tendency is tailored in different breeds (or lines within breeds) to the type of stock herded. Fragile stock such as ducks or sheep may require a threat or a very inhibited pinch, but feral cattle or cattle defending calves may be uncontrollable and lethal to the dog unless it has the courage and ability to bite hard. This bite is equally useful when herding dogs decide to control human movement, and even when inhibited it can be a very hard pinch. Herding breeds need careful testing to see whether they will bite people, determining whether they are stimulated to bite by running or quick movements as well as for all the other usual doggie reasons.

Initiative: variable. This trait ranges from low, as in the case of some Border Collies selected for constant and tight control by the handler, to very high, as in the case of the Australian Cattle Dog. This latter breed is sometimes expected to seek out semi-feral cattle and herd them to a holding area entirely on its own.

Fearfulness: high. Some fearfulness helps the dog to be cautious and to avoid injury from stock. Because most herding dogs live in rural areas and may stay on one farm their entire lives, fearfulness of strangers and new places does not affect their herding ability, so this is not selected against. Most fearfulness in herding function dogs is probably due to selection for alarm traits.

Dominance/submission: variable. Herding functions that require a dog to work independently and control aggressive stock seem to favor dominant temperaments, and those that involve a shepherd's tight control over a dog herding delicate stock seem to favor submissive temperaments. A dual guard function increases dominance.

Other-dog aggression: variable. Responses range from ignoring other dogs (strongly desirable in herding dogs that work together with other dogs), to intense other-dog aggression (strongly desirable in herding dogs with a dual alarm/guard function of protecting livestock from predatory canids such as wolves, dingoes, coyotes, or stray dogs).

It should be noted that very high intelligence is vital for herding work. The dog depends on strong instincts, the expression and focus of which are shaped by training, but its work is never by rote. The dog must learn many commands, and generalize its herding strategies to adapt to constantly varying situations of weather, terrain, different tasks, and livestock behavior. Although the presence of conceptual thinking is debatable in dogs, I believe herding function dogs at least approach this level of thought. Herding is a function in which it would take a less intelligent dog years of intensive training by rote to cope with all the situations it encounters.

In looking for a Hearing Dog among herding group dogs, we are attracted by their intense social interactiveness, rapid learning and generalization, activity, and submissiveness (although the latter is seen less often in the cattle-herding dogs.) High levels of reactivity and sky-high levels of activity may be hard to live with, and predatory aggression may be hard to control, but the real obstacle to Hearing Dog roles is fearfulness of strangers, new places, and most importantly, sound shyness. Socialization can make a huge difference in the behavior of herding dogs. When born with a less fearful temperament, puppies of these breeds can be socialized to the point that they can handle public access roles. Shelter dogs, however, have rarely been sufficiently socialized, and what might be sufficient socialization for an outgoing retriever pup is only a fraction of what is needed to make most herding function puppies equally outgoing and confident in public places. For this reason, it is hard to find herding function shelter dogs that pass public access suitability tests. Herding purebreds had a low 19% graduation rate at the Hearing Dog Program.

Herding breed temperaments can also vary widely depending whether the dog has a dual purpose as a guard or alarm dog. Dogs without these dual purposes are more suitable. Of these, the best are those individuals from breeders who are selecting for the outgoing, confident temperaments needed for obedience competition dogs. The following is offered for consideration.

Herding/Guard

Dogs that have traditionally been all-purpose farm guard/herding dogs show herding ability combined with a predatory and territorial attitude towards human intruders. Several herding/guard breeds (such as the German Shepherd and Belgian Malinois) have been selectively bred in this century to serve even more of a guard function than originally intended, and are now used extensively for police and military work. The predatory instinct of herding dogs is used as a motivation for searching for criminals, drugs, and explosives. Territoriality and barrier aggression allow these dogs to be area guards as well. Unlike the traditional guard breeds, which are territorial but not predatory, herding/guard dogs tend to chase moving people or children. Their predatory herding instincts, when combined with reaction to territorial threat, can result in aggression towards strangers. Herding/guard temperaments can be modified by heavy socialization to strangers combined with expert training to control aggression. In this group, the Australian Cattle Dog and Corgi fall closer to the herding function and the Rottweiler and Bouvier des Flanders are closer to the guard function.

Herding/Alarm

Many herding breeds serve as alarm function dogs that may or may not back up their alarm with biting, depending on their proportion of fearfulness to aggression. Extremely heavy socialization to strangers, strange places and to loud noises can mask the basic temperament. Shetland Sheepdogs, and some Australian Shepherds, have dual functions as alarm dogs.

Herding/Companion/Show

Another category consists of breeds that have become popular as show dogs or pets and lost much of their herding function temperament. These are far less reactive and active than most other herding breeds. They often show a temperament closer to companion function dogs. Rough and Smooth Collies are an example of this type.

Hearing Dog suitability:
- For sound alerting role: variable, depending on fear of sounds.
- For companion role: moderate.
- For public access role: low, unless extensively socialized.

Blueprint for a Retriever

A retriever function dog works under human control to retrieve shot game birds. The temperament ideal for this work coincidentally also fits well with the requirements for companion function, with the exception of their high activity level and predatory instinct. Since predatory instinct is incomplete—tailored to select only the behavior of retrieving prey back to a safe place or to its waiting puppies—this strong fragment of instinct is acceptable or even welcome in a family dog. The inhibited bite used for gently retrieving birds lowers its potential to bite people as well. A few retriever breeds have a dual function as guard, which changes their profile.

Reactivity: low to medium. Hunting involves quick response to commands, but the dog does not need the same amount of reactivity as a dog designed to herd stock or kill prey. Moderate reactivity is sufficient to deal with wounded or escaping birds. Long periods of waiting quietly in a boat or blind for birds to approach also favor a less reactive dog.

Sound reactivity: low to moderate. The dog should be reactive to verbal and whistled commands, but should not overreact to gunshots. Breeding for low reaction to gunshots may produce a dog with low sound reactivity overall.

Activity: high. It should be active enough to do water retrieves for hours. Its activity should be controllable, however, as the dog must wait calmly at times.

Interactivity: high. The dog works closely with its owner, following many commands, and since retrievers must be comfortable around other hunters in the same area and are sometimes loaned to other hunters, it should have a high interactivity with strangers.

Territoriality: low. Since hunting often involves different locales, the dog must be comfortable enough to work away from home. Breeders that select for companion function actively select against territorial aggression. Retrievers often show an excited, non-aggressive territoriality that is sufficient to alert owners, but ceases once visitors are admitted.

Predatory instinct: moderate. Aggression is minimized, since the dog is not expected to kill, but only to gently retrieve dead or wounded birds.

Biting: low. An inhibited bite ("soft mouth") is desired, although when not in retrieving mode, the dog may show a bite hard enough to injure people if it also possesses any form of aggression.

Initiative: low to moderate. The dog must do some problem solving on its own at a great distance from the hunter, but it also must be responsive to commands at a distance.

Fearfulness: low. It should have no fear of strangers, gunshots, or new environments. Lack of fear results in a dog that is easily socialized and remains flexible in its ability to accept the unfamiliar.

Dominance/submission: submissive. It needs to be both easy to control at a distance and "eager to please." This term does not really mean that the dog has some selfless desire to help people, just that it desires to be part of a pack so strongly that it will alter its behavior to get social rewards and prevent painful social exclusion. Retrievers are considered "easy to train" because of this inherent motivation to cooperate with humans. Retrieving also involves more training of non-instinctive behaviors than other hunting function dogs, because they must be taught to follow directional signals and retrieve in specific ways.

Other-dog aggression: low. Retriever function demands that dogs work around other hunting dogs and ignore them. Hunting dogs are often kenneled while training and other-dog aggression is not wanted. Dogs with dual guard function may be exceptions.

There is a huge dichotomy between hunting-bred retrievers, particularly those suitable for field trials, and those bred for companion or show qualities and intended as pets. Those bred for field trials usually have the initiative and activity level needed in a Hearing Dog, but tend to be powerful, intense dogs that do not fit the lifestyle of most people. Conversely, the companion type excels in public, but may be impossible to motivate in sound alerting. Those retriever individuals that do possess talent in sound alerting can make excellent Hearing Dogs. Purebred retrievers graduated at a 33% rate from the HDP.

Retriever breeds are recognized for their high percentage of individuals that show suitability for service dog functions. Service dog trainers search or selectively breed for extremely submissive, interactive dogs with as little initiative as possible that will wait for commands. Low activity and reactivity levels are essential. The dog should always be easily controllable, even when the dog knows there will be no physical correction if it does not obey. Dogs that can perform dual functions as service and Hearing Dogs are obviously hard to find, due to the conflicting nature of the desired temperaments.

Hearing Dog suitability:
- For sound alerting role: low to moderate
- For public access role: high
- For companion role: high

Blueprint for a Terrier

To create a dog that will hunt and kill small prey that sometimes hides underground, we need to start with a dog small enough to get inside burrows and small spaces. It needs to either flush out the prey, or kill it underground where humans and larger dogs cannot reach it.

Reactivity: high. The dog needs very high overall reactivity, as it must have reflexes faster than that of the prey it hunts.

Sound reactivity: high. To locate prey, the dog must use all of its senses, but hearing is especially vital to locate underground or hidden animals that cannot be precisely targeted by scent.

Activity: high. It should be able to hunt all day. High activity levels also give it great persistence in digging towards inaccessible prey for long periods.

Interactivity: moderate. Many people would indignantly describe their terrier as highly interactive, but the definition depends on whether their dog would prefer interacting with them to hunting a mouse. Terriers are often described as dogs that truly enjoy being with their owner as long as the owner participates in activities that the terrier likes. If a dual function as alarm dog exists, low interactivity with strangers then results.

Territoriality: variable. Territoriality is not relevant to terrier function, but dual functions such as alarm or guard may exist.

Predatory instinct: high. Very high predatory aggression is required; not only is this dog killing other animals that can bite back, it is killing them when they are cornered and fighting for their lives. The prey is often similar in size to the dog. High curiosity helps the dog investigate hunting opportunities.

Biting: high. It must have an uninhibited, full-force bite that can kill quickly before the dog is injured. Although aggression to humans is not necessary to terrier function, the terrier's lack of interest in being directed and controlled, its uninhibited bite, and its high reactivity all combine to create a dog with high potential for biting people.

Initiative: high. It must be independent and strong willed to make its own decisions, since the human owner is not able to direct or help a dog working underground. Other dogs that hunt prey of equal or larger size almost never tackle it alone, but work in packs to gradually weaken the prey. Terriers must work alone, since there is not room for more than one in the confined spaces where their prey is found. Independence results from a combination of high initiative and lower social interactivity.

Fearfulness: low. Retreating from pain or threat would cancel its value as a hunter. Killing prey that is sometimes its own size requires an unnatural level of fearlessness, since survival instincts alone would dictate a more sensible attitude of retreat. Many terriers are described as being fearless to the point of being foolhardy.

Dominance/submission: variable. Terriers are often described as tending to be dominant, yet their dominance is more toward dogs than humans; some are quite submissive to people. Since terriers are often injured while hunting, submissiveness to people can help them be easier to handle and treat.

Other-dog aggression: variable, but often high. High other-dog aggression in terriers is not due to overall high predatory aggression; most behavior researchers classify social aggression as a totally separate behavior than predatory aggression. More likely, other-dog aggression is due to the long history in Great Britain of dog fighting as a dual function for all terriers, not just the bull terrier types commonly associated with this activity. Other-dog aggression levels can also depend on whether the dog was designed to hunt alone, semi-cooperatively with other terriers, or with whole packs of foxhounds.

It is easy to predict that the average terrier will be too independent and not interactive enough for our purposes. It will prefer to explore and hunt rather than stay with its owner, and its high predatory aggression will be a problem. It may show aggression to people and dogs. On the plus side, it will have fantastic sound reactivity, backed up with a high activity level and curiosity, giving it good potential in sound alerting. Its smaller size makes its high activity level easier to live with.

However, because some terrier function dogs have been bred for companion traits in this century, and some of their aggression has been eliminated, it is possible to find purebred terriers that are suitable as Hearing Dogs. Cairn Terriers are a good example; some have a temperament closer to a poodle than to a terrier. A wide individual range in temperament is seen in some breeds. Unlike these, the Jack Russell Terrier still remains close to the original terrier blueprint; too much potential in sound alerting, and too little for the other two roles. Jack Russell owners often describe intensely sound-reactive behavior with a strongly aggressive component; attacking ringing telephones and biting owners as they run to them, for instance.

Hearing Dog suitability:
- For sound alerting: high
- For companion role: moderate
- For public access role: low

Blueprint for an Alarm Dog

This type of dog is usually termed "watchdog," but I prefer "alarm dog," since many people use "watchdog" and "guard dog" interchangeably. There is a continuous gradient between alarm and guard functions, and many breeds fall somewhere in between. Bonnie Wilcox, DVM, and Chris Walkowicz give an interesting comparison between alarm and guard dog function in *The Atlas of Dog Breeds of the World*. It describes the Brazilian Terrier, a small dog descended from the Jack Russell Terrier and others. The Brazilian Terrier "is most common on the outlying ranches and estates. With his alert bearing and bark, he warns of strangers. Lest intruders think they have only to deal with a noisy twenty-pound terrier, the barking serves to wake up the tough one-hundred pound Filas which answer the alarm and handle any threat."

Many alarm-function dogs also have a dual role as companion dogs. Specific breeds are often hard to classify, since alarm dogs have a xenophobic quality that does not affect their ability to be good companions to their own family. Within most breeds individual variation is great, depending on aggression and fearfulness levels. It's possible to encounter the unexpected, from a suspicious, reactive Pug to a calm, non-territorial Schipperke.

The desired behavior in an alarm dog is an instant alert to anything out of the ordinary with barking and activity. Since the dog's only duty is to alert, not to follow up through aggression, it is more useful to have it be too wired, just as any alarm system operates better when too sensitive; twenty false alarms are worthwhile if one real one saves lives. Likewise, missing that one real crisis through insensitivity makes the whole alarm system useless. It is up to humans to respond to the alarm function dog's alert, and then decide whether to act upon it or not.

Reactivity: high. In order to function as a good alarm when danger is sensed, such a dog needs to be highly reactive overall. Waking up easily from sleep is characteristic of reactive dogs, and alarm function dogs must be useful at all hours.

Sound reactivity: high. This dog must be highly sound reactive to all sounds, with a strong tendency to approach them, albeit cautiously. This approach behavior informs its owners about the location of potential danger. It should also be reactive to visual and olfactory stimuli. Slow habituation enhances the overall sensitivity of its alerts to danger.

Activity: high. A very high activity level will enable it to constantly patrol the territorial boundaries. Rapid movement makes its alerts easy to notice.

Interactivity: high. Reactivity, fearfulness, and aggression in this dog are balanced by extremely high social interactivity within its human pack. Its interactivity keeps it near enough to humans for them to note its reactions to danger. Whether submissive or dominant with its family, it is constantly interacting, playful, and active. Its social interactivity with strangers is low. As in guard function dogs, all strangers are guilty until proven innocent.

Territoriality: high. Alarm function dogs need high territoriality both to perceive the boundaries to be patrolled, as well as to stay safely within them. They may have high territorial aggression similar to that of a guard function dog, but it is usually inhibited by fearfulness. Alarm dogs whose temperament is closer to companion dogs display a happily excited but not aggressive territoriality. Extreme curiosity motivates the dog to investigate anything unusual in its territory.

Predatory instinct: moderate to high. Other animals can also be classified as unwanted intruders and are alerted to. Many alarm dogs are well suited for a dual function as terriers, killing small animals such as rats and mice, nor is it uncommon to hear about small alarm dogs chasing off huge animals like bears.

Biting: high. Since the dog is going to react to almost everything that happens around it, it is more likely to bite than a calm, non-reactive guard type. One safety catch that can minimize this problem is for the dog to be small. Its bites will not do as much damage as those of a larger dog's will. It needs to be able to bite strongly to defend its frail little body in the event that a burglar or predator attacks it, but it will probably not bite unless approached, preferring to escape—and continue sounding the alarm. If it does attack, biting by rushing up behind the threat and then fearfully retreating is often its chosen strategy (hence, the derogatory term "ankle biter" used for many small alarm breeds).

Initiative: moderate. An alarm dog needs initiative in order to act on its own to any danger that arises without being inhibited by any human activities going on. On the other hand, too much initiative will cause it to behave too independently, and it may stray away from its family; it should stay close, both for its own safety and for the family's awareness of its alerts.

Fearfulness: high. By breeding for small size for this function, we now have a dog that puts its life in danger if it approaches the threat it is alerting to. Moderate to high levels of fearfulness, and a lowered ability to be socialized past puppyhood, ensures that it is cautious and wary, circling far around an intruder.

Dominance/submission: variable. Although dominance helps in the alarm role, submission helps in the companion role of these dogs.

Other-dog aggression: variable. The temperament traits of alarm function dogs tend to create the same problem behaviors with strange dogs as seen towards strange people. Frustrated, hysterical behavior with mingled components of fear and aggression is intensified by the fact that these dogs must be picked up or kept on tight leashes to protect them from being killed by larger dogs that become aggravated by their provoking behavior.

In the alarm group we find many of the ingredients that make up a good Hearing Dog. High activity, reactivity, initiative, curiosity, and interactiveness all make for top potential. Small size is another plus, since most people wanting a Hearing Dog prefer small dogs. The ingredients we don't want are the high fearfulness, aggression, and territoriality, which affect their abilities to handle public access. An uninhibited bite may be delivered when threatened by strangers reaching out to pet them; a good survival strategy when confronting intruders, but a poor one for Hearing Dogs.

Hearing Dog suitability:
- For sound alerting role: high.
- For companion role: moderate.
- For public access role: low.

Blueprint for a Companion Dog

Many people imagine that any dog they acquire will become their companion. This is true to some extent, but most dogs have been bred for some other primary purpose than to interact with humans. Their drive to engage in other instinctive behaviors is strongly present and they will be happy with people only as a second-best activity.

My definition of a companion dog is one that prefers interaction with people to other activities, craves inclusion in a social group, and develops strong relationships with its owners. It is necessary to breed out all the primeval survival behaviors. We are willing to be responsible for this dog's survival, so it won't need them. Besides, we certainly don't want a dog that practices its survival techniques on us. The few instincts left are those relating to social relationships. These are the most important features of a good companion. The social rewards that we get back from this dog are well worth the extra effort needed to care for it.

Companion dogs show a wide range of reactivity and activity levels, because only a few breeds exist that have been designed solely for companion purposes. Most also double as alarm dogs, or have retriever or spaniel functions that coincidentally fit in well with companion specifications. The gradations between companion and alarm functions mean that the following profile applies only to dogs that are true companion function dogs with no alarm tendencies. Dogs with dual functions show a temperament somewhere between the two.

Reactivity: low. Reactivity is detrimental to companion function. The less reactive the dog is, the more cuddly, passive, and childlike its behavior.

Sound reactivity: low. Excessive reaction to sounds interferes with having a calm, adaptable companion. Companion function requires that dogs quickly habituate to the unfamiliar, which includes sounds.

Activity: low to moderate. People prefer a pet that has enough energy to play or exercise when they have time, but is happy to laze about when nothing is going on.

Interactivity: very high. Our companion should be sensitive, emotionally and communicatively. It must be good with children, so we need high interactivity. It shouldn't need special training to be a good pet. Removing so many instinctive survival behaviors except for social behavior makes this easy, because most "obedience" training has nothing to do with obedience itself, but is designed to suppress instinctive behaviors and substitute other more acceptable ones. With this dog, there is little instinctive behavior to suppress. By increasing the desire for social interaction with humans, the dog is cooperative when we try to influence its behavior. Its interactivity with strangers is also high. Most people who desire companion temperament have lifestyles involving kids and visitors, and require a dog that can coexist peacefully without aggression or fearfulness. Such dogs have a "World Pack" mentality.

Territoriality: Low or nonexistent. Some excited but non-aggressive recognition of territorial intrusion is useful.

Predatory instinct: Low or nonexistent. Removing this instinct prevents the dog from reacting aggressively to running, screaming children or other pets. It also prefers interaction with its owner to any type of hunting behavior. A little predatory behavior is acceptable—divorced from aggression—because we enjoy a playful dog that "hunts" its toys.

Biting: Low or nonexistent.

Initiative: low. An ideal companion waits for people to give cues instead of constantly trying to make things happen.

Fearfulness: Low or nonexistent. Lack of fearfulness creates a dog that is easily socialized and retains flexibility in adjusting to change throughout its life. Strangers, dogs, and unfamiliar environments are accepted with little difficulty.

Dominance/submission: submissive. A very submissive dog is easiest to control, and tends to challenge people less, even if people act submissively to it by treating it as they would a human infant. Because most companion function dogs are small, when aggression does appear it is less of a problem—or is just taken less seriously!

Other-dog aggression: low. This dog should have more interest in people than in other dogs. Poodles, for instance, tend to prefer to bond with people even if raised in a house full of other dogs. By lowering the intensity of so many natural behaviors, we may have also altered the social signals that companionship dogs use to communicate with each other, making their relationships with other dogs less intense and communicative.

When searching for Hearing Dogs among the companion function dogs, we note their eminent suitability for public access and of course companion roles. They may lack sound reactivity and activity, but many of those with dual functions as alarm dogs can show the most desirable features of both groups, sometimes lacking all the undesirable ones. Among the dogs categorized as companion/alarm function, 36% of purebreds graduated, but an astonishing 43% of purebred Poodles made it.

Hearing Dog suitability:
- For sound alerting role: low.
- For companion role: high.
- For public access role: high.

Blueprint for a Spaniel

This dog locates hidden birds by scent or sound, indicates their position, can be inhibited from flushing them until the hunter is ready to shoot, and then retrieves them without damaging their edibility. It often has a dual function as a companion dog, probably a coincidental role that the spaniel temperament fulfills.

Reactivity: high. Quick response to commands and bird movements is necessary. While actively searching for birds, high reactivity enables the dog to indicate birds instantly.

Sound reactivity: moderate. A spaniel function dog listens for bird sounds when it cannot scent them, and must also respond to whistled or verbal commands from the hunter. It should not react fearfully to sounds, since it will be exposed to gunfire. Perhaps because of this effort to breed a dog that ignores gunfire, some spaniels show very low sound reactivity.

Activity: high. Spaniels must be able to hunt for hours in varied terrain. Their quartering behavior while searching requires constant activity.

Interactivity: high. This dog works closely with its owner, following many commands as well as its own instinctive behaviors. Since hunters often hunt with other people or loan dogs to friends for hunting, high sociability with strangers is desirable.

Territoriality: low. Territoriality is not relevant to hunting birds. Spaniels need to confidently range out in new areas, and do not need to protect or remain at their home base.

Predatory instinct: high. Spaniels need strong predatory instinct that ends after the chasing and catching part of the sequence. Lack of killing behavior helps lead to an inhibited bite.

Biting: low. To gently retrieve birds, this dog needs a bite with inhibited pressure.

Initiative: moderate. A balance is needed between control by the hunter and independent decision-making to search for birds.

Fearfulness: low to moderate. The dog should show enough caution for self-preservation while out hunting. It should not be fearful of strange environments because hunting involves traveling to new places and freely exploring them. Poor breeding of the more popular spaniel breeds produces many individuals with very high fearfulness, so most spaniels show higher fear than would be expected from this profile. Spaniels bred specifically for hunting and field trials or for companion temperament show less fearfulness.

Dominance/submission: variable, often submissive. Its hunting behavior involves rapid quartering of an area, directed by the hunter, so it must be submissive and responsive to commands. To balance the strength of the powerful hunting instincts that motivate it, it must be submissive from a distance. As a result, overly submissive spaniels can often be seen. In particular, the dog that is so perfectly controllable at a distance may be overwhelmed by dominant human body language or voice when up close, and show submissive urination problems. On the other hand, a dog hunting for long hours under hard conditions needs resiliency and determination. Such dogs may be difficult to control by nontrainers. Different breeding programs designed to produce pets, hobby hunting dogs, or field trial competition dogs result in widely differing temperaments both between and within breeds.

Other-dog aggression: low. Hunting dogs need to coexist and ignore other dogs when hunting.

The spaniel group shows high potential for all three Hearing Dog roles. Some individual dogs show sound reactivity, submissiveness, interactivity, inhibited bite, sociability with strangers, and high activity levels. An intriguing breed, which I've never personally seen, is the field trial version of the English Cocker Spaniel, which looks nothing like an English Cocker. It resembles a small Cocker mix, and is reputed to preserve the classic spaniel temperament.

The most often seen spaniels in shelters are the Cocker Spaniel and the Springer Spaniel. Due to their health problems and temperament anomalies, it's hard to find a suitable one. I sometimes see what appear to be throwbacks to the old type of Cocker; short body coat with long feathering and curly ears, a happy, outgoing, non-biting nature, and normal-appearing eyes and ear canals. A few of these have turned out to be good Hearing Dogs. But it is cocker mixes that interest me more. Some sort of alchemy happens, and a dog appears that bears some physical resemblance to a Cocker Spaniel, yet has the gentle, energetic temperament most people think a Cocker Spaniel has. At the HDP, Spaniel mixes graduated at a very high 39% rate compared to 17% of purebred Spaniels.

Hearing Dog suitability:
- For sound alerting role: high.
- For public access role: high.
- For companion role: high.

Designing a Hearing Dog

Hearing Dogs need to help their partners with three basic survival needs:
1. communicating with other people (by assisting with door and telephone)
2. personal safety issues (by alerting to smoke alarms and other danger signals)
3. social needs (both by companionship as well as being a social facilitator for interaction with other people)

One would think that "designing" a Hearing Dog would be easy. But simply taking the desirable traits and combining them does not fit the way temperament works. For instance, high reactivity is detrimental to companion suitability, unless submissiveness is also present and all aggression and fearfulness removed.

Reactivity: moderate to high. High reactivity enables the dog to shine in the sound-alerting role. Low or moderate reactivity is more desirable for companion and public access roles.

Sound reactivity: high. High sound reactivity is usually a factor of high overall reactivity, but there are ways to avoid designing a dog that is too reactive overall. Just as scenthounds may have a lower overall reactivity level but an intense reactivity to scent, Hearing Dogs are sometimes found with moderate overall reactivity and a high reactivity to sounds. Selective breeding could be used to intensify this combination of traits.

The mystery is whether the sensory reactions seen in scenthounds, sighthounds, and herding dogs are achieved by intensifying reactions to certain senses or by blocking input from other senses, or both. When scenting, scenthounds appear to notice nothing else around them, but when not scenting, they react normally to all stimuli.

Activity: moderate. The desirable activity level depends on its balance with sound reactivity. Too active, and all but the strongest reactions to sounds are overpowered. Too inactive, and the active physical alert to sounds is lost. Owner preference is another factor; the lower the activity level, the more suitable the dog is for companion and public access.

Interactivity: high. The more interactive, the better, for all three roles. Interactivity with strangers, though, should be moderate. It is interesting that poodles often have a perfect attitude for public access. They show a combination of a reserved, disinterested reaction towards strangers with intense interactivity with familiar people. Their attitude towards strangers is often without aggression or fear, just rather remote. This behavior may be why poodles have been labeled "snooty."

Territoriality: Low or nonexistent. At most, excited, non-aggressive alerts to territorial intrusion are acceptable. If territoriality is any higher, then the partner must have an equally high ability to control the dog's behavior. Although being alerted to intruders is a survival issue for the partner, the higher territoriality becomes, the more it affects the dog's performance of the public access role.

Predatory instinct: low to moderate. In spite of the advantage that this trait seems to give in sound alerting, it can be detrimental to the other two roles.

Biting: low.

Initiative: moderate to high. Higher initiative is essential for sound alerting, yet low initiative is desirable for the other two roles.

Fearfulness: low or nonexistent. Not only must the dog be fearless of strangers, new environments, and all other stimuli, it must be adaptable enough to adjust to anything new or unusual that it encounters. To be able to do this, it must retain its potential to be socialized throughout its life. It should not need constant exposure to the same situations to remain free of fear.

Dominance/submissiveness: submissive. Submissiveness helps to counteract many of the challenges presented by reactive temperaments. Unwanted survival instincts may be acceptable at a higher level if the dog is submissive and easily controlled. An acquiescent dog that will accept any status in its human pack, as long as it can be included, fits in better with most people's lifestyles.

Other-dog aggression: low or nonexistent. Owners of Hearing Dogs that show other-dog aggression are often inhibited from using control measures in public for fear that people will perceive them as abusing their dog. Other-dog aggression in public is a difficult problem for all assistance dogs.

Perfect Hearing Dog temperament, with all its conflicts between the ideals for each role, is as unattainable as all the ideals specified in any other blueprint, but it is a goal to work toward. Knowing which functional groups Hearing Dog temperament derives from is a step towards selecting purebreds and mixed breeds for testing, as well as selecting breeding stock to create a Hearing Dog. Dogs are not recipes, and genetics is not a simple matter of mixing ingredients, but looking at Hearing Dogs in these very simplistic terms provides a starting point.

The companion, retriever, and spaniel groups have temperaments that are suitable for companion and public access roles, but tend to lack sound reactivity and initiative, and some lack high enough activity levels as well.

The terrier, herding, and alarm groups possess the sound reactivity, initiative, and high activity levels needed for sound alerting, but are hindered in companion and public access roles by varying amounts of aggression, territoriality, biting tendency, fearfulness, dominance, independence, and lack of sociability with strangers.

Excluding the Dachshund that shows a terrier/alarm temperament, the guard, primeval, hound, and sled group temperaments have more unwanted traits than wanted ones. They can offer initiative and sometimes activity levels, however.

The fact that all of the functional groups show both desirable and undesirable traits is a clue to why mixed breeds often show Hearing Dog temperament. Theoretically, mixes with parents from different groups should have more potential than those with parents from the same functional group. Crossing within a group (such as a Springer Spaniel and a Cocker Spaniel) might intensify the undesirable traits as easily as the desirable ones, but crossing between groups that do not share the same faults might give better results. If dogs from any two different groups were bred together (such as any terrier with any spaniel), the resulting offspring would have a wider range of temperament. Some pups could be expected to show a combination of the worst traits, and some the best. Even if the "best" offspring were rare, they still represent a new combination that was unattainable by limiting breeding within a functional group.

Looking at the possible inheritance a dog could receive from different groups allows one to speculate wildly that there should be combinations that would produce more Hearing Dogs than others would. The companion, spaniel, and retriever groups could contribute their outstanding social interactivity, whereas the terrier, alarm, and herding groups could be a source of high activity levels and sound reactivity. As noted in the Appendix, these six groups did indeed show the most success for the Hearing Dog Program.

When randomly bred, dogs revert to primeval appearance, and possibly also revert to primeval temperament. Fearfulness and other survival instincts reappear unless a domesticated temperament is constantly selected for. If companions, spaniels, and retrievers are part of a mix, their influence tends to counteract this trend.

Selecting Purebreds from Shelters or Rescue Groups

Selecting a purebred dog that can be suitable for Hearing Dog roles is complicated even when the breed selected seems to have potential. The adopter needs to be aware of the following issues:

The purebreds seen in shelters consist of very high numbers of unsuitable breeds, although the occasionally suitable Labradors, Cockers, and Poodles are among the top ten most common shelter breeds.

Information published on breed temperaments can be very misleading. Often descriptions that should be warnings in bold red type are instead phrased in vague, euphemistic terms in order to avoid offending fans or breeders. For instance, the statement, "The South Bay Ratsnatcher is affectionate to its family's children if they are taught to respect its need for occasional privacy. Like all Ratsnatchers, its personality is best brought out by socialization with strangers and strange children throughout puppyhood" *really* means, "The South Bay Ratsnatcher will snap at or bite the family's children if they bother it. If not extensively socialized, it may bite any strangers or children that might be visiting." One excellent book that is bluntly truthful about breeds is *Choosing the Right Dog* by Nancy Baer and Steve Duno.

Because breed temperament descriptions assume that the dog started out with the correct breed temperament and was then raised correctly, they are usually useless when dealing with any adult purebred. Even starting with the right temperament, a badly raised dog might not fit the breed description. Herding breeds are a case in point. With extensive puppy socialization to strange places and strange people, most herding breed adult dogs show only slight fearfulness, often displaying all of the best traits of the herding breeds. Raised without socialization and sensitive training, however, they behave as if more closely related to coyotes than to dogs. Fearful, panicky, and sometimes aggressive, they are the ones I see cowering in shelters, traumatized at being separated from their owners and in a state of shock at being in a terrifyingly strange place. Finding a socialized, fearless, outgoing herding purebred in a shelter is a wonderful surprise, more the exception than the rule.

Breeds that have been popularized also become changed in temperament, often to the point of being mentally disabled. Selection of breeding stock for fertility alone lets other traits fall by the wayside. The new temperament becomes that of the majority of the breed, and the fact that a few dedicated breeders are still producing dogs with the original ideal breed temperament becomes almost irrelevant. These dogs are now a tiny minority, and the average puppy buyer is not aware that they must find these breeders if they want a dog like the descriptions they've read.

The variability caused by poor breeding can actually work in favor of finding purebred Hearing Dogs. A dog may have incorrect temperament for its breed, such as an overly outgoing and non-suspicious alarm individual, but coincidentally be perfect for a Hearing Dog. It doesn't really matter if the average Lapland Lingerlonger is a sluggish little snapper, if you happen to find the only active, friendly one ever born.

Of the hundreds of breeds in the world today, very few can fit into modern lifestyles, let alone fill the public access role of a Hearing Dog. Many very specialized or primeval breeds are publicized as potential family pets, with the caveat that they must be raised and trained in certain ways that usually involve hundreds of extra hours of effort beyond what a more suitable breed might require for the same end result. The more special techniques a breed needs, the less chance there is that the individual seen in a shelter has received all that special attention.

Breeds or individual dogs with companion temperaments survive shelter life and other environments that would make basket cases out of other dogs. They do not require special

These unrelated dogs are from many shelters, but share that elusive quality, Hearing Dog temperament. (Photo by Mike Rowell, SF-SPCA)

raising techniques to emerge without damage from substandard puppyhoods. The average person or family can raise a dog with companion temperament successfully by simply letting it grow up with good care.

Chapter Five
Animal Shelters

Animal shelters can be confusing and stressful places not just for animals, but for those who visit them. Although they often look like simple concrete buildings with kennels and cages and workers in rubber boots, they are strange worlds of their own with complex politics and mysterious rules and regulations. Employees often seem either angry and unhelpful to visitors, or so obsessed with animals that people don't seem real to them. Their jobs are hard, and if they stick it out more than a year or so, some of them develop coping mechanisms that may make them appear hardhearted and cold. In reality, they wouldn't have lasted so long in the job if they didn't love animals. But when they are forced to kill them, whether in person or in the abstract, they naturally turn their guilt and anger towards the public who abandoned their pets at the shelter—who in turn redirect their own guilt about surrendering their pets by becoming angry at the animal shelter employees for being unable to find homes for them.

This atmosphere was common in shelters when I started working at the Hearing Dog Program in 1989, but new trends in the animal control industry have since changed shelters for the better for both animals and people. Many shelters are now built and managed in ways that control disease (thereby reducing euthanasia rates), provide an attractive, friendly atmosphere, and keep animals comfortable. Still, it only takes one or two bad experiences with the old, "dungeon" type of shelters for many people to swear that they will never again willingly visit an animal shelter. The common refrain is, "It makes me too sad."

I would urge anyone interested in adopting a hearing dog from a shelter to either grit their teeth and go and get to know the local animal shelters (and maybe be pleasantly surprised), or else find a qualified person to select a dog for them. More and more shelters now have volunteer programs, and volunteers can provide a great interface between the public and the staff. They can see the point of view of both groups, and know how to find their way through the intricate regulations that both protect animals and sometimes make it complicated to adopt them. Volunteers are also good contacts for dog trainers, breed rescue groups, and any other information that the overworked shelter staff does not have time to provide.

Animal Shelter Types

There are two main types of animal shelters: usually designated "open door" and "no-kill," although most shelters do not fit these categories so neatly. This distinction reflects more than euthanasia policy. This distinction reflects more than euthanasia policy. Open-door shelters are those that accept *all* animals in need regardless of their condition and then make a judgment on the animal's potential for adoption. In the end, the animal is either euthanized or placed for adoption. These are usually shelters that perform stray animal control duties as part of the city or county administrative system. They are always severely under funded and are forced to euthanize many adoptable in addition to the unadoptable animals.

Because animal control shelters are required by local law to accept all animals brought to them, they receive many that are terminally ill, feral, or have severe behavior problems that make them unable to be rehabili-

Does this gloomy place hide the dog of a lifetime? This small, underfunded rural shelter provides many wonderful dogs to the Hearing Dog Program. Caring employees try to save the dogs they feel are the best pets in spite of severe space and financial limitations.

tated. They have no choice but to euthanize the most severe of these cases. Depending on the amount of funding, some can afford medical or behavioral treatment to make animals adoptable, or keep adoptable animals for long periods of time until adopted. Most rely on volunteers who socialize, foster, and train animals, and local vets who donate medical care such as low-cost sterilization services. Animal control shelters are often run as a division of the local law-enforcement sector and may have rather rigid policies.

The other types of shelter, dubbed " no-kill," are private nonprofit organizations that are supported by donations. These shelters do not euthanize animals except in what they consider emergency situations, but they manage to avoid most euthanasia by only accepting animals that they deem adoptable. Since owners whose animals are rejected by the no-kill shelters then take them to an open-door shelter where they might be euthanized, some critics of no-kill shelters claim that the overall euthanasia rates are not much affected. These policy differences create bad feelings between the two types of shelters; the no-kill shelters attract donation money, but the open-door shelters feel that they must do all the euthanasia and then get blamed unfairly for it. Their resentment is compounded by the fact that if they too could attract financial donations, they could keep adoptable animals much longer, and lower their euthanasia numbers. No-kill shelters may err on the side of keeping animals so long that their quality of life becomes debatable; dogs kept in shelter kennels for months may show severe stress and their behavior may degenerate to the point where they are no longer adoptable.

Dealing with Shelter Employees and Policies

Both types of shelters are usually eager to place dogs with qualified owners or trainers to become hearing dogs, but making good contacts with shelter employees and long-time volunteers is essential for the best success in finding a dog. Being able to bypass voice-mail labyrinths, or even to receive a phone call from a shelter saying that "Dog Number 34599 was not reclaimed by the owner and will be available for adoption at 3 p.m." can make all the difference.

The best way to have a good relationship with an animal shelter is to behave differently from the other visitors. It seems nobody ever enters an animal shelter in a calm, rational mood. People are desperately searching for lost pets, trying to reclaim animals confiscated for biting, irritated at having to pay fines, or trying to adopt an animal without crying too hard for all the others they can't take. Employees explain and argue about shelter rules and policies hundreds of times a day to frustrated, anxious, or angry pet owners. When these employees encounter a polite, calm, well informed, professionally behaving person (hopefully like you!), it is quite a pleasant shock to them. Learning each shelter's policies, hours, and hierarchies and writing them down is essential. Each one is like a separate little kingdom with absolute and unbreakable rules. Showing respect for and knowledge of policies will set you apart from the average person who makes the difficult job of shelter employee still harder. For instance, instead of approaching a counter clerk with a statement like, "I want that brown spaniel mix you have, don't kill it yet because I can take it home later today," you would receive far better service and information by saying, "I see that the dog with tag number 348 in Kennel 12 came in on the fifth, and I hope she's available to adopt today. Could you please check that out for me?" Hear the difference?

Tester Reactions to Shelters

Few people willingly visit animal shelters. Nobody wants to see a sad dungeon full of doomed dogs and cats. And it's true; some shelters are like that. Anyone who loves animals is naturally going to be affected by seeing them in such sad conditions. In spite of all the dedicated volunteers and shelter employees at every shelter, the fact is that many die for no reason other than lack of funding. And all this death is not just a remote concept; visiting shelters in off hours, one may see tables three deep in dead cats, or dumpster loads of dead dogs being tipped into the renderer's truck. All I can say is that one must focus on the positive, look at every dog, try to notify rescue groups about adoptable purebreds, look for potential drug detection and police K9s, and find hearing dogs. It's always personally rewarding to bring back dogs that failed testing, yet would be good pets, for our own shelter to adopt out.

The San Francisco SPCA is at the opposite end of the spectrum. It is a no-kill type of shelter with programs for grooming, training, medical treatment, and exercising for animals waiting to be adopted. Training programs for people, who are the root of the animal overpopulation problem, include humane education for children, a sterilization clinic, dog training classes, owner counseling, grief counseling, animal-assisted therapy, outreach adoption, and others. Working there, it is quite a shock to drive four hours to a rural shelter and see desperate volunteers trying to care for 17 puppies in a 6x6 dirt pen, and no adopters in sight. It was a still greater shock to return to this shelter a few months later and learn that the volunteers had been kicked out and all animals were being euthanized after the minimum legal holding period, so I didn't even have 17 runny-nosed puppies to pick from.

I could focus on the sadness of this situation, the waste of human effort and dog's lives. Or, I can focus on Nutmeg, one of the runny-nosed ones I adopted. She resembled a ten-pound Cavalier King Charles Spaniel, was great at sound alerting but terrified of traffic, and although she dropped out, was adopted as a pet by a couple who already had a hearing dog. She alerts to sounds, and is so devoted that they nicknamed her "The Limpet."

To feel helpful to all these dogs in shelters, sometimes one needs to do all this sideline rescuing, because hearing dogs are few and far between. It's not uncommon to travel to five shelters in a day-long trip, see 300 dogs, and not find a single hearing dog candidate.

Shelter Personnel Input

Experienced shelter personnel often have good input on the dogs in their shelter. They might not know what the tester is looking for and suggest "that real mellow Golden over there," but they do know the difference between the poor or average dog and the really great ones. Dogs that exhibit exceptional sociability in particular will attract their attention, since they have to deal with so many dogs that only want to interact by biting. Some newer shelter employees and volunteers select the most maladapted, pathetic, or sickly dogs to try to save. In particular, they often confuse fearful or aggressive temperaments with the effects of abuse, and wish to rescue these dogs most of all. Their motives are admirable, but it's already emotionally difficult enough to test shelter dogs without being made even guiltier by someone determined to offer you their least-adoptable dogs.

Shelter personnel also know about dogs that may not be on public view, such as those in a hospital area, sterilization clinic, foster care home, or protective custody ward. Custody-ward dogs are not always abused dogs that would fail testing. They often are neglected, yet trusting, or their owners may have gone to jail for unrelated offenses. Many shelters have volunteers who foster sick or pregnant dogs at their own homes. Any of these dogs may be available for adoption immediately or at a later date. Dogs scheduled for euthanasia that day might be held in a separate area. Shelley Monson visited one shelter and rescued Kristen, an American Eskimo, right off the euthanasia table. Since then, Kristen has climbed Mount Whitney many times with her partner, who is a backpacking instructor, and provided much peace of mind for her on camping trips, since she knows Kristen will warn her of approaching bears or other wildlife at night.

Although you may not always find the next "wonder dog" of hearing dogs, these kinds of success stories make the failures that much easier to take.

Most of the more suitable functional groups are behind the ancestry of these mixed breeds. (Photo by SF-SPCA)

Chapter Six
Shelter Dog Behavior

Animal shelters can have negative effects on a dog's behavior, but this should not be used as an excuse for temperament problems or bad test results. Instead, the shelter environment gives the tester an opportunity to evaluate many traits that cannot be seen when testing an owned dog in a home environment.

The dog's behavior in a shelter is one of the best predictors of its ability to handle the stressful or exciting things that a dog with public access rights can encounter. Any dog that can be abandoned by its owner, housed in a noisy place with slamming metal gates and constantly barking dogs, stared at by strangers while confined in a small kennel, live in these conditions for weeks on end, and still be sociable, playful, trusting, and confident, is an amazing dog that will probably be happy and confident in any situation imaginable. Such a dog is not going to be stressed by a little adventure like a trip on an airplane with its partner. In addition, for dogs that must spend their training period in a kennel situation, shelter behavior will help predict whether they can adjust, or whether they need a calmer home environment immediately.

From a dog's point of view, being enclosed in a small space with no escape route is a dangerous situation. Any shelter kennel, even the largest, can still make a dog feel that its survival is endangered. Dogs with little fearfulness do not feel endangered by most of the scary aspects of an animal shelter. They show little reaction to stressors that make most dogs upset. This is why testing while dogs are inside as well as outside their kennels is so informative. The dog's temperament is exposed, and it is up to the tester to decide its relevance to the real world.

Barrier Frustration and Territoriality

A common sight at animal shelters is dogs that seem to be attacking from inside their cages; they may even bite the bars. A commonly heard refrain at shelters is, "Oh, he's just like that in the cage, he's fine when he's out." This may sometimes be true, but there are several reasons for this behavior, and all of them indicate unsuitable temperaments for Hearing Dogs. Dogs may protect territory, and be blocked by a barrier such as a fence, which causes frustration. They also may be eager to get closer to a dog or person to interact in a non-aggressive way, but become frustrated when blocked from a goal. Whatever their goal, the stress of frustration than causes anger and aggression—*if* these traits are present in the personality in the first place.

Many dogs that seem aggressive in a kennel are not frustrated at all, but terrified and feeling trapped inside their kennel. They would escape if they could, but instead must deal with the "threat" (in their mind) of an approaching person by coming forward aggressively. They may or may not be bluffing; whether they would run away if free could only be judged if the dog was set loose. This kennel behavior has very strong predictive value for the dog's behavior in other enclosed situations that trigger frustration, territoriality, or fear. We might not recognize these situations easily but to dogs, being in a car, a yard, the front hallway of a house, the corner of a classroom, under a restaurant table, in a small airport lounge, being surrounded by a group of people, or, for some dogs, just being "trapped" on a leash with a stranger innocently approaching, are all barrier situations.

Some fearful dogs actually appear friendlier in their small cage. They gain security from discovering that people do not cross their safety barrier. Once the door is opened, or the dog is taken out of this little territory, it becomes terrified, only to recover when placed back in its kennel.

Upon seeing any form of aggression or severe fearfulness at all behind a barrier, the tester should move on to the next dog. Further testing on such a dog will not benefit dog or tester, and only people experienced with shelter dogs and aggression should be dealing with them.

Sniffing

Because scenting is so important to dogs, and forms a part of their social greeting behavior, the way they react to the scent of a stranger is informative. Sniffing behavior before making or allowing any physical contact indicates suspicion. It is commonly accepted that dogs need to sniff people to "get to know" them. This is only true in the case of dogs that are categorizing unknown people as strangers. Dogs that are very socially interactive and do not perceive pack versus non-pack distinctions do not need to

Above - Tail up, ears forward, and making intense eye contact, a male German Shepherd evaluates the tester...

Below - ...and comes to a conclusion.

get to know anyone; they behave as though they know and trust strangers already. These dogs often make friendly contact first and sniff later.

Eye Signals

Eye contact in dogs has many functions and dogs are very sensitive to canine eye signals. Dogs gain information by quick glances that assess the other dog's eye and body signals, not by prolonged staring. Therefore, staring is a threat behavior. It is possible that our eyes, showing extensive white, which resembles the expression of a fearful dog, make our glances even more noticeable and significant to dogs. When stared at, dogs have several options: they can threaten back aggressively, they can escape fearfully, they can show displacement behavior such as sniffing the ground or grooming to avoid dealing with the threat, or they can exhibit submissive behavior, accepting the human's "right" to threaten them. There is one more option, the most desirable for Hearing Dogs; if the dog lacks fearfulness and aggression in its temperament, then it cannot perceive eye contact as threatening, and shows no reaction at all. Displacement, submissive behavior, or no response at all indicates good potential. Fearfulness or aggression indicate future problems in the companion and public access roles.

When a dog reacts negatively to eye contact, its eyes show changes in pupil size and eyelid positions, which send complicated signals about the dog's emotional state. When it

 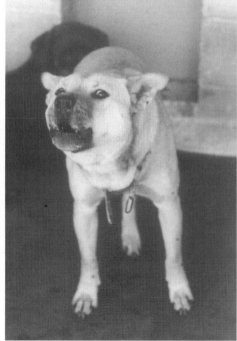

Left - This Shar Pei mix shows several unacceptable behaviors: he is raising his head to sniff the air without approaching, his legs show that he is ready to retreat, his head and neck are stiff while his eyes track the tester, and his mouth purses up in the beginnings of a fearful alarm bark. Right - He jumps slightly backwards as he barks fearfully, eyes wide. This mouth position is absolutely unacceptable.

freezes and stiffens its neck, it is prepared for danger. While staying ready to react, it allows its eyes to monitor the source of the danger. This means that the eyes must move alone, without accompanying movement of the head. Such eye movements cause the whites of a dog's eyes to show dramatically in the stressed expression described by Sue Sternberg as "whale eye." During play, the whites of the eyes are flashed briefly, but fearful dogs show it for at least several seconds at a time.

Puppy Jinx feels threatened and is not correctly reading Keeshond Bigia's very exaggerated play signals. Bigia's eye markings emphasize the wide open eyes, which flash white for an instant before she looks away. Bigia holds her head high so as not to directly threaten, and pants with a mock-fearful mouth, lips retracted. She play-bows as she prepares to bounce away in pretend terror.

Merely seeing the whites of a dog's eyes does not indicate much; very calm dogs may not bother to move their heads along with their eye movements, and dogs often assume a communicative stance, then watch for a reaction. Dilated pupils signify stress or fear. Wide eyes indicate threat or fear, and narrowed eyes indicate submission or relaxation. These many signals all interact in complex ways, and no single one can be used to define a dog's emotional state. However, if I see any eye movement combined with a stiff neck and rigid body, especially eyes that track my progress while the dog remains still, I do not interact with that dog, even to test it while it is still in the cage. The dog is showing strong fearfulness, and it is constantly calculating its trajectory for escape—or attack—relative to my movements. Whether it escapes, remains passively fearful, or attacks depends on many factors that I prefer not to investigate.

Because humans show far more white in their eyes than dogs do, one might expect that dogs would continuously misinterpret human expressions, and yet dogs are able to interpret human eye signals as well. Perhaps undersocialized dogs are so fearful of people because they have not learned to ignore the constantly showing whites of our eyes and our insensitive use of eye contact. Dogs that are heavily socialized with people can learn to tolerate and invite prolonged friendly eye contact.

Dogs that interact aggressively, without much fearfulness, show a different type of eye contact and movement. Unlike the rigid, fearfully frozen dog that moves only its eyes, these more confident dogs move their head in synch with their eyes, maintaining eye contact. If a dog is staring at me and moving its head along with its gaze, almost like a stalking movement of the head, yet shows no relaxed and playful body language in response to my efforts to appear non-threatening and friendly, I do not interact with that dog. My presence alone is causing a negative reaction; any attempt to interact may trigger aggressive behavior. If I tried, I know I could establish a reasonably friendly relationship with most dogs that behave this way, but there is no point; I now know that this dog reacts badly to strangers.

Obviously, a dog's reaction to eye contact has high relevance to its suitability for public access when they perceive strangers staring at them. And stare they will! People are often curious about a dog in a place where dogs are not usually present; they may be trying to read lettering on a leash or vest to find out what this dog is for; they may be fearful and "keeping an eye on it" in case they are attacked; or they may want to pet it but are trying to assess the dog's friendliness first. The stranger may be a child whose eyes are closer to the dog's level and therefore more threatening, or they may be the idiot who is surreptitiously staring and barking or growling to get a rise out of the dog.

Because the Hearing Dog in public attracts attention, and not always positive attention, any dog in a shelter that shows attack, threat, or escape responses to eye contact will have problems in public.

Multiple Dogs in One Cage

The interactions between two or more dogs may make evaluation difficult. In crowded shelter kennels, dominant dogs who prevent others from approaching doors, food bowls, or visitors often intimidate other dogs from showing any reaction to the tester. These bullies usually require that the other dogs sit passively in corners and show no strong emotions. The tester might need to be aware that the dog in the corner that is faintly smiling and wagging its tail unobtrusively might simply be inhibited from approaching by the presence of the dominant dog. The friendly dog enjoying its chance to get all the attention from the tester at the cage front might in reality be the bully that is inhibiting the others.

Dogs who interact with the other dogs instead of approaching the front of the cage to meet the tester are showing that they prefer interacting with dogs over people, and are unsuitable for the companion role of a Hearing Dog. Dogs that are fence fighting with the dog next door will most likely show the same behavior in a yard, car, or on leash around other dogs.

Groups of dogs will react differently to eye contact testing than will sin-

Above - The two most dominant males of this litter gang up to pounce on their sister, the most submissive pup. In crowded shelter kennels, this kind of behavior can inhibit otherwise suitable dogs, making testing difficult.

Below - Testing dogs that are this crowded is difficult. As I walked another dog down the aisle, all these dogs became agitated. The Pit Bull mix attacked the escaping dog to the left, the white-faced dog continued to bark at the strange dog, and the dog on the left interrupted his barking to worry about the fighting.

gle dogs. Often one dog will erupt in a frenzy of aggression or a panicked alarm barking at the slightest hint of eye contact from the tester, affecting the composure of all the others. The special dog that is oblivious to the fuss, and continues to act friendly in spite of a furious kennelmate, is showing excellent potential.

Length of Time Spent in Shelter

Decisions must be usually made according to the dog's behavior on that particular day. Often I'm told, "Oh, she's improved so much, she was terrified when she came in a few days ago and look at her now, so sweet." I used to be impressed, but now I shy away from that dog. I know that it is actually showing poor potential. Although it has somewhat recovered, it has already demonstrated a lack of resilience and will not be able to adjust easily to future stressful changes.

Is this Herding mix fearful of the tester or of the other dogs? Spilled food on the floor suggests a previous fight, but only further testing will tell.

Dogs that show increasing aggression or fearfulness after several weeks in a shelter are feeling the effects of stress or the buildup of territoriality. In dogs that have a predisposition to be aggressive to strangers, the constant parade of people and dogs by their kennel may appear threatening. The mere act of walking toward the dog's kennel, then seeming to flee as they walk away from the barking dog is sufficient to reinforce aggressive behavior. Unfortunately, such "training" is not easily reversible. Dogs that might previously have been fearful and avoided strangers can learn to use aggression to drive away people. Confident, dominant dogs may discover that threatening humans is good sport, reinforced every time people walk away from them. No intentional teasing or abuse is needed to create these behaviors; these are normal reactions to a caged situation.

Dogs that remain friendly to strangers under these conditions are showing very desirable temperament for Hearing Dogs.

Bonding Effects

I came across a really adorable dog in the Alameda County shelter, a tiny 12-pound blue-speckled dog that seemed to be part Chihuahua and part Australian Cattle Dog. I was surprised when she instantly liked me, and jumped up on everyone else as well, since both these breeds are often shy of strangers. I had expected her to at least act reserved. I took her back to the Hearing Dog Program in a crate in my car, and put her into a kennel with some food and worm medication. I then went home for the weekend. On Monday I was out doing interviews, and was surprised when the other trainers informed me that "the new dog" was screaming in fear and urinating when anyone went near her kennel. "Nonsense, that dog's perfectly friendly to everyone. What happened to her?" "Nothing, we've been trying to make friends but she's terrified!" I marched up indignantly to the kennels. The little dog was ecstatic to see me, happy and playful. I walked her around, put her back, and watched hidden as the other trainers approached. Screams, hysterical spinning, and urination. It looked like I was her chosen owner—even though I had spent a total of 40 minutes with her three days before.

She had probably been apart from her former owner long enough to lose the old bond. She was equally friendly to everyone at the shelter, because without a bonded relationship, her lonely little heart couldn't recognize the concept of "stranger." She then spent 40 minutes with me (not particularly positive minutes, either; a walk, put in a crate, a car trip, picked up briefly, and fed), which was all it took. Once bonded to me, there was no place for anyone else, and her previously repressed fear of strangers took over. I felt sorry for the poor dog, but I couldn't have another dog, and I knew that it was not some mystical partnership that was fated to be, but simply an intense need to bond to a single person. Intense loyalty to one person, combined with suspicion of strangers, is often seen in both Australian Cattle Dogs and Chihuahuas and this dog seemed to have gotten a double dose! I tried to stay away from her so that she wouldn't attach herself even more to me, as we desperately searched for a home for our "Toy Blue Heeler." She was shy at first with her new owner, a gentle man, but after a few days he reported that she was the most loving and loyal dog he had ever had.

Had I seen this dog a few days previously, I too might have seen a stressed-out dog urinating and shrieking at the sight of me. As it was, I met her during a small window of opportunity. I've seen many dogs react similarly to this one, although less dramatically. Most formed a strong bond gradually with a trainer, then progressively became less and less friendly to strangers.

Adopting an owned dog can be difficult if a sudden transfer is necessary. The dog may actually associate its feelings of depression and loss with the new owner. Dogs re-bond best if they have nobody for a few weeks, then find a new owner after they are ready to bond again. I wouldn't want to do this on purpose, since it would mean the dog would be unhappy temporarily, but being placed into a shelter kennel with minimal attention breaks old bonds quickly and makes the dog totally open to an intense new bond. People often feel that shelter dogs bond more strongly than dogs adopted in other ways. They interpret this phenomenon by believing that the dog knows that its life has been saved, and they are not far from wrong. The contrast between the shelter and the loving new owner is so dramatic to the dog that is open to a new social relationship that the effect is just as strong as if the dog was really conscious of the concepts of future and death.

Shelter Design

An understanding of the general setup of the shelter kennels will allow the tester to predict any unusual effects on the dog's behavior. Most shelters have solid walls between cages to prevent fence-fighting, but these also prevent dogs from perceiving that visitors are approaching until they are quite close; to the dog, they appear out of nowhere in a startling way. Other dogs being walked past appear suddenly as well. Kennels with glass fronts are the most stressful; the dog is frightened and disoriented when it is unable to smell the person approaching it. At the San Francisco SPCA's Maddie Center, all kennels are glass, but "sniff holes" at dog level allow access to the air outside the kennel. One can see just how important scenting is to the dog by the fact that it is almost impossible to persuade dogs to leave their sniff holes when trying to interact with them from outside. Even the friendliest dogs stand as if glued to them, eager to know more about who's outside.

Small cages stress dogs more, as does having no escape route to an outdoor section. Proximity to sections where the more aggressive dogs have been quarantined for biting or in-fighting will upset those dogs closest to them. Most modern shelter kennels are now built in small, quiet sections with no visual access to other dogs, and adequate space for the dog to feel comfortable meeting prospective adopters. After saying all this, I must reiterate that a good Hearing Dog candidate

Kennels are often badly designed in that the dog has no visual clue that a visitor is approaching. Dogs get a surprise with every person that walks by.

could care less about all these factors and shows at least some potential regardless.

Effects of the Tester upon Dog Behavior

Response to strangers is seen as soon as the dog senses the tester's approach. Therefore, the tester needs to be aware of the impact that different types of approaches may have. Because I carry a gym bag containing testing materials, this changes my body outline and forces the dog to classify me into a different category than "Normal Human Outline." I try to consistently carry my bag so that all dogs are exposed to the same version of me. Dogs that are afraid this different outline are showing suspicion and/or lack of socialization.

Because I am a woman, dogs react more trustingly than if I were a man. A dog that is somewhat fearful of humans in general is often willing to trust the least frightening ones—women. However, testers need to be able to role-play and mimic the opposite sex to thoroughly test dogs—if nobody's watching!

Merely being a dog owner will affect how dogs react to you. Dogs live with their owners, who then smell like the dog, and are more likely to be approached and socialized by other dog owners, who also smell like dogs in addition to their normal human scent. For example, dog trainers who mainly socialize their puppies with their friends and at gatherings of other dog owners, such as parks or dog shows, often run into a puzzling problem when their normally trusting puppy seems to randomly select strangers to be afraid of. This is caused by the fact that humans who have no dog odor are a whole different class of beings to a dog, and this difference is intensified when the puppy realizes that non-dog owners often act differently than dog people do. Additionally, they are more likely to be (and smell) apprehensive, and even if they mean well they often do not know how to behave appropriately when making friends with a dog.

It's interesting to note that dogs sometimes react negatively to tall or wide people or anyone who is notably different in some way from the person they're accustomed to. Therefore, it's always good to ask people of different shapes, sizes, etc., to interact with the dog. I once walked into the isolation kennel at the Hearing Dog Program and was puzzled when a new dog freaked out in fearful barking at me. How had it ever passed Shelley's testing? It soon became obvious that the dog trusted blondes and was fearful of anyone with dark hair.

Play Behavior and Communication

When a dog wishes to stimulate a person into play behavior, it may show intense but non-threatening eye contact. This may be confused with threatening eye contact. The difference is that playful eye contact is brief, lasting only long enough to get a reaction, and then quickly shifts away into a submissive head-turn to entice the other to approach. Dogs that know each other well may show very intense eye contact in predatory stalking games.

Determining whether a dog's behavior is playful or aggressive can be difficult. Understanding the playful body language of one's own pet does not automatically allow a person to understand that of a strange dog. This is understandable since play behavior contains many components of aggressive behavior, although with more relaxed body language and incomplete behavior sequences. In both dogs and humans, one of the functions of play is to determine social status and cement relationships without the permanent consequences of "serious" behavior. For humans, the rules of behavior within a

Above - Playful or threatening? This is Jekyll's playful expression but if I saw this face while testing in a shelter, I'd be very leery. Looking closely at this photo reveals that his mouth is open and relaxed, and his eyes are relaxed with no brow wrinkles. In real life, a tester has only a split second to notice such fleeting expressions in a dark kennel.

Tall Ibizan hound pup, Samba, gives the younger puppy the confidence to raise its tail and play by lowering herself in a play posture. She puts her head below that of the puppy.

relationship can be negotiated by joking and teasing, until both people feel secure and know they can trust each other. An aggressive undertone is often present as people feel out how acquiescent or assertive (submissive or dominant) the other person is. The same applies in dog-to-dog interaction, and even dog-to-human interaction.

In both species, interactions are cautious and restrained at first, and advances and retreats occur before friendly or antagonistic relationships are formed. Many of us have major trouble determining whether unfamiliar humans are behaving playfully or aggressively. Teasing and joking are human play behaviors that are so easily misinterpreted that it is risky to engage in them with strangers. Just as I would never playfully poke or insult a stranger, I never make "jokes" with strange dogs!

For instance, a friend adopted an ex-police K9 Malinois who had by a complicated turn of events ended up at an animal shelter. The dog seemed very stable, and was let out onto a patio area off leash while being watched by his new owner. A co-worker walked by the dog at a distance, but suddenly whipped around, brandished some papers at the dog, and jumped into a playfully threatening stance. We observers just stood there, stunned, and the dog's new owner froze as well, not daring to give any command lest the dog misinterpret her. The dog raised his head slowly, leaned forward, and grew suddenly taller, locking a freezing gaze onto this audacious man. As the man froze too, realizing from our silence that something was wrong, the owner then called the dog to her; luckily, he responded. She told the man, "You know, I was really nervous. This dog is trained to bite." "Oh," he said. "Would he have nipped me?"

Health Factors that Affect Test Results

Tracheobronchitis

"Kennel Cough" is almost universal in crowded conditions such as shelters. Few shelters have modern air circulation systems that eliminate airflow between individual dogs, and this is a disease spread by contact and aerosol contamination of the air by coughing and sneezing. Tracheobronchitis is usually mild, lasts several weeks in otherwise healthy dogs, and rarely is fatal—except in animal shelters that euthanize all coughing dogs. Shelters often have no money for treatment, no quarantine facilities, and don't want other dogs in the shelter also coming down with kennel cough, reducing their chances for adoption.

Determining whether a dog has tracheobronchitis or a more serious disease, such as distemper, is made harder by the fact that shelter dogs often show more severe symptoms than do pets. Complications like bronchitis and pneumonia, or heavy eye and nasal discharge, often occur, probably due to poor nutrition prior to arrival and stress from the change in conditions. Some shelters can only afford to spend money to vaccinate animals that have been evaluated as having a good chance for adoption. This may be too late, if the dog has already been exposed to disease.

Antibiotics can help with the secondary infections that often occur. Before temperament testing a dog, it is important to find out whether it is being treated for tracheobronchitis, because some medications affect behavior. Antibiotics may affect food motivation, and Torbutrol, a cough suppressant, makes many dogs appear calm and sedate.

It can be difficult to evaluate temperament in a sick dog, but not impossible. I once adopted a four-pound, six-month-old Yorkadoodle (a cross between a Toy Poodle and

Yorkie), that appeared weak and sick. I adopted him mostly out of pity, but was secretly hopeful that his illness was masking his great potential, so I named him "Arrow." He had tested well on interactivity and sounds, if you can call jumping on me between coughing fits and weakly turning his head at noises "testing well." I had faith that no Yorkadoodle could really have such a blah personality as this poor guy seemed to. He recovered from pneumonia, and turned out to be a dynamic, determined dog that once gave his partner a black eye while ricocheting around the house, but sustained no injuries himself.

Many dogs with Hearing Dog temperament are so active and exuberant that they show only coughing, without depression, when sick with tracheobronchitis. In reality, they probably are showing some depression, but if one doesn't know their actual activity levels when healthy, they may simply seem to be an average dog. They may continue to bounce around, and those with high food drive will continue to eat. Their vigor and intense personalities can actually cover up how sick they really are, so x-raying and antibiotics should be considered. I've seen many dogs that seemed only mildly ill, but when x-rayed turned out to have severe bronchitis or borderline pneumonia. Such active dogs do not rest, but stay active and aggravate their disease.

Giardia

Giardia does not often have severe symptoms in adult dogs except for intermittent diarrhea, and some loss of appetite when having an attack. Dogs seen in a shelter with diarrhea therefore do not necessarily have parvovirus, and the tester can decide whether or not to test them. If the dog is being treated with metronidazole (Flagyl), it may appear nauseated and will not test well for food motivation. Giardia is very prevalent in dogs in California.

Sterilization Surgery

Many shelters spay and neuter dogs before adoption, so the tester needs to be aware that recent surgery may lower their energy level, especially if they were sick at the time of the surgery. Many dogs with Hearing Dog temperament are relatively unaffected and maintain a high activity level and good attitude. Dogs that have been altered within a day of testing should be handled carefully. If they show strong pain reactions, they either have a problem stemming from the surgery or they are overly sensitive to pain. About 90% of dogs that had passed the Hearing Dog Program discomfort tolerance tests beforehand have shown no awareness of pain or discomfort the day after being spayed or neutered, and have to be kept quiet and confined for their own good.

Spayed females show a greater tendency to marking and leg-lifting behavior, and studies indicate that they often show higher aggression. In females that were not very aggressive anyway, there does not seem to be a noticeable change. Neutered males show some loss of activity level overall, but this is perhaps compensated for by increased interactivity with people and less interest in urine marking, sniffing, and other male behaviors. I mostly notice improvement in male dogs that were hypersexual or obsessive urine markers prior to neutering. I have never seen males that were too aggressive to dogs or people before their surgery show a significant enough change afterwards to be suitable as Hearing Dogs.

When looking at Hearing Dogs as a group, there is very little difference between the sexes in behavior, although non-Hearing Dogs show dramatic differences. When compared to non-Hearing Dogs, I see huge differences between the sexes. I believe this is because the dogs at the Hearing Dog Program were selected for low aggression, high submission, and social interactivity, so that the typical "male" traits are not so evident. Interestingly, Hearing Dog males and females seem to have more in common with each other than with non-Hearing Dogs of the same sex.

PART THREE:

TESTING POTENTIAL HEARING DOGS

Chapter Seven
Temperament Testing Concepts

Dogs with high potential as Hearing Dogs make temperament testing seem simple. These superstars ace every test, and show an obvious desire to be something more than a couch potato. Such dogs are interactive and non-aggressive *no matter what*, attracted to sounds *no matter what*, and happily confident *no matter what*. So why should testing be so complex? Because there are very few dogs that test this well, and not everyone wants such a high-powered workaholic dog. Testing the remaining dogs is much more difficult, because temperament testing is much better at screening out the dogs that have no potential than it is at selecting those with high potential. This is because temperament tests are not objective and cannot provide firm answers about a dog's temperament. Instead, they bring up questions, which suggest further tests, which bring up further questions, and so on. Their main value is in giving the tester a frame of reference to work within and in developing the tester's ability to read dog behavior.

What is a Temperament Test?

A temperament test is a series of procedures designed to trigger behaviors in a dog so that it can be systematically evaluated, with the ultimate goal of gauging the dog's aptitudes and predicting its behavior. This behavior is graded by matching it to one of a list of possible behaviors that different dogs might exhibit.

The words "temperament test" conjure up an image of an orderly process that easily reveals all the hidden facets of a dog's personality. Nothing could be farther from the truth. Although this is a worthy goal, the realities of testing present many obstacles. The results evaluate the dog's level of various temperament traits, or, in some tests, its suitability for some specific role such as police work.

All scientific experiments are tests of some sort, and the "scientific method" is a set of guidelines for understanding how to create a valid experiment. While a temperament test may not follow the true scientific method—since it relies in part on a tester's "gut feeling"—the most crucial scientific guideline that it adheres to is that only one variable should be tested at a time. Otherwise, there is no way to know which variable affected the result. Testing shelter dogs probably involves thousands of variables, a few of which are: the dog's previous experiences, instincts, age, length of time in shelter, and on and on. Many other factors are also at work that cannot be tested at a shelter: whether the dog will become territorially aggressive as it matures, has genetic health problems, or will become stressed by living in a kennel while being trained. In addition, no two testers ever administer a temperament test in exactly the same way, no two testers generate the same reactions in dogs, and no two shelter environments affect dogs in the same way. Therefore, the results of one temperament test should not be considered conclusive.

At the San Francisco SPCA Hearing Dog Program, 31% of dogs adopted graduate. At a shelter, one can determine whether the dog shows enough potential to warrant adoption and further testing and training at the Hearing Dog Program, but I have learned that I cannot predict whether it will graduate in the end. A temperament test is just the first step in the dog's long journey towards becoming a successful Hearing Dog. Ralph Dennard, director of the Hearing Dog Program, has made the astute comment, "The temperament test is over when the dog is doing well with its new partner."

Although temperament tests are not a scientific experiment, and do not reveal all the hidden facets of a dog's temperament, they do have great value for other reasons. The test is a mental framework that serves to organize the tester's thoughts and impressions about a dog, and develops the tester's ability to "read" dog behavior. The tester should understand that the better they know themselves, the better their testing will be. After ten years, I know a lot of my faults and prejudices as a tester. Although I can't change my feelings, I do know how to compensate for the kind of misinterpretations I make if not careful and when to listen to that little voice saying a dog is too good to be true.

Tests cannot enable someone to read dog behavior if they do not already understand it. I've been around dogs for a long time, and it is hard for me to comprehend how a person could be unable tell the difference between a fearful and a challenging bark, or not realize that a dog is about to bite them. But understanding dog language is exactly like learning a foreign language, only harder, since this is the language of another species. In her book, *On Behavior*, Karen Pryor describes the biologist George Schaller explaining that to understand an animal species' communication, you need "5,000-hour eyeballs." He was referring to the amount of observation time necessary for a human to begin to see and interpret animal communication signals. Beyond this mere familiarity with basic signals lies the ultimate skill shown by the person who is fluent in both reading a dog's behavior and communicating back.

Objectivity and Subjectivity

Testing dogs involves decisions based both on objectivity and subjectivity; it's necessary to evaluate dogs in both modes. Objectivity is needed to avoid slipping into fantasy, and subjectivity is needed to see beyond superficial test results.

Staying focused on the reality of the moment is essential. The minute the tester begins to slip into a fantasy world, excuses start to be made for the dog's behavior. Let's say a dog appears very stressed by the tester, and snaps at her. The fantasy may be, "He snapped because he probably was abused by a dark-haired woman who looked like you; after all, he likes blonde women." The reality is, "This dog snapped. That is not acceptable behavior." While excuses are easy to screen out when babbled by ignorant people, they are harder to ignore when they arise within our own minds.

Subjectivity is not the same as slipping into a fantasy world. Being really subjective involves being in touch with all of the unconscious thoughts that a dog's behavior triggers in us and seeing where they lead. Once you go into this subjective mode, try to identify why those vague, seemingly irrational feelings about a dog come up, and switch to an objective assessment of them. I ask myself, does my good feeling about a dog relate to its temperament, or to its physical resemblance to a favorite dog that died? Does a bad feeling come from its behavior, or to the fact that it resembles a breed that has never yet passed testing?

I once got an uncomfortable feeling about a Springer mix who seemed friendly, but, for a few seconds, an odd expression that I couldn't identify passed over his face and then vanished. I evaluated him only to please a concerned volunteer, but he passed all the tests, so I adopted him for the Hearing Dog Program. He was happy and friendly in the crate in my truck. At the next stop I got out of the truck and was talking to him, when I noticed him staring at me and growling, then exploding into all-out aggression inside the crate. His glazed eyes were completely alien to the dog he had been before, and reassuring him that it was just me had no effect as he bit furiously at the crate door. I walked away slowly, feeling stunned at what had happened. After a few minutes I cautiously returned. Panting, he wagged and sweetly looked at me with gentle, trusting eyes. My initial bad feeling had been very perceptive. That fleeting expression that had initially clouded his face was a real warning of something terrible lurking inside, and the experience made me decide to never again test a dog that I didn't feel good about. I returned him to the shelter and warned them that he might have the mysterious disorder called "rage syndrome."

Objectivity helps keep the tester on track. I know that if I have driven a few hundred miles, looked at three hundred dogs in five shelters and found no prospective Hearing Dogs, each subsequent dog starts looking better and better to me. I find myself mentally willing dogs to pass, and myriads of excuses pop up in my mind. Even in well-designed scientific experiments with controlled variables, the experimenter's expectations have been shown to have a mysterious but real effect on the results. In the most famous of these, researchers who were told that one group of maze-running rats were from a more intelligent strain than the other found that the "intelligent" rats performed better. In reality, the rat groups were randomly selected. Guidelines were then designed to avoid this effect, setting up "double-blind" experiments in which researchers cannot predict results.

In a non-scientific temperament test, these effects are far stronger. Switching into objective mode helps you to remember that dogs that are skinny and don't want treats are not just sick or full, but probably have low food motivation. If you realize that you like a dog that is not passing, then you can decide to take it anyway to place as a pet or give to a rescue group, but not delude yourself that it can be a Hearing Dog. There's nothing wrong with deliberately trying to train a less-suitable dog and preparing to spend extra training time to make up for lack of socialization or natural talent. What *is* wrong is when you fool yourself about the test results. It's easy to do.

I now find it hard to believe that when I started this job, I adopted some very cute dogs that I couldn't train. I kept working with them, and I know I was prejudiced in favor of their appearance. But eventually I came to feel that nothing could be uglier than a beautiful dog lying on the couch while the phone rings and rings—and while the exhausted trainer leaps up and down like a monkey waving treats and chattering encouraging words. I also realized that nothing was more gorgeous than the sight of an undershot, grayish little mutt with a coat like old laundry lint ricocheting off me on his sixth trip to the door, ignoring my treats because he's so caught up in the fun of his work.

Facing Reality

Two inspirational sayings form the basis of many success stories of dogs rescued from shelters. "Love conquers all," and "Time heals all wounds." Unfortunately, for most shelter dogs, all the love and time in the world are not enough to help them become a Hearing

Dog. Poor or unsuitable genetics and bad puppyhood conditions are irreparable strikes against many of them. Because people go to shelters with the idea of rescuing animals, they accept that the dog they bring home will need some help to overcome problems. This mindset is essential for success, but when applied to selecting Hearing Dogs, it needs to be balanced with the thought that Hearing Dogs are probably born, not made. Looking for Hearing Dogs means looking for dogs that already have Hearing Dog temperament, not dogs that the adopter feels sorry for because their poor temperament or socialization makes it obvious that nobody else is going to adopt them.

Putting a mental template of a Hearing Dog onto an unsuitable dog requires quite a bit of denial. In past years, I often tried to cure these dogs by a process of intense love, hard work, and willpower. If I loved them so much, and they loved me back, then they *must* be good dogs. They were, but they were not Hearing Dogs. Some of the dogs that were capable of intense love were also capable of equally intense fear and hatred. After placing my most treasured dog, one that the other trainers had often warned me showed fear of strangers and children, I had to return within two days after she bit a visiting child in the ankle as he left the house. The dog's new partner was so heartbroken at giving up this dog she had already fallen in love with that I had to wake from my delusions and see the damage I had done to her. It seemed so strange to me that all my love for this little dog could have hurt someone so badly.

Flexibility

The tester must be flexible and creative rather than sticking rigidly to the test procedure. It is not always possible to perform each test, since every testing situation presents different opportunities and challenges. There are many ways to reach a goal, as the numerous warring faiths within the subculture of dog trainers prove. Test results cannot be rigidly quantified to produce an answer, because many mysterious factors affect a dog's behavior.

I once encountered a situation where it would have been a bad idea to go "by the book." In the distance I saw a Chow in a kennel, and what attracted my notice was its wagging tail and the fact that it was leaning against the bars trustingly rather than positioning itself farther back. Most Chows do not pass Hearing Dog tests; even the few that are very friendly to strangers are calm and independent, with very low reactivity and activity levels. People sometimes label Chows "treacherous" because they often permit people to come quite close before biting. However, this behavior is actually the product of the very small personal space of a few inches that many Chows place around themselves, whereas most dogs defend a personal space measured in yards and will get upset and show warning behavior long before a person gets dangerously close. Obviously a tiny personal distance that is aggressively defended is quite dangerous, since the person might get about one inch away from the calm, watchful Chow before, at three quarters of an inch, the dog punishes the crossing of the boundary.

Still, this Chow intrigued me. Its tail was not curled up like a Chow's; it hung down, and swished submissively at the tip like a Golden Retriever's. I decided that the dog must be a mix, and approached closer. As I did so, the tail wagged harder, and the whole rear end accompanied it. I love dogs that wag with their whole body. But the dog's expression bothered me. Chows have mask-like faces that are hard to read, but this one's face seemed unusually stiff, with no panting or movement. In fact, it held its head still while its eyes followed my movements—a very bad sign.

However, the waving tail was enticing me closer and closer. Suddenly the dog gave a warning bark and showed a definitely threatening expression. It was then that I realized that the wagging tail and rear were the product of some kind of constant tremor, probably the result of surviving distemper. The dog had "wagged" its tail harder as I approached because the stress made the tremor intensify. It was leaning against the bars, not because it was inviting close contact, but because its weakened rear end needed support. I should have remembered that friendly Chows do not press submissively against kennel bars; they usually stand directly facing me or jump up, alertly wagging their tail and hoping to be approached respectfully. Going strictly by test results, a wagging dog pressed against the bars of a kennel should be let out for further testing—usually!

Safe Testing

Mindful of my role as a professional trainer, I have often fallen into the trap of being too proud to admit difficulties with a dog to the shelter employees lest I tarnish my competent image, and perhaps make them leery of trusting me to safely test dogs. After being cornered for several minutes in a kennel ward by an angry Lhasa Apso, I decided that perhaps the kennel attendants were better trained in dealing with difficult dogs than I was, and began to swallow my pride and ask for help more often.

Over the years, I've learned to read the danger signals dogs give, particularly if I feel or see any stiffening by the dog. Most importantly, I no longer interact with any dog that acts neutral. Neutral behavior is a danger signal in itself, a message that the dog does not wish to interact. How it would behave if forced to interact is not something I want to find out. I now require that the dog actively display both trust and affection towards me before I take it out of a kennel, and at the first signs that trust and affection are diminishing, I try to build the dog back up to a happier state, then replace it in the kennel and move on to test another dog. A dog that does not desire to establish a friendly relationship with me has no reason not to bite me. Understanding dog behavior is not always easy for me, but I can safely

Do not ever corner dogs! Dachshund mix Frisco crouches submissively when cornered and reached for. He is fearful of strangers, but luckily, he passively submits to any handling by them..

say that I at least know when I am getting in over my head with a certain dog, and can back out of difficult situations.

If the dog gets too pushy, especially if it is large, the tester should remain neutral and defuse the situation, not attempt to correct it. Correcting a strange dog may backfire. Previous owners who always became intimidated and backed off when the dog protested any attempt to control its behavior might have already accidentally trained the dog to become aggressive when corrected. Other dogs have been taught to respect any human control, and will never challenge a human who corrects them. Still others

Unsafe testing: the tester hugs this fearful dog, whose head direction, tense ears, and paw show he is trying to get away; his "smile" actually is caused by the nervous drawing back of the corners of his mouth. This tester has no way to avoid being bitten.

naturally have a strong defensive response to aggression by people and respond in kind. I'd rather not try to find out by trial and error which category a dog belongs to! If the dog shows any aggression, the proper course of action in a shelter is to stop testing immediately, inform the behaviorist or other personnel, and safely return the dog to a kennel.

I know of one trainer who learned the hard way not to correct strange dogs. The owner of a young adult male guard breed told the trainer that the dog jumped on people, and when the dog rested his paws on the trainer's chest and stared at her, she tried a technique that sometimes discourages overly enthusiastic puppies from jumping up; she gently squeezed his front paws and didn't let go. The dog corrected this disrespectful behavior by biting her severely on the stomach. Had she been more experienced, she would have set up a training program to deal with a dominant, aggressive dog, instead of giving the dog the opportunity to learn that attacking people is an easy way to control them. The next trainer who was called in had a doubly difficult task ahead of her! Although this situation happened with an owned dog rather than a shelter dog, the point is that the trainer got herself into major trouble by interpreting the dog's behavior as that of a playful puppy rather than a bossy adult dog. Even worse, she had no backup help in case her method didn't work, and no way to protect herself. If she had been alone in a noisy kennel, it might have been a long time before someone would have known that she was being attacked. Safety should always be the tester's first priority.

Humane Testing

Humane testing dictates that the dog should find testing a positive or at least neutral experience. Testing should improve the dog's chance of adoption, not be a stressful experience that makes the dog show itself more poorly in the future. Although I feel strongly that potentially dangerous dogs should not be adopted out, I do not want to make any dogs more dangerous than they actually are, especially if they are strays who may yet be reclaimed. For this reason, I stop testing before a dog intensifies minor signs of undesirable behavior. There is no point in continuing testing on a fearful or aggressive dog. If I were searching for a protection dog, I would try to test appropriately for the type of aggression I desired, but in searching for Hearing Dogs, I need not be in the position of dealing with any dog who shows this behavior. I used to continue testing until I had absolutely proved to myself that a dog could not pass, but now that I know what behaviors predict later failure, I can stop testing earlier in the game, sparing dogs from tests they cannot handle.

Who Should Temperament Test Dogs?

There are few experts in temperament testing. Even people who are experienced in testing litters of puppies may be at a loss when confronted with a kennel full of shelter dogs. All of the best testers I know freely admit that they often misjudge dogs, and are always trying to improve their skills. Several categories of people have the potential ability to test shelter dogs:

- People who have trained many dogs of different breeds
- Obedience trainers who have experience in teaching classes with varied breeds
- Shelter employees who constantly handle shelter dogs
- Shelter behaviorists or trainers with shelter dog experience
- People with experience in breed rescue

Who Should not Test Dogs?

There are no legal standards for dog trainers or behaviorists. All it takes to be one is enough money to buy a set of business cards with "Top Trainer to the Stars" printed on them. It's a lucrative field for those with the talent to be good con artists. Since most people don't know much about dogs or training, they are easy to dupe. To avoid these smooth-talking know-it-alls, insist on references from clients, veterinarians, shelters, and other trainers. Search the Assistance Dogs International web site for excellent information on evaluating trainers. Try to find a trainer who is enthusiastic about communicating with people, but be aware that these people are not guaranteed to also be good at communicating with dogs.

Avoid trainers who swear by one method or philosophy of training, especially if the method is secret or has a really fancy name. The real "secret" to dog training is reading dog behavior accurately and understanding how dogs learn, which takes time. As good trainers grow in experience, they become more flexible in their training techniques, not less, as they come to appreciate the variety of individual dog personalities and learning styles. Trainers who promote very rigid methods that are applied equally to all dogs are either hucksters or not very experienced.

Some trainers may be of the "armchair" variety rather than rich with experience of dealing with actual dogs and owners. "Book larnin'" and experience with other species of animals can help anyone understand dogs better but does not necessarily confer the ability to evaluate dog temperament.

Most people who do rescue work, dog training, or work at shelters are firmly grounded in the harsh reality of dealing with dog temperament problems and are well suited to help select Hearing Dogs. A few, however, live in an illusory world where all dogs are basically good, and all temperament problems are the result of abuse by humans, who should be prepared to become martyrs to adopted problem dogs in order to atone for the sins of others. It is essential to identify and avoid these people. Neglect and abuse of dogs is bad enough, but it is equally bad to excuse behavior problems which, if allowed to continue, will result in euthanasia. Adopting dangerous dogs to the public is abusive to the human victims of dog bites—usually children. Anyone who cares far more about dogs than they do about their potential owners is not qualified to test Hearing Dogs.

Choosing a Hearing Dog

If you fall in love with a dog that cannot handle public access situations without stress, then your Hearing Dog must be limited to being a companion that works in the home. If the dog cannot alert to sounds, then you may end up with a companion that is just a pet. If the dog lacks companion qualities, it may be a source of stress rather than happiness. Therefore, potential partners need to think ahead and examine their attitudes. If the dog did not work out as a full Hearing Dog, what would you do? Would you be able to abandon your dream of a dog that can alert to sounds and go everywhere with you? Would you find a good home for the dog, and try again with another dog? Would you euthanize a dangerous dog? Would you spend money on behavioral counseling for a problem dog? The clearer you are about your own goals, the easier it will be to select a dog.

You are probably the best-qualified person in the world to decide whether a particular dog is the right one for you. That where-has-this-dog-been-all-my-life feeling is valid. But for your own safety and to avoid the trauma of falling in love with a dog that is unsuitable in some other way, you may want professional assistance. Many shelters now have behaviorists on staff that can assist in testing, or can recommend trainers that have experience with shelter dogs. The companion role is the bottom line for both dog and human partner, but the dog needs to also fill the public access and sound alerting roles, and dogs that can do all three are few and far between. Once a dog has shown that it has this potential, that is the time to evaluate whether it is the right companion for you.

Tailoring Goals for Personalized Testing

When testing for another person, it is important to stay objective and keep that person's needs in mind. For example, the dog that will be trained in a home environment can have a slightly less resilient temperament than the dog that must spend several months in a training kennel. Likewise, the dog that will be taken to work and on business trips must be fearless, as opposed to the dog that will live a stay-at-home life in a small town.

For these reasons, selecting a dog for another person requires that the tester have a thorough knowledge of that potential partner's personality and needs. The new partner's dominance level, activity level, and lifestyle will be important factors in selecting a dog, and the trainer must be knowledgeable enough to train a dog with a different temperament than they might pick for themselves. Trainers who might prefer very submissive dogs need to realize that a loud, assertive person needs a thick-skinned, resilient dog that will not become intimidated by aggressive voice and body language however well intended. Selecting a dog to match someone's personality is a great art, and a serious responsibility.

A woman had brought her Irish Wolfhound to obedience class where I was assisting. He was full grown and completely untrained. She said that this wasn't a problem except that when she tried to show him in conformation shows, he fought the leash by rearing up like a circus horse. Predictably, the dog was too unruly to fit in with the class program. He was completely gentle and friendly, but had no idea that people might want something from him. The trainer asked me to take the owner aside and talk to her. She explained that she and her husband loved the dog, but they could not walk him, take him in the car easily, or even lie down in the house to watch TV; the dog would literally walk right on them. I explained that he would be happier if he could at least learn enough to go places with them or take a walk, but she kept worrying about "breaking his spirit." After awhile I tired of being polite and said, " You know, you're lucky you picked an Irish Wolfhound. He's the sweetest dog, and he's not going to bite you no matter what. But if you had gotten a German Shepherd and treated it like this, it would have bitten you by now and you would have had to put it to sleep." Her eyes widened. "Oh!" she said, "But we *did* have a German Shepherd! And we *did* have to put him to sleep! Do you know what he did? He *bit* me!"

When testing for oneself, excessive subjectivity is not always a problem. The more emotionally and irrationally attracted the tester is to the dog, the more emotional energy he or she will find available to deal with any problems that occur. When I first met my American Eskimo, Snap, Kathy O'Brien, who had adopted her for the Hearing Dog Program, warned me that she jumped up. I thought this was silly; after all, I *am* a dog trainer! But as I opened the kennel door, a white furry thing rocketed up and glued itself against my face like the creature from *Alien*, and while sharp claws gashed my lip open. Startled, I screamed and threw up my arms, and she fell to the ground. When I bent over the poor creature to see if she was hurt, I got a glimpse of a laughing little face before the world went white again. Before I could get clawed again I grabbed her tightly, suddenly remembering in horror that American Eskimos hate to be grabbed by strangersæbut all I felt was a happy dog licking my face. Not everyone would have considered this a good experience, but I fell in love with that dog right there—her ebullience, dynamic personality, and total love for people. I was ecstatic when she dropped out of the program because of several health problems so that I was able to adopt her and train her for myself. I would not have been motivated to adopt any other dog with health problems, but I liked her so much that I decided that even if she couldn't live a long life, I'd rather have a short time with her than a longer time with some other dog.

Trainers who select a dog for themselves also have more flexibility in dealing with temperament problems. Socializing can proceed at the dog's pace, and if it takes months for the dog to be comfortable in public situations, it doesn't really matter, as long as the owner is happy with the progress. After I adopted Snap, she became devoted to me and less attracted to strangers. Fearfulness of men, especially with beards, took about a year to overcome. When one day she sat smiling at a Lion's Club demo, surrounded by big men reaching to pat her, I was really proud.

Nell: an Unsuitable Dog

Nell was a small Border Collie. Placed in a rural shelter because of normal Border Collie behavior (escaping from her yard to chase cattle), she was not adopted, and was taken to the euthanasia room to be put to sleep. Nell had exceptional direct eye contact, as do many Border Collies, but hers was extremely personal and emotive, unlike the usual manipulating stare. The shelter employee could not bear to put her down, and when she was finished euthanizing the other cats and dogs, decided to keep Nell around the shelter as a semi-pet, hoping to avoid the inevitable day. When I turned up at the shelter looking for Hearing Dogs, Nell turned that gaze on me, and although she failed Hearing Dog testing by being overly submissive and inhibited and appearing to have been beaten (she seemed trusting until I opened the kennel door, then fled in panic when I moved the leash in my hand), I could not resist her. I thought I would take her and call my Border Collie Rescue friends to find her a home. After all, she hadn't failed the testing *that* badly. She would not bite, and seemed eager to meet people; it turned out that she was just afraid of throwing or hitting motions, not people themselves. She was not afraid of sounds although she was slightly inhibited by them, and she was interested in food. Once I got her back to San Francisco, she was not as fearful of the city traffic and noise as I had expected a little country Border Collie to be, fellow trainer Kathy O'Brien advised me to give her a try as a Hearing Dog after all. Perhaps she could work out; she was not as active as most Border Collies, and would make a good companion.

She adjusted to the city, and seemed to enjoy her new life at the Hearing Dog Program with lots of different people giving her attention, but I was having trouble with her sound training. I couldn't find a way to motivate her. She didn't want food enough to approach the telephone ring, which she was a bit wary of. She was very inhibited on a leash, so she didn't enjoy being guided to sounds. Obviously, nobody had ever played with her, because she interpreted a thrown tennis ball as a punishing missile. I felt frustrated by the usual dilemma—here was such an empathetic, interactive dog with so much to offer, but if she wasn't going to offer sound alerting she was just going to have to drop out and be a pet for someone. It was hard to believe that this meek, inhibited dog had ever boldly chased cattle.

That gave me an idea. I talked to Nell excitedly, then ran away from her. She looked interested. After a few times, she ran with me. Then she suddenly began to chase me. It was as if some crust of ice around her had melted, and for the first time she began to play. I was worried that I'd be teaching her to chase and nip people or kids, but she was still sufficiently inhibited not to do that. I began running to the ringing phone, and she was now eager to eat the treats there. When I would stop short before getting to the phone, she started to continue on towards it. Once her inhibitions had broken down a bit, she realized that running to sounds was fun. Like many Border Collies, she had simply needed "permission" to work. Amazingly, she became one of the fastest workers I've ever trained, deliriously happy as she flew back and forth, alerting her new partner, retired nurse Glenys Wilson.

Nell fit in well in her new home. She was good with the grandkids and walked for miles every day with Glenys. I still worried, however, that her success was fragile and that her alerting might be affected by her sensitivity. Sure enough, Glenys called and said that everything was fine, but she mentioned that because she didn't permit Nell on the other furniture, now Nell would no longer get on the bed to alert to the burglar and fire alarms when Glenys was sleeping. I offered to help re-train her, but Glenys just laughed. "Oh no, that won't be necessary! Nell figured it out herself- she just bumps the bed frame with her shoulder!"

All the tests that could be invented could not have predicted Nell's future. She makes me wonder just how many other "unsuitable dogs" I've left behind at shelters, and keeps me aware that any temperament test is only as good as the person using it.

Chapter Eight
Temperament Tests for Hearing Dog Suitability

These tests are designed to be performed only on shelter dogs by professional trainers and shelter employees. While I hope that other people can benefit from reading this chapter, most shelters will not permit the general public to test dogs. They want to protect their dogs from stress and the public from injury. Many shelters have behavior counselors on staff, or can recommend a trainer they trust to test their dogs.

No one should test their own dog. Such a test is invalid; Hearing Dogs must tolerate strangers, so the test must be performed *by* a stranger. In addition, these tests are designed for shelter dogs and are difficult to adapt to dogs not in shelters. As humans, we are often are blind to the faults of those we love. Dogs are not, however, and most dog bites are to their owners. Doing unaccustomed things to one's own dog during testing may cause resentment.

Testing dogs owned by other people is another job for professionals; although anyone who wants to give away or sell a dog has some knowledge of its temperament and life experiences, he or she also may be motivated to conceal or be in denial of its problems. Remember that the younger a puppy is, the less valid the tests are. Aggression and fearfulness may increase and/or decrease temporarily or permanently during a dog's development, and not stabilize until maturation. Pups five months or older test a little better and are less likely to have serious diseases than younger pups.

The chart on the following page is one way to screen out the most unsuitable dogs quickly. The tests in this book are loosely arranged with this strategy in mind.

Designing Testing Order

The order in which temperament tests are performed affects the dog's reactions to both the tester and to the subsequent test. The tests should be arranged with the goal of eliminating the least suitable dogs early in the testing process. Each level of testing is a gradual increase in stress, so dogs that cannot handle even low levels are released from the testing situation before it gets to be too much for them. In looking for such a rare combination of traits, many dogs must be quickly and efficiently screened out in order to concentrate on the few suitable dogs. By following this testing sequence, the dogs should encounter less stress than they would from anyone else visiting the shelter and taking the dog out to get acquainted with it.

All of the dog's reactions during testing are interesting and relevant, even if the tester has no idea of what is triggering a behavior. Nothing the dog does is accidental or random so it is up to the tester to make the right conclusion about what it is reacting to, and why. It is not easy.

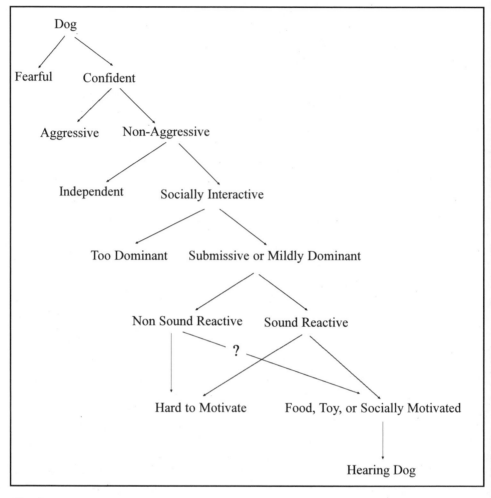

Goals

Without definite goals, temperament tests are useless. The test is designed to reveal some aspect of temperament, but it may or may not do so, depending on many circumstances. If the test is not working, then the tester needs to think of another way to meet the goal of the test. The tester also needs to have a mental picture of the optimal reaction a dog can show to each test. This theoretical perfect dog's performance can be compared to the real dog's reactions to test stimuli. Without constantly referring back to a mental picture, I often get mired in a world of "good enough." If a dog tests poorly overall, but gives one or two reactions that are better than the rest, I tend to be impressed. That is when I refer to my mental image of perfection. It's easy to see what a dog is giving you, but harder to notice everything that it is *not* showing you. Often I realize that the dog I am testing is nowhere near my mental ideal, but just looks good by comparison with all the other dogs I've tested that day. Only then can I decide objectively whether its behavior is acceptable even if not ideal.

General observation plays an important part in any temperament test. There are many traits that are not easily quantified by any one specific test. They should be observed during the entire testing procedure. Activity level, reactivity, resiliency, initiative, social interactivity, and visual communication are grouped at the end of the testing as part of the final evaluation of the dog. By that time, the tester should have already gathered enough clues about these elusive traits to form some ideas.

The tester should find out as much as possible about the dog before testing it. Cage cards have some information, but the shelter desk may have a surrender questionnaire from the owner or some report on behavior from whomever brought the dog in. Some reasons given by former owners who are surrendering a dog have secret meanings that must be translated:

- Moving – When people move, they take their valuables and get rid of their unwanted junk. It's up to the tester to discover whether the problems that made the owners treat their dog like a disposable item are simple training problems or severe temperament problems.
- Digs, barks, or jumps the fence – The dog was probably left out in the yard, neglected and unsocialized, enough to develop problems. So what problems did it originally have that made it no longer welcome in the house?
- Too big – Never trained, so its behavior became proportionately more difficult as it grew larger and stronger.
- Mouthy – Sometimes means gently biting playfully, sometimes this is a euphemism for real biting.

Wrong information can be worse than none at all. I recently let my guard down because the dog was on leash with its owners, who told me it was friendly. Stupidly, I ignored a tiny growl that immediately escalated into a snapping lunge at my face—on a Flexi-leash! I would never have ignored a growl if testing a shelter dog.

John Rogerson, a British behaviorist, has done extensive work on improving shelter conditions, evaluating dogs, and solving behavior problems, and has published many excellent books and videos. Some of the tests used or adapted here were developed by him to assist in selecting potential assistance dogs from shelters. Trainer and shelter consultant Sue Sternberg has done groundbreaking work on evaluating pet or working suitability in shelter dogs, and I recommend her excellent video and temperament tests to anyone handling or testing dogs. Write to Sue Sternberg, Rondout Kennels, 4628 Route 209, Accord, NY 12404.

I would also highly recommend the videos, "What's Behind Dog's Aggression?" by Ivan Balabanov and "The Dominant Dog" by John Rogerson, and the book *Know Your Dog* by Bruce Fogle. These have valuable visual information on recognizing dog communication signals.

TESTS WITH DOG INSIDE KENNEL

Neutral Stranger

Goal: The dog should be friendly and approach the tester. Dogs that react badly to someone neutral and harmless will probably fail any subsequent tests. Dogs that approach the front of their kennels without obvious fear or aggression should be noted for further testing.

Method: The tester should take a moment to get into the Neutral Stranger frame of mind, to appear polite, non-threatening, and respectful. Dogs evaluate each other's levels of threat or playfulness partly by levels of body rigidity and relaxation. Rigidity indicates preparation for the sudden movements of attack or escape, so the tester must appear relaxed, yet not goofy. No direct eye contact or frontal approach toward the dog is made. Instead, the tester can gaze slightly upwards, using peripheral vision and quick glances to check reactions. Approaches should be curved or slightly sideways, with the head slightly turned the other way in order to negate the impression of advancing. Meandering calmly, as if one could care less about a bunch of barking dogs, produces near invisibility: it is important that the dogs feel that the tester is no danger to their existence. As stated earlier, shelter kennels sometimes prevent dogs from gradually becoming aware of a visitor due to noise and visual barriers. For this reason, the tester should talk casually so that dogs are aware of someone coming. The ideal dog is thrilled to be surprised by a visitor, but others may react badly.

The best prospects come to the front of the cage. Those that run away or attack the cage front are immediately eliminated from consideration. The remaining dogs either show less obvious negative behavior or are actively friendly, but some of them show stiff, fearful body language, while their eyes track the tester's movements. They should not be tested further either. Dogs that appear friendly are approached indirectly and casually by the tester, who drifts sideways to the kennel and hangs a hand a few inches from the cage front for the dog to sniff.

Because this test is designed not to overexcite the dogs, some suitable dogs will not show intense desire to interact until other tests are performed.

Note: The Neutral Stranger fail and pass behaviors that follow are also used for some of the other following tests. "Fail" only means that the dog fails that particular test, and is highly likely to fail subsequent tests, although the tester needs to decide whether the dog should be tested further or not.

Fail if dog:
- Holds tail high, wagging/vibrating it stiffly in an arc of a few inches(unless it's a breed with a tail naturally over the back). Remains at the cage front but looks stiffly frozen, or holds head rigidly while its eyes follow the tester's movements.
- Runs away and hides in back of kennel.
- Remains in the back sniffing the air with head up or cautiously approaches the front.
- Growls or barks aggressively.
- Exhibits fearful alarm barking, such as barks that run together ("Barararararar" or "Boowoowoowoo," or a soft alarm, "boof."
- Attacks the front of kennel.
- Fights, fence-fights, or is so focused on any interaction with other dogs that it doesn't prefer to notice the tester.
- Remains rigidly stiff and still while staring at the tester.

Pass if dog:
- Is not actively showing obvious fear or aggression.
- Shows relaxed body language.
- Presses against bars trustingly or jumps at cage front.

A good indication of trust and desire for contact: this Aussie presses trustingly against the bars and welcomes the hand petting him. He does not feel a need to face the tester in order to feel safe..

- Shows attention-getting barking, whining, yapping.
- Makes eye contact with loose, floppy body language.
- Acts excited and happy no matter what the tester does.

These behaviors allow the dog to go on to the next stage of the testing. Neutral behavior is usually a signal that a dog may punish attempts to interact, but the dog needs to be given a chance in the next test to show some positive atttraction to the tester.

Friendly Stranger ("Dog Person")

Goal: Dog shows friendliness to people who know how to relate positively to dogs.

Method: Tester switches behavior from neutral to interactive. The tester should approach a dog which passed the previous test and make a sideways, casual approach toward kennel, turn frontally rather suddenly, then start talking to the dog—crouching down if necessary—and coaxing the dog to interact. If the dog wants to be touched and presses its cheek, neck, or side against the cage front, scratch or pet it and note the reaction. Do *not* pet the muzzle. Move a hand to different parts of the cage front to see if the dog follows the hand and continues to want petting. This indicates that it wants contact, not just to escape from the cage. Vary behavior from calming and soothing to excited and playful. If possible, get a member of the opposite sex to approach the kennel to make sure the dog relates well to both men and women.

Reactions: The dog should ideally be trusting. The dog should match the excitement level of the tester, even if the tester gets very silly. Submissive dogs may become excitedly submissive, and even if very inhibited should show their response to the tester by friendly glances or a little tail wagging. They should not be fearful of a happy person. By the end of this test, about half of all shelter dogs over five months old will have shown failing responses.

Fail if dog:
- Shows any of the same fail behaviors as in Neutral Stranger test.
- Sniffs toward tester but will not come close enough to be petted through cage front.
- Withdraws if it feels a touch.

Pass if dog:
- Shows the Neutral Stranger pass behaviors.
- Becomes either calm or excited when touched, but shows desire for more physical contact, not less.
- Hops constantly or paws at the cage front.
- Presses the side of its face or body against the cage for petting.

Friendly stranger ("Ignoramus")

The tester should take on the characteristics of a blustering man, a giggly woman, or a child. The dog that tests well might either be well socialized with people who are inept at handling dogs, or it might have so little fear that it does not perceive the inappropriate human behaviors in the test as threatening. Either way, a dog that is friendly to this bozo is unlikely to be panicked when approached by the real ones it will inevitably encounter in its life as a Hearing Dog.

Goal: The dog is comfortable even with humans who behave insensitively and use human cues of friendly intentions rather than dog cues.

Method: The tester should switch into a more abrasive personality, someone who is eager to get the dog's attention. My mental image is that of a cheerfully obnoxious guy who's had a few beers and thinks he knows how to get dogs to like him. The switch must be gradual to avoid startling the dog. The tester's voice can be growly and loud, or giggling and screechy, and body language should be on the clumsy side. Some rude commands can be given, "sit! sit! sit!" in a friendly bossy way or "C'mere! Hey!" in a scolding voice, and so on. Clapping hands to attract the dog should be done, but very gently at first, as some dogs have learned that a hand clap is a correction. Hand movements similar to "loud" American Sign Language conversations should be done.

Reactions: All of the actions of the "ignoramus" should either excite and stimulate the dog to equally silly interaction, or it should become a little submissive and squeeze up against the bars trying to interact in spite of its slight apprehension. Quick crouching or backing away is acceptable, if the dog immediately forgives whatever the tester did, and tries again to interact.

Fail if dog:
- Shows any of the Neutral Stranger fail behaviors.
- Freezes and does not recover.

Pass if dog:
- Quietly watches tester, perhaps freezes briefly, then recovers and eagerly interacts when tester calms.
- Shows excitedly friendly behavior, jumping, wagging, play bowing; intensity of behavior escalates with that of tester.

Initial Screening for Slight Threat, Knocking Sound, Raised Object

Goal: The dog is unafraid of an arm raised above it, a slight knocking sound, and a raised object.

Method: The tester raises their arm above head level and gently pretends to knock or wave at the cage front. The motion is not a hit, and is done at normal speed, not fast. Friendly body language is essential. Dogs that are not reassured by the body language and are still frightened after the hand is withdrawn have failed the test. If the dog acts fearful, the voice should continue cheerfully in order to jolly the dog up as soon as the hand is withdrawn. If the dog shows no fear or even notice of the action, or jumps up playfully, the test should be repeated more abruptly.

If this test is successful, the tester then raises an object such as a gym bag or clipboard up past shoulder height and lets it rest against the cage front. The dog should show no fearfulness, although it may crouch slightly and then recover instantly.

The tester raises their arm and knocks lightly on the cage front or a clipboard to see if the dog is afraid of a slight noise. Strong fearfulness of the knocking indicates that the dog is too fearful of sounds to be subjected to further sound testing, and testing should be halted for this dog. Jolly the dog up if it shows any fear.

Fail if dog:
- Shows any Neutral Stranger fail behaviors.
- Freezes fearfully at the raised hand.
- Freezes fearfully or runs away from the knocking sound.
- Acts fearful when an object is held high, and does not recover afterwards.

Pass if dog:
- Shows any of the Neutral Stranger pass behaviors.
- Crouches for an instant, then quickly recovers and ignores arm movements thereafter.
- Gets excited and tries harder to interact with the tester.
- Leaps up to claw and mouth at the hand through the bars, gets very excited, or does not calm down when tester withdraws hand. (This dog may prove hard to handle in later testing.)
- Acts curious and orients to or ignores the knocking sound.
- Gets excited when the object is held up. Any initial fear should be quickly lost.

If the dog seems a little nervous, but crouches rather than runs away, and is eagerly showing submissive appeasement behavior, I would continue on to the next test. This dog may be showing the effects of being previously hit or threatened, but its trust is undamaged, as shown by its eagerness to interact.

Eye Contact

The majority of dogs at this point will ignore, submit, or show displacement activity when eye contact is made. Shelter dogs should not be stared at unnecessarily; the general public already does it enough! The few dogs that respond badly to eye contact during this test are showing that they enjoy other types of interaction, but draw the line at threat by eye contact. The ancient doctors' credo, "Physician, do no harm" should be remembered here. On the average, half of the dogs in most shelters will be euthanized. If the tester stresses the dog and impairs it's adoptability, so that it does not show itself well to the next person that comes along, it may mean the difference between life and death for that dog. For two reasons, if at any point in eye contact testing the dog appears fearful or aggressive, the tester must immediately stop the test:

1. The dog must not be stressed, and needs to be left friendlier than when the tester arrived. Efforts should be made to return to the previous friendly relationship.
2. The test must stop because any strong negative reaction to eye contact means that the dog is unsuitable for the role of Hearing Dog. There is no point in further testing.

To ensure that a dog is safe enough to take out of the kennel, the eye contact test must only be done while it is still inside. About a third of previously "friendly" dogs fail the eye contact test.

Goal: Suitable dogs do not perceive eye contact as a threat or they submit to it by ignoring it or looking away. Undesirable reactions to eye contact or body language in a cage situation are a predictor of possible problem behavior at some point in the dog's public or companion roles.

Eye contact. This dog reacted well. (Photo by Drake)

Method: The tester first gets the dog's attention with a quiet cough or bark (similar to a "boof" warning bark), then stares mildly at the dog, and establishes that the dog noticed the stare. Dogs often have strong reactions to eye contact, so the tester should try a very brief stare at first, almost a glance. If this elicits no reaction, he or she can stare a little longer. If the dog returns the stare, the tester stares back until some definite reaction is seen. If no immediate reaction is seen, the tester maintains the eye contact and suddenly changes body position to provide a mild threat, such as leaning forward abruptly. Do not jump at the dog, raise your arms, or yell. The tester maintains the stare until some definite reaction is seen. The tester should then use a friendly voice and body language to distract the dog from the previous eye contact and alleviate any anxiety.

Fail if dog:
- Shows any of the Neutral Stranger fail behaviors.
- Stares back, evaluating the situation. Its body may stiffen, and it freezes in position. It may begin to growl softly. At this point a fearful dog may give a soft alarm bark, a "boof," and begin to back away slowly, ready to bolt and escape if the tester shows any movement towards the dog.
- Stares back, while slowly moving its body upward to stand taller and leaning forward slightly. It may growl, bark, attack, or remain silent while maintaining eye contact with the tester.
- Shows any undesirable reaction of fearfulness or aggression, but immediately recovers when eye contact stops. It might then seem just as trusting as before. It still fails! The question must be asked: Why was the relationship so easily disrupted? Perhaps the dog is not as trusting as it previously seemed.

Pass if dog:
- Shows any of the Neutral Stranger pass behaviors.
- Briefly meets eye contact, breaks it off, and either crouches or squirms submissively on the floor. Although the dog was slightly startled and intimidated by the

tester's sudden behavior change, it maintains its initial trust.

- Briefly meets the eye contact, showing that it did indeed perceive it, then immediately looks away and tries to solicit friendly or playful interaction, glancing upwards to see whether the tester is responding. This dog is trying to defuse a tense situation playfully and submissively.
- Seems oblivious to eye contact. It does not perceive that eye contact is a threat. It appears that there is no fearfulness or aggression inside the dog to be elicited. This is common in very domesticated companion-temperament dogs.

Children

Test location: Dog *inside* kennel, children *outside* kennel.

Goal: Dog does not react aggressively or fearfully to children while it is in the kennel, and ideally shows an active desire to be touched by them.

Method: The tester observes dog reactions to any children visiting the shelter. If children are purposely brought near the kennel, this should be done only after the dog has passed eye contact testing by the adult tester.

Reactions: Any undesirable reactions should bar the dog from any further testing. DO NOT TEST DOGS OUTSIDE OF A KENNEL WITH YOUR CHILDREN OR OTHERS' AT A SHELTER UNLESS SHELTER PERSONNEL HAVE A SUPERVISED SYSTEM TO INTRODUCE DOGS AND KIDS AS PART OF THEIR POLICY.

Fail if dog:

- Shows any of the fail behaviors in Neutral Stranger.
- Approaches, wags, is eager to be petted, but shows any fearful behavior such as freezing or backing away at any point due to actions by the child.
- Ignores children. Dogs that merely tolerate children are not showing friendly behavior. In dogs, "neutral" behavior signals a desire to be left alone. Children almost always escalate their behavior when interacting with a dog. If the dog accepts petting, they grow bolder and often want to hug the dog. It is very hard at this point to stop kids from hugging without physically grabbing them, which will upset the parents as well as the dog. Ignoring children in public is desirable in the dog, but it should be a trained behavior, not an avoidance behavior.
- Leaps, claws, mouths at children playfully behind the bars, or becomes more excited if they jump away or scream. This dog may like children in the sense that they are a great squeaky toy.

Pass if dog:

- Shows any of the Neutral Stranger pass behaviors.
- Actively seeks out any strange children, does not sniff warily first or need to "make friends," and appears to want to instantly sink into a sea of children as the high point of its life. Nothing children do can make this dog suspicious. When touched, the dog melts and relaxes into a puddle of fur to attract more petting. When the children escalate their excitement, the dog may wriggle and move about, but does not begin playing roughly or mouthing. It avoids bumping into kids. Total trust and tolerance are obvious. This dog might seem a rare creature. It is. Usually, only obtaining a puppy with an appropriate temperament for children and raising it correctly with kids can produce this behavior. Few people invest this effort or accidentally get the perfect dog for their perfect situation. Perhaps such a dog is less

This pup shows a good response by climbing over a ledge to get out of the kennel. (Photo by SF-SPCA)

As the door is opened, the collar is ready. This dog approaches a bit warily. (Photo by Drake)

This dog was only interested in other dogs, not me. (Photo by Drake)

likely than others to end up in a shelter are, but they do.

TESTS WITH DOG OUTSIDE OF KENNEL

Reaction to Open Kennel Door and Being Leashed

Goal: The dog should confidently explore the unfamiliar space outside of its kennel. A dog that enjoys exploring new places will leave the safety of its kennel. It might be hesitant, but if it can make this giant step, it is testing well. When the barrier (the door) is no longer present, the dog should not be suddenly fearful of the tester. The dog should accept the leash calmly, or run about unaware of it, fighting the leash briefly if it tightens, but showing no fear or panic when it does. It also may freeze, then walk for brief distances, but should not be terrified to the point of total immobility.

Method: The first priority is safety. Prevent escapes by being prepared for any reaction to the open door, especially if there is more than one dog in the kennel. For safety, I prefer to use any type of slip collar or leash (except the nylon rope nooses used at shelters). Whatever is used, it should be strong, ready to get on the dog's neck easily, and large enough that it can be removed quickly if needed. The test should stop and the dog replaced at the first sign of fearfulness or aggression.

Ideally, the door should be opened slowly and the dog carefully observed as it realizes that the situation is changing. This crucial moment gives many clues about the dog's temperament. The tester blocks the doorway, crouching if the dog is small. Blocking the doorway prevents escapes and ensures that only dogs that are willing to approach the tester are let out of the kennel. The collar and leash should be slipped on unobtrusively as the dog pushes out the door. Once the leash is on and the dog outside the kennel, the tester should watch its reactions very carefully; the first few seconds are very revealing. If the dog mouths and leaps on the tester, it may be showing aggression caused by frustration at being restrained on leash.

When I am trying to calm a large, boisterous dog that tries to overpower me instead of mirroring my controlled quiet behavior, I know I have a problem. This dog did not want to come out of the kennel to be with me, or it would be enjoying contact with me, not fighting it. It either wants to escape all restraint—and fast—or it only likes people to pet it, not attempt to control it. It sees me as an obstacle to overcome, not a friend to be made. This dog may or may not bite to get away, but it certainly has no reason *not* to bite. Dogs that are trying to get free may resist being put back into the kennel even more strongly, and begin to mouth the tester. If this happens, the tester should remain calm and locate a shelter employee.

Reactions: The tester should realize that the dog that is eager to come out but "can't," usually also "can't" do a lot of other things that it will need to do as a Hearing Dog. It must be said that shelter aisles can be terrifying places—the inevitable other-dog aggressive dogs in the other kennels begin roaring and crashing at the bars the moment they see a dog in the aisle. Still, many dogs hop out of the kennel and prance down the aisle, ecstatically unaware of the monsters on all sides.

Fail if dog:
- Shows the Neutral Stranger fail behaviors.

- Panics at any point.
- Approaches warily and allows itself to be handled, but retreats at any sudden movement. It should be remembered that the dog with the desired temperament loves to be caught. By now, a suitable dog should be showing increased trust, not less.
- Charges out the door, but only because it is trying to escape the kennel. Once outside, it becomes unruly and struggles with the tester.

Pass if dog:

- Shows the Neutral Stranger pass behaviors.
- Appears eager to exit, but refuses because it seems to be afraid to hop over a gutter or other small obstacle in the doorway. It should be given the benefit of the doubt and helped out of the kennel.
- Is fearful when on leash, but seeks the tester for rescue.
- Exits kennel confidently, allows itself to be leashed, and although slightly fearful, can walk hesitantly with the tester.
- Exits confidently, interacts with the tester, is eager to make contact, struggles slightly against leash. This dog shows no panic or escape behavior, just occasional bewilderment at its situation.
- Shows that it is used to being leashed by pulling steadily, accepting that it must tow a human wherever it goes.

Testing Area – Dog Observed Neutrally

Once in a suitable testing area, the dog can be walked around casually, allowed to toilet, and its reactions to the environment noted. I must say that I've rarely found a "suitable" testing area. Some of the most unusual have had features such as a leaking dead horse, dead skunks in barrels, or live emus running in a corral. At least I gained valuable information about a dog's reactions to these things!

Recall and Leash Jerk

Note: Once the dog is out of its kennel, the tester discovers whether it wanted to get out of its kennel to be with a person or simply to escape. The two extremes will both present big training challenges. The clingy one may be hard to motivate to investigate sounds, and the independent roamer will lack the interactive qualities needed.

Walking a dog to the testing area can be a major test of the tester's strength and cunning. While trying to keep the dog from tangling, escaping, and leaping on people or other dogs, it's important to keep a mental notation of the dog's behavior. These first minutes out on leash should be giving some indication of areas that should be further tested. Sue Sternberg points out that when moving shelter dogs, the leash should be kept short at a constant tension, not loose, as most testers may have been taught to do in obedience classes. A loose leash allows the dog to tangle, jump up, or scare itself by ricocheting to the end only to come to a sudden stop.

Goal: Recall test – The dog shows enough confidence to leave the tester, but when called comes back to the tester.

Leash jerk test – Dog should not be frightened by an unexpected tug on leash and remains trusting and interactive with the tester. In other words, it's forgiving and doesn't

Although it may not look it, this is actually a good reaction from a dog that is unaccustomed to being on leash or on a slip collar. She runs off, reaches the end, and looks frustrated and surprised, but not fearful or inhibited. The dog's reaction to the sensation of a slip collar displays informative reactions to restraint. (Photo by Drake)

Young Aussie mix is called while facing away...

...and rushes excitedly to make contact. Very importantly, she ignores three dogs in the kennels that are barking at her. (Photos by Drake)

sulk.

Method: Recall test – The leash must be completely loose, since a taut leash may cue the dog to come or to resist; the tester should move along with the dog while calling it (without giving it the feeling it is being chased). When it is not looking at the tester, it should be called with friendly ("Puppy, puppy!") and enticing body language, not a formal command the dog might obey or avoid. Once the dog responds to the call, it should be petted and praised, then allowed to go away, then called again. Multiple recalls can be revealing for another reason; I prefer a dog who still comes to me for several consecutive recalls even after it has found out that I don't have food or toys.

Reactions: When called, a strong positive reaction to a human voice may indicate socialization, sound reactivity, or both. The dog should show actively submissive and friendly behavior.

Leash jerk test: This test for resilience is given *after* the recall test is completed. The dog is allowed to wander on a loose leash, and once its attention is distracted, the tester gives a tug, then observes the dog's reaction. This tug is not a correction for anything, and is given silently. The tug should not be painful and be appropriate for the dog's temperament.

Reaction: The dog should not panic at the sensation of a small tug on a leash.

Fail if dog:

- Ignores the call, continuing its previous activity. It might look towards the tester, then ignore him or her.
- Notices the leash jerk, then becomes very fearful and tries to escape or to avoid the tester, and does not recover.
- Ignores the leash jerk, even if it is repeated harder. This dog may be hard to control.

Pass if dog:

- Rushes toward the tester and tries to make some contact. A very good reaction is for the dog to throw itself into the tester's arms as if it had just rejoined a long-lost owner. Equally acceptable is the dog that scurries submissively and rolls over when it gets there. The dog should show desire to be touched.
- Stays with the tester and does not leave. This is acceptable if the dog is also interested in sounds. It must be determined whether the dog prefers to be with the tester, and keeps interacting, or is just seeking safety from a scary environment and using the tester as a security blanket.
- Notices the leash jerk, acts inhibited, returns to tester and interacts submissively.
- Notices the leash jerk, returns excitedly and interacts with tester.

Understanding Restraint Tests

Reactions to restraint reveal a lot about a dog's socialization as well as its temperamental suitability for a companion role. Reactive dogs complicate the issue by showing many reactions that might be easily interpreted the wrong way. They often struggle frantically and may panic if not accustomed to handling. Dogs with the desired temperament will eventually relax when they realize they are not being harmed. Tests such as holding a dog firmly on its back may seem pretty straightforward; surely a dominant dog would show dislike of such treatment. In general, dominant dogs tend to do things to people, and resent people doing things to them. But dominant dogs react according to their life experience as well as to their temperament. If the tester acts confident and in control, some dominant dogs might challenge the tester, while others might feel intimidated and show submission to the tester's perceived greater dominance. If the tester acts submissive and hesitant, some dominant dogs might react aggressively, but some might remain tolerant until they feel seriously challenged. It is easy to make major misinterpretations in this area of testing.

Evaluating Different Reactions to All the Restraint Tests
Fail if dog:
- Goes into a state of "playing dead" and remains frozen and stressed when released. It shows no motivation to bite, as there is no aggression in its temperament. This temperament is too submissive or fearful for Hearing Dog roles.
- Panics, screams, or urinates.
- Tolerates handling but shows no signs of enjoyment. It may appear distant, or it may be focused on some other stimulus such as other dogs in the distance. When released, it does not acknowledge the tester's presence.
- Stiffens, growls, snaps, or bites when handled. It may show a rolling eye looking toward the tester's hand combined with a stiff body and neck.
- Mouths hard when restrained. Dogs that mouth do not necessarily bite. The soft chewing used to protest the restraint may escalate to harder chewing and rapid pinching, but it is a different behavior sequence from the rigid threatening that leads to a warning snap. The snapping dog attempts to scare the tester away and stop *all* interaction, whereas the mouthing dog may just want to change the rules of the interaction and gain a little control.
- Screams easily. This is a problem, even if the dog seems okay otherwise. Whether the dog is naturally a "screamer," has learned the behavior to avoid handling, or has been abused, it is not suitable. For hearing impaired partners of Hearing Dogs, sometimes only the angry glares of other people inform them that their dog has screamed for some reason. This is hard on the partner, since they naturally worry both about their dog's feelings and that observers will assume that they have been abusing their dog.
- Struggles so energetically that the tester cannot place it in any position. The test may be tried again after the dog is calmed and handled for a while. The dog may be dominant, overly reactive, or actually hyperactive due to some brain abnormality.
- Appears wary and mistrustful when freed from restraint.

Pass if dog:
- Shows a very passive, relaxed response to restraint. Dogs showing no resistance to restraint are showing good companion qualities and potential to be good with children.
- Struggles with intent to get away, but turns its head away from the tester's hand and does not even open its mouth. Its intent is clearly to avoid even giving the impression of a threat.
- Mouths gently, but when it discovers after a few seconds that mouthing does not produce freedom, it abruptly stops and either relaxes or tries a new strategy. It does not try mouthing again.

When his handler pushed on his rump, Marco arched his back and resisted so that she could not get him into a sit position. He then whirled around and began biting the leash.

Marco struggles to get away, pushing against the tester with all four feet. Pointing his head away from the restraining hand indicates that he is not thinking about biting. Chain collars are controversial training aids, but provide safety for both dog and tester. Strong nylon slip collars are also safe; do not use buckle collars or one-piece rope slip leashes when testing dogs. Always use a slip collar large enough to remove easily and quickly when replacing the dog.

Marco finally accepts being placed on his back, but his rigid body indicates he is very uncomfortable in this position, even though the tester is now scratching his chest. He remained like this for only a few seconds before resuming his struggling.

- Wiggles happily, shows loose relaxed body language and seems to enjoy the handling.
- Struggles frantically, but settles when it realizes that its struggling is not effective.
- Acts relieved and excited to be set free after the test, and still also wants to interact, perhaps in an excitedly submissive way.

Initial Screening for Handling Sensitivities

Goal: To screen out dogs that are unsafe to handle in further testing.

Method: The dog should be on a slip collar for safety; one hand holds the collar and leash firmly in order to keep the dog at arm's length if necessary. I prefer to crouch or stand next to the dog rather than bend over it. Bending over a dog is threatening and puts the tester's face too close to the dog for safety. The tester needs to be in a position to hold the dog out and away if any bad reactions occur. The dog is petted on the head. If it acts eager to be petted, the tester pets neck, shoulders, and strokes the back and then other parts of the body, carefully feeling for stiffening of dog's body. If the dog freezes rigidly at any point, it is placed back into its kennel. Crouching submissively or rolling over and lying still do not constitute stiffening. Dogs that stiffen are usually bracing their legs as well, and begin rolling their eyes back to watch the intrusive hand of the tester.

Fail if dog:
- Shows Restraint fail behaviors.

Pass if dog:
- Shows Restraint pass behaviors.

Restraint to Sit and Down Positions

Goal: The goal is not to ascertain whether the dog will sit or down, but to test its reactions to being handled in a sensitive area, the rear, and to being dominated by pressure on the shoulders.

Method: If the dog shows no resentment, the back and rear should be petted, then gently massaged. If the dog tolerates this handling, the rear can be gently pressed to place the dog into a sitting position. If the sit position is tolerated, the dog can gently be pushed on the shoulders into a down position. The tester then progresses to gently rolling the dog over onto its back. If the dog strongly resists, it should not be flipped or thrown down, but replaced in the kennel. A dog that cannot be firmly and gently rolled over is showing problems. The dog needs to be held at least thirty seconds, but the goal is to hold it gently but firmly down (not scratching its tummy or cooing to it) until some definite responses are seen. Its behavior after it is let up will help evaluate its resiliency and forgiveness.

Reactions: Dogs tend to protect their rears from intrusive sniffing or mounting by other dogs. Being pushed on the rear by a person is similar to the feeling of being mounted by another dog. The feeling of being pushed into a down is similar to the dominant move of a dog pressing its head on another dog's shoulders to see whether it tolerates this prelude to mounting or fighting. If dogs are too wiggly to get into any position, but show no fear or aggression, an effort should be made to see if they become easier to handle as they gain experience during the testing, or become more difficult, showing a temperament problem such as hyperactivity.

Fail if dog:
- Shows any Restraint fail behaviors.

Pass if dog:
- Shows the Restraint pass behaviors

Foot Restraint

The purpose of this test is to slightly annoy the dog without dominating it. Many dogs get snappy if annoyed by someone they perceive as submissive, so it is essential that the tester does not act controlling, firm, or dominant. The dog must feel free to react naturally to the problem presented to it.

Goal: The dog calmly accepts that it cannot free its gently held foot.

Method: The tester holds the dog's front paw very gently, but just firmly enough that the dog cannot yank it away. The hand should be as if glued to the foot. If the dog wants to move its paw, the tester's hand goes freely along with it.

Fail if dog:
- Shows Restraint fail behaviors.

Pass if dog:
- Shows Restraint pass behaviors.

Restraint – Handling Head and Mouth

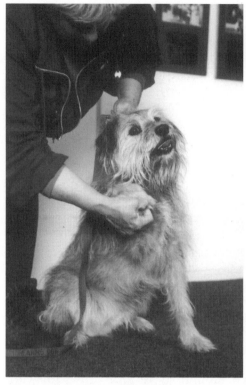

Terrier mix is about to bite. His panting and wide eyes show he is stressed by having his paw handled. He bit the tester on the hand immediately after this.

Regardless of how much mouth handling the owner plans to do, intense reluctance to allow the mouth to be handled is a strong indicator of potential problems with handling in general.

Goal: The dog permits its mouth to be opened, touched, and examined.

Method: While petting the head, the tester starts petting the lips and muzzle, massages lips gently, pulls them up to look at teeth, opens mouth and rubs gums. A happy voice and body language are helpful ("Oh, such beautiful teeth!"). The tester should attempt to examine the mouth long enough to determine age and any tooth or gum problems.

Reactions: Most dogs find this process annoying and will struggle away. Very few dogs will relax and passively allow their mouth to be handled, so to expect them to do so would be unrealistic. If the teeth can be briefly examined during the struggling, and the dog remains cheerful and interactive after the mouth handling is finished, that is an optimum response. Dogs that resist strongly and are suspicious of attempts to handle their mouth are not suitable. They will become progressively more and more difficult to handle, and begin to forcefully whip their head away or threaten approaching hands.

Fail if dog:

- Shows Restraint fail behaviors.

Pass if dog:

- Shows Restraint pass behaviors.
- Struggles briefly but the teeth can be glanced at.
- Passively allows mouth to be handled.

Restraining Mouth

In watching films of wolf behavior, dominant wolves can be seen to sometimes grab another's muzzle and press downwards. The submissive wolf offers its muzzle as part of the ritual of active submission. Both cooperate because, as pack members, they already have a relationship established. For a human to do this to a strange dog is rude and antagonistic. Therefore, this test must be done *only* to dogs that have easily passed the other handling and restraint tests. Do not do this with dogs that the tester even *suspects* may snap or bite. This test offers a good indication of response to dominating behavior as well as to repeated unwanted touching. It should be done slowly and non-threateningly, as if petting.

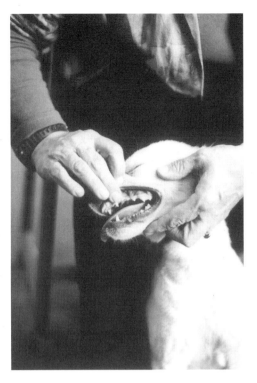

This dog passively allows his teeth to be examined without any resistance; an unusually good reaction.

Goal: The dog allows both dominant behavior and restraint from the tester.

Method: The tester gently and slowly reaches for the muzzle, holds it shut very gently but exerts a little pressure to move the muzzle up and down, then releases the muzzle and slowly withdraws hand about a foot away. Wait two seconds and repeat. This is not a quick grabbing motion, and the dog must see the hand coming. After four or five repetitions the dog will realize that the hand is again coming to restrain its muzzle. Its reactions give a good clue as to how it feels about gentle but unwanted handling. The issue here is not the dog's reaction to grabbing, but the fact that the dog after a few times anticipates that it will be restrained gently yet again. How does the dog deal with the approaching hand?

Fail if dog:

- Moves sharply to avoid hand on muzzle and tester is unable to touch muzzle again. If it threatens as the hand approaches, put the dog back in its kennel.
- Tolerates a few holds on muzzle but then acts "fed up" and avoids hand. If the tester keeps trying and the dog snaps, stiffens, or whips its head away sharply, put it back in its kennel.

Pass if dog:

- Gets very wiggly and avoids hand, but once muzzle is held, tolerates the holding. Dog is still friendly and interactive after test stops. Submissive behavior is okay.
- Might wiggle, but does not resist strongly. It allows the muzzle restraint over and

over. This dog is still friendly and interactive after the test stops.

Note: After the test, evaluate dog's attitude towards tester. Has it changed? If so, jolly the dog up with happy voice, body language, and whatever contact the dog enjoys most to erase any negative feelings about the muzzle holding.

Play Interaction

The Play Interaction test is done before the next test in order to give the dog a break from the other restraint tests.

Goal: Dog may or may not be comfortable playing with the tester, but should not become fearful or aggressive.

Method: A cheerful voice and body language can entice the dog to play. If it responds by bouncing playfully, the tester pats his or her knees mimicking the patting of the front feet by a dog in a play-bow. The tester tries to appear submissive, and very gently pushes the dog away, then quickly withdraws hands. When the tester stops the game and becomes still, the dog's reactions should be noted. At any fear or hesitation the test should stop and the dog gently cheered up.

Excellent reaction to restraint: this little spaniel mix is relaxed and trusting as his muzzle is restrained gently.

Fail if dog:
- Is frightened and tries to escape. When tester stops, dog will not interact again.
- Interprets attempts at play as a threat and growls, stiffens, or shows "whale eye."
- Plays back forcefully, escalating the play until unacceptably rough. When the tester stops playing, the dog continues to play and cannot be stopped easily.
- Plays, but then stiffens or snaps or escalates play biting to nipping when the tester gets a little rough.

Pass if dog:
- Plays rougher and rougher but shows inhibited mouthing, and matches the tester's intensity. When the tester stops, the dog calms.
- Makes a few intention movements of playfulness but is too inhibited to actually play. When the tester stops, the dog acts relieved and rushes up to interact.
- Is intimidated by play attempts and crouches submissively but does not run away. When the tester stops, dog creeps up to interact.

Note: All of the temperament tests in this book are designed to favor dogs that show submissive behavior. This means that most dogs that do well overall will prove to be too inhibited or submissive to play with a stranger during this test. Most will play later when they get to know a person. Dogs that are eager to play with an unfamiliar tester during the testing situation are actually quite bold and fearless, and need additional testing to determine just how rough they will get, how hard to handle they are, and whether they will chase running or screaming people and children.

Discomfort Tolerance

The tester needs to now assume the role of a submissive or at least neutral person. If the tester is perceived as submissive, the dog is more likely to bite or snap than at a dominant, controlling tester. Acting hesitant or scared can make many dogs feel free to bite; the tester's own judgment of who will be ultimately handling the dog should determine the level of dominance shown by the tester. I personally act quite hesitant and wimpy. Because the dogs that I test are going to live with very loving people who usually do not have a lot of dog handling experience, I really want to screen out snappy dogs. It is best to do this test after a dog has passed other handling tests to avoid being bitten. If a dog has performed well on all others, it is unlikely that it will bite seriously if it feels a minimal amount of discomfort.

Goal: The dog tolerates slight pressure between the skin of its toes. This discomfort at its most intense should only be equivalent to real-life situations such as nail-clipping, medicating an injury, removal of burrs or splinters, or accidentally being lightly stepped on or pulled at by a child.

Method: The tester holds the collar gently with one hand so that any snapping can be directed away from the face. With the other, he or she massages the dog's front paw and

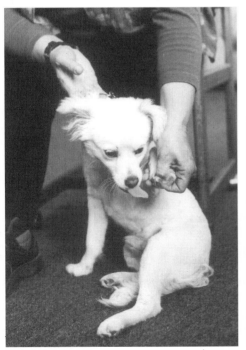 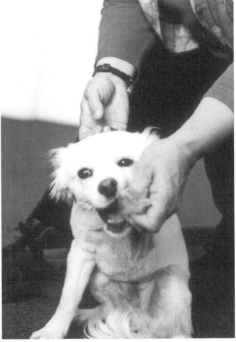

Left - Spaniel mix licks in protest at the slight pressure on his toe webbing... Right - ...then mouths gently at the hand. After mouthing was not effective to free his paw, he turned his head away and stopped protesting.

the skin between the toes. If it tolerates this, the skin should be pinched, very lightly at first, and with increasing pressure until the dog reacts in some way more than just pulling the foot away. The tester needs to know what the dog does when it realizes that pulling its foot away does not stop the discomfort.

Fail if dog:
- Shows Restraint fail behaviors.

Pass if dog:
- Shows Restraint pass behaviors.
- Shows no reaction to pressure from pinch. Needs further testing to evaluate tolerance versus low pain sensitivity.

After this test, play with the dog to erase any negative impressions the tester has created.

Tie Out – Neutral Observation and Approach

Goal: The dog feels reasonably secure if tied up alone, not showing panicked or trapped reactions. It shows friendly behavior if the tester walks towards it.

Method: The dog is tied on a five-foot leash, left alone, and observed from a hiding place for about two minutes. Do not do this test with dogs that are afraid to be on leash or start to struggle and tangle in it. If the dog seems comfortable, the tester waits about one minute, steps out from hiding, stares at the dog for a few seconds, then walks briskly directly toward the dog while carrying a bag or other object near shoulder level.

Fail if dog:
- Shows any of the Neutral Stranger fail behaviors.
- Acts fearful when the tester approaches carrying a bag or object on his or her shoulder.

Pass if dog:
- Is inhibited or slightly fearful when first left tied up, but relaxes and looks around with interest. Neutral or friendly reactions to distant people.
- Is active, tests leash, restless, looks for tester, wags tail if it sees people in distance.
- Barks and whines, looks for tester, howls, seems anxious. May have separation anxiety or is just a very vocal dog.
- Is eager to approach the returning tester or shows submission without fear.

Predatory Aggression

Note: If dog has shown *any* aggression during previous tests, *do not* do this test.

Goal: Dog does not attempt to bite or intensely chase moving objects or people.

Method:

Dog is held on a strong leash by a helper who keeps the dog safely at a distance. The tester drags a towel at a safe distance by an attached rope past the dog in a teasing way, staying twenty feet away at all times. Next, without the towel the tester then runs back and forth, still at a safe distance, past the dog while mimicking excited childlike behavior. Finally, the tester runs with the dog on leash for a short distance.

Reactions: These tests are not very conclusive, because the tester is artificially imitating the role of prey animal, jogger, and child so the dog should not be failed or passed based solely on its results. The best that can be expected is some indication that further testing in real-life situations is needed.

Fail if dog:

- Bites and tugs on towel, holds it, rips it up, shows intense behavior and cannot be refocused away from the prey object. Tester should later determine whether the dog is accustomed to tug games or really wants to bite anything small that moves rapidly.
- Leaps, attempts to chase, and nips at tester's skin or clothing when tester runs past. Dog cannot be refocused away from the person. Tester needs to later determine whether dog is playing rough but is easily controlled, or really wants to chase and bite any moving person.
- Leaps to nip skin or clothing when running alongside the tester. Further testing is needed to determine whether the dog's behavior is easily controlled or is dangerous.

Pass if dog:

- Shows mild interest, pouncing at towel or person. When movement stops, dog calms and loses interest. The dog should be refocused easily away from its goal by the tester or a third person.
- Shows no interest in chasing towel or person. Nevertheless, this does not mean the dog has no problems in this area; it should still be later observed in more appropriate situations for predatory aggression.

Food Motivation

Giving dogs food is traditionally a good way to "make friends." This can be counterproductive when trying to test the dog's reactions to a stranger. During tests where the tester wants to play the role of a stranger, or is still actually a stranger to the dog, giving food should be avoided. The tester should give food as a conscious decision to change the relationship and be aware that from then on, the dog's attitude will be a little different.

Goal: The dog should have high food motivation and eat as if every crumb is its last. It eats any kind of food offered in any situation no matter how full its stomach is. High food motivation means that the dog has a fanatical, intense focus on food, and expends great amounts of energy to get it. If the trainer keeps food away by closing it in their hand, the dog should not give up passively, but continue to root and search for a way to get the food from the hand. Dogs that cheerfully plod towards their food rewards, then amble around looking for more, are not showing enough drive for sound alerting work. If they move this slowly when they know a treat is there, imagine how slowly they will move (or not move) when they know the treat might possibly *not* be there! The ideal attitude for training with food suggests that the dog believes that finding food is a life-and-death situation, with death from starvation right around the corner.

Method: Offer several kinds of treats while the dog is in the kennel. Later, when dog is outside, offer the treats again. If the dog eats them, keep the treats in a closed hand and observe if the dog makes efforts to get to the food. Move the hand around to observe if the dog will follow the hand. Toss a treat on the ground.

Fail if dog:

- Refuses all types of food.
- Mouths and drops food.

Pass if dog:

- Accepts food or accepts one type of food.

- Is eager to get the food and shows great persistence in nudging and searching for it. When food is eaten, the dog continues to search for more.
- Upon seeing a non-moving treat on the floor, even with no other competitors for it around, the dog rushes and pounces on the treat with the same intensity it would show toward a running mouse.

Loud Noises

Goal: Dog hears a loud crash, but turns to investigate rather than avoiding in fear. It should quickly approach and sniff, not warily creep up to it.

Method: A metal dog bowl or other object is dropped on the ground about six feet behind the dog, not towards the dog. The tester remains silent and motionless and observes the dog.

Fail if dog:
- Crouches, remains fearful, does not approach bowl.
- Bolts away and does not return.
- Bolts or startles, observes bowl, creeps up to it to sniff it, backs away, avoids it subsequently. Many people mistakenly categorize this response as "recovery." It is not "recovering" unless the dog recovers its former confident attitude.
- Totally ignores sound. Test further for deafness or lack of sound reactivity. Deaf dogs may feel the vibrations as the bowl hits the ground or see it moving with their peripheral vision, and give the impression of testing well.

Pass if dog:
- Startles at sound, investigates the bowl hesitantly, then behaves exactly as before.
- Turns at the sound, immediately runs to investigate bowl, acts confident and curious.
- Looks toward the bowl, then ignores it.

Umbrella

This test observes the dog's attitude towards a startling visual stimulus.

Goal: Dog recovers and approaches/investigates after being slightly startled by an umbrella popping open. When the umbrella is held overhead, mimicking the effect of a large hat, the dog shows no fear and is willing to approach the tester trustingly.

Method: A pop-up umbrella is pointed downwards about six feet in front of the dog and released to open as it hits the ground; after waiting about thirty seconds, the tester then slowly picks up the umbrella and holds it overhead.

Fail if dog:
- Bolts away and will not approach umbrella. (Do not proceed to holding the umbrella overhead.)
- Shows any of the Loud Noise fail behaviors.

Pass if dog:
- Shows any of the Loud Noise pass behaviors.
- Jumps on the umbrella, walks around on it, or bites it playfully. When the umbrella is held overhead, the dog leaps to nip or play, or confidently jumps on the tester. This dog is showing plenty of confidence, but may be hard for the average person to handle; it needs further testing to assess predatory aggression.

Mechanical Toys

Goal: Dog is not overly fearful or aggressive toward unusual objects to demonstrate that it does not show high predatory aggression.

Method: The dog is exposed to an deactivated mechanical toy dog or animal about six feet away from it, and its reactions observed. If it is confident and investigative, the test may be repeated with the toy turned on. Each time, the toy is at a distance and the dog allowed to approach on its own. The toy should not be suddenly plunked down in front of it.

Fail if dog:
- Avoids the toy and tries to bolt or hide. Does not ever recover and investigate.
- Circles fearfully with barking and escape behavior.
- Attacks toy while mechanical part is turned on, "kills" it, rips at it. Tester must make the difficult decision about whether the dog is accustomed to playing this way with toys or is treating the toy as it would a small live animal.

Pass if dog:
- Is fearful and wary, but is comfortable at a distance from the toy. Does not approach closely.
- Approaches warily, sniffs the toy, then avoids it without fearful behavior.
- Approaches, sniffs toy, then ignores or bites at it gently.
- Ignores toy

Other-dog Aggression

Most of the behavior called "other-dog aggression" is motivated by fearfulness, but I am using this term for practical purposes. Growling, lunging, and barking is unacceptable behavior for Hearing Dogs no matter what the inner motivation.

Goal: The dog shows no fearful or aggressive behavior with other dogs, even if they show aggression. It should prefer human company to interacting with other dogs.

Method: The dog should be observed (1) inside a kennel and seeing a leashed dog outside, (2) on leash and seeing a dog inside a kennel, and (3) encountering another dog on leash.

Dogs should be kept from getting close enough to injure each other, and the test should be stopped as soon as some definite reaction is seen. If the dog is showing aggression, the handler may be in danger from redirected aggression. Allowing dogs to lunge and bark at other dogs constitutes a training session for intensifying other-dog aggression. "But he only does it on leash" is a poor excuse. Hearing Dogs in public places should always be on leash.

Fail if dog:
- Lunges forward at the other dog while growling, barking, or snapping. Stares rigidly at the other dog, tail up and wagging stiffly, or slowly walking toward dog. Return the dog to the kennel; the tester is in danger from redirected aggression. Ask for help if needed.
- Makes escape attempts with panic and hysterical behavior and/or backing up with barking and growling. Return the dog to the kennel.
- Shows playful barking and leaping that is so intense that the tester cannot redirect the dog's focus back to the tester. The behavior might be playful, not aggressive, but if the dog is that interested in other dogs, it is not sufficiently oriented towards

As this scary monkey rolls his eyes and claps his cymbals, Summer cautiously approaches to sniff from the rear. An acceptable reaction to such a difficult test. This toy was used for photos, but is too frightening to get meaningful test results with. A plush dog is a better tool.

If, on the other hand, a dog is bold enough to bite and shake a mechanical toy, it is a sign that it may be high in predatory aggression. It should be further tested.

Confident investigation with tail up and ears forward; a Malinois pup approaches a plush terrier.

people to be a good companion or easy to handle in public.

Pass if dog:
- Ignores other dogs. Needs further testing to evaluate actual attitude. The dog may simply prefer people, or it might show aggressive or fearful behavior only if approached closely by a dog.
- Shows extreme submission; crawling forward, spinning, urinating, face licking. Young dogs sometimes outgrow these behaviors. If the dog cannot be refocused onto the tester, the dog may be too dog-oriented and should be further tested to evaluate people-orientation.
- Shows eager playfulness (play-bows, whining, loose bouncy body language, frisking), but its focus can be redirected to the tester.
- Shows mild interest that is easily redirected to the tester.

Food Guarding

Although dogs should be tested for this problem, it is risky to test strange shelter dogs. Only do this test if the dog has passes all the previous ones. Do not do this test with a dog that has shown any "fail" or even less-than-optimal behaviors in any previous tests. Stop the test if the dog freezes, stops eating with head held rigidly over the bowl, or growls.

Method: Tie the dog securely, and offer it a bowl of food that it will eat. Once it is eating, stay out of range and attempt to pull the bowl away with a broom or other long object. Alternately, use Sue Sternberg's "Assess-a-Hand," a lifelike artificial arm. If the dog shows no growling or freezing, then use the item to gently push its muzzle away from the food bowl.

Fail if dog:
- Growls.
- Stops eating and holds head rigid over bowl.
- Freezes rigidly and stops eating.
- Snaps at the object interfering with its food.

Pass if dog:
- Continues eating, ignoring the object.
- Leaves food when bowl is moved or muzzle pushed away.

This test only gives an indication of a tendency to guard food. Passing it does not mean there is no problem; many factors influence this behavior, and doing this test in a shelter is not very informative.

Traffic Sights and Sounds

Goal: Dog shows that it is not overly fearful of traffic sights and sounds.

Method: Dog is walked near any available traffic and observed for fearfulness or car-chasing tendencies. Excuses for extreme fearfulness such as "perhaps the dog was hit by a car" are not always valid: many streetwise dogs have had bad experiences and learned to be cautious and avoid cars, not become panicked. Panicked fearfulness should alert the tester to the possibility of a temperament that can develop phobias. As in all types of fearfulness, a major point is the dog's ability to respond with increased confidence to jollying and confident behavior on the part of the tester. Dogs that find security in relating to a person have a way out of their fears. Evaluate the dog using the fail/pass behaviors in the following "Interiors and Stairs" test.

Interiors and Stairs

Goal: Dog is either confident inside buildings or shows signs that it can adjust. It's hard to predict which dogs will improve in traffic and interior environments and which will stay the same or grow worse. Some improvement should be seen during the testing.

Method: Dog is walked inside buildings and introduced to stairs or uneven surfaces. It is observed for signs of fearfulness and whether it recovers with jollying by the tester.

Fail if dog:

- Remains still and cannot move or walk, even with jollying.
- Tries to escape in panic.
- Wants to escape from both the tester and the traffic or interior environment.

Pass if dog:

- Will go up one or two stairs with coaxing after sitting with the tester on the stairs for a few minutes.
- Starts to walk when jollied.
- Clings and stays with the tester in spite of fearfulness of interiors or traffic.
- Walks hesitantly but improves over a few minutes time.
- Shows confident exploration and no fear.

SOUND TESTING

It should be noted that several breeds (or mixes derived from them) have a higher incidence of hearing impairments, most notably Dalmatians, Australian Cattle Dogs, and English Bull Terriers. The latter two breeds are claimed to have some Dalmatian ancestry. The most frequent cause of deafness in mixed breeds is inheritance from breeds with known incidence of deafness, or a product of breeding two blue or red merle dogs together, producing "Double Merles." Luckily these are often easily recognizable by white coloration with a few diluted merle markings of a pale pastel tan or gray color, lack of pigment on nose and around eyes, and blue eyes. The more white coloring a dog shows, pale diluted merling, or any sign of Dalmatian or Australian Cattle Dog heritage, the more suspiciously I test its hearing.

Totally *eaf dogs are often asleep in a noisy shelter, hard to wake up, and when alert, rarely move their ears. Their ears may have a sort of "dead" quality from lack of use of the muscles that move them. They often compensate by showing very high visual reactivity, and this can make it difficult to assess their hearing. I once almost adopted a totally deaf Terrier mix that not only had fantastic temperament, but had great responses on all the sound tests as well. I was about to adopt her when I noticed that her ears were very slack, and she did not respond to sounds behind her. She was fascinated by any movement I made, and was responding to my hands when they held the sound gadgets, not to the sounds themselves. (I now hold sounds behind me or set them to ring after being placed somewhere.) This dog was really great and could have learned unlimited signs. Luckily, the shelter considered her adoptable.

Occasionally, dogs with normal hearing may appear deaf. Shelley Monson once adopted a young Springer who tested well. Once back at the SPCA, the pup pointed and stared at moving shadows, and we could not get a response to sounds from it; clapping hands or even the ring of a smoke alarm had no effect. Loud sounds a few inches from its ears didn't even cause them to twitch backwards. When the pup was not entranced by moving shadows, it responded normally to all sounds. It was diagnosed with a neurological problem.

Many dogs with normal hearing could not care less about any sounds that are not relevant to them, and show no response. They may flick their ears backwards briefly if a sound is behind them, and respond to a meaningful sound such as their name, the click of the opening kennel or bang of a food dish, but that is it. It's hard to believe that they are not deaf, but they might as well be, in terms of aptitude for sound alerting.

The dogs that pose the most problems for the tester are those with partial hearing. Often deaf in one ear, or with different losses in each ear, they can hear, but have trouble locating the direction sounds come from.

Since hearing-impaired dogs have difficulty locating sounds, and cannot hear certain frequencies, sound alerting is problematic, although dogs that become deaf through aging often continue to work as long as they can hear the sounds. I once visited a household with the loudest phone ringer I had ever heard. The Deaf owners explained that they could not hear the ring, but they had purchased the ringer to help their aging Hearing Dog.

BAER hearing testing for dogs is available through specialists or teaching veterinary universities.

How Dogs React to Different Sounds

From a dog's point of view, certain sounds that we wish dogs to alert us to are inherently exciting while others are inhibiting. High-pitched repetitive sounds, such as loud beeping, stimulate movement in dogs, and low, descending, growling tones inhibit them. It is easy to teach dogs to alert to high-pitched sounds, much harder to teach them to alert to low-pitched sounds. Office telephones designed not to annoy people also do not excite dogs, but louder and more excitatory phone rings such as those designed for the hard-of-hearing are relatively easy to train dogs to alert to. These differences in responses can help to identify dogs that are highly sound reactive. The ideal dog reacts strongly to a wide range of sounds, whereas other dogs might only respond to the more exciting sounds.

Sound Testing Procedures

The optimal reactions for Hearing Dogs is to run quickly to the sound and bite, scratch, or jump at it. They are equally interested if the sound is repeated a second or third time. They are distracted away from other activities by sounds. They do not show fear of loud sounds; they actually get more excited the louder sounds get, and the smoke alarm gets them really excited. One would think it must be painful to their sensitive hearing, yet some dogs jam their nose right up to it, simply fascinated.

I test when the dog is calm and not particularly focused on any one goal, and also when it is distracted. I highly value the dog that turns around to investigate a sound, even while very focused on something else.

Sound reactivity testing has three goals:

1. to establish that the dog can hear (not that easy!)
2. to find its level of sound reactivity
3. to find out whether its sound reactivity is easily overshadowed by other senses

Methods of Testing Sounds

Testing for sound reactivity is done when the dog is facing away or not focused on the gadget producing the sound. Sounds are produced, then the dog's reactions observed. Some guidelines must be followed to avoid actions that actually make dogs fearful of the sounds they might otherwise have tested well on:

Sounds that consist of one short sound are not repeated until the dog has shown a reaction and its interest is once again elsewhere

Sounds that are continuous are continued without interruption until the dog shows a definite reaction

Repeating or restarting a sound as the dog is approaching will frighten even confident dogs. If the sound suddenly re-occurs while the dog is investigating its source, it is as if the sound attacked the dog. The dog is in effect being trained that this particular sound is a threat, although it may still have no fear of any other sounds. Everyone has seen this effect when a dog investigates any mysterious object such as a rolling paper bag. When the bag stops moving, the dog may approach, but if it blows suddenly toward the dog, it jumps back as if attacked, because dogs are genetically programmed to understand that unfamiliar things may attack. Dogs react to sounds in the same way. Testing for sound reactivity has nothing to do with testing for the dog's reaction to being suddenly startled. Other tests should have revealed this already. While the dogs with the highest potential are positively interested in sounds no matter what, and therefore less affected by mistakes in testing, the majority of dogs can be negatively affected.

Method: The dog is on leash, and allowed to relax and ignore the tester if it wants to. If it wants to interact, it should be ignored. The dog should not be strongly focused on a distraction. The tester unobtrusively hides the sound gadget by holding it out of the dog's sight. Care must be taken that the act of concealing the gadget is not interpreted by the dog as a teasing game of "hide the toy." This causes dogs that are deaf or just playful to appear to be searching for the sound source. The sound is started and the dog observed until it shows a definite reaction. If it shows no reaction and is focused elsewhere, the test can be restarted, and this time, the sound gadget can slowly be brought behind it and moved closer to its ears while producing the sound. If the dog turns, orients, but then loses interest, the sound should be tried again. If it habituates rapidly when the sound is repeated, and no longer orients, it may possibly not have much sound reactivity.

General Reactions to Sound Testing

The following reactions hold true for all of the sound reactivity tests.
Fail if dog:

- Shows an immediate halt to tail movement, a slowing of body movement and moves away. Inhibition from fearfulness causes a wary, stressed appearance. If the sound is repeated the dog attempts to leave the area or to cling to the tester.
- Freezes and focuses on the sound in a way which can be at first misinterpreted as a curious orienting reflex, but its subsequent reactions are to avoid the sound rather than approach it.
- Approaches the sound, but with wary, fearful body language. The legs are slanted backwards ready to escape, and the whole body leans backwards. The neck is stretched out and the dog is sniffing with chin held high. The dog may approach directly or in a slightly arced path. This is not an acceptable response. The dog is

physically and mentally prepared to flee. If it does finally accept the sound as not dangerous and then relaxes, it has still shown that it is fearful of new sounds, and will not be suitable in public places or in sound alerting. It may never show a strong positive response to sounds.

- Orients, approaches sound, investigates, then slightly avoids the sound.
- Ignores the sound after a brief orientation. Moving the sound behind its head produces a flick backwards of the ears, but no head turning or other acknowledgment of the sound.

Questionable if dog:

- Responds well to all voice sounds but ignores other sounds. This dog is possibly a well socialized dog with low sound reactivity. Its responses to voice tones are learned, not natural. It is showing good companion potential, but may have difficulty in sound alerting.
- Tests well on most sounds, but appears fearful of the smoke alarm. Dogs that test well on all other sounds and show only slight avoidance of the smoke alarm are still showing potential. Further testing and training will reveal whether the dog can learn to have a positive attitude about the smoke alarm or is too fearful of loud sounds in general to function in public or in sound alerting.

Pass if dog:

- Orients to the sound, but does not approach. Upon hearing the sound again, may or may not orient again, but does not avoid the sound or look fearful.
- Orients to sound, then approaches confidently, body leaning forwards, body relaxed, sniffs in an eager way when it gets all the way to the source (not pausing to sniff from a distance fearfully).
- Responds to some sounds but totally ignores others. This is normal behavior even in dogs with high potential.
- Appears fascinated and obsessed with investigating all sounds produced by the tester, and orients to or investigates any other environmental sounds that occur. Ear, head, and body movements all are easily triggered by sounds. If the tester conceals a gadget on their body, the dog jumps and paws when it sounds, eagerly searching for it. If the tester is making unusual vocal noises, the dog jumps up or wriggles looking upwards. It responds to voices with instant excitement. When sounds are repeated, the dog again responds rather than ignoring them. The tester gets the feeling that simply by watching this dog's behavior, he or she would be aware of everything going on around them. Given a suitable temperament for its other roles, this dog is the ideal Hearing Dog.

SOUND REACTIVITY TESTS

"Oddball" sounds

Method: The sound should be less loud than a smoke alarm, but not faint. Starting with a very loud sound may stress a sound-shy dog, so it's better to work up slowly to loud sounds. Starting with a very minimal sound is not the answer; often the dog does not give a clear response. The tester must ensure that the sound source is concealed from the dog's sight when it is sounded, and give no body or verbal cues that would affect the dog's reactions. Suitable sounds include beepers, wild animal call makers, and a tape recording of a crying baby.

Reactions: "Oddball" sounds often elicit excitement, curiosity, and surprised interest. See Fail/Pass above.

Smoke Alarm

Goal: Dog approaches and investigates smoke alarm eagerly, shows no avoidance.

Method: Smoke alarm is concealed behind the tester, both to avoid letting the dog see it and to muffle the loud sound somewhat. Ninety decibels can damage both human and dog hearing. I keep it pressed inwards against my body or jacket, or muffle the sound with some tissue in the little horn that can be seen when the cover is off. The test button is pressed and the sound continued until the dog shows a definite reaction. As the dog approaches, the sound should stop if the dog hesitates, but continue if the dog is still moving forward. If the dog reaches the alarm, the sound is stopped to avoid any discomfort.

Reactions: Reactions specific to the smoke alarm range from fearfulness to intense investigation and interest. See Fail/Pass above.

Whistle

Goal: The dog is aware that the sound comes from the tester, but still trustingly approaches or orients toward the tester. The body language necessary to blow the whistle probably makes the dog more aware that the whistle sound emanates from the tester.

Method: The tester blows the whistle when the dog is facing away from the tester, continuing to blow as the dog looks around at the tester. The whistle is blown long enough so that the dog realizes that the sound is coming from the tester, but ceases when the dog starts to approach. If it is continued during the approach, it may frighten the dog. The tester then remains neutral and observes the dog. The whistle is blown again if the dog runs up and acts confident.

Reactions: Because this is a loud sound, the dog that turns with interest, realizes that the sound is coming from the tester, and nevertheless approaches is showing both high sound reactivity and trust in the tester. Dogs that react fearfully to the whistle and then also seem afraid of the tester are showing a lack of trust and interactivity. See Fail/Pass above.

Timer (high-pitched continuous kitchen timer).

Goal: Dog approaches a faint sound on the ground.

Method: The timer is set to go off in about thirty seconds or so, placed on the ground in a place visible to the dog. The timer is set for this time length so that dog has time to sniff it, classify it as irrelevant, and then ignore it. The only reason to place the timer on the ground is that the other sounds must be held and operated by the tester, and some of the dog's responses may be affected by desire to interact with the tester. Placing the sound on the ground allows a little more objectivity in judging sound reactivity.

Reactions: Timers sound more like prey animals than some other sounds, so some predatory responses can be expected. The dog ideally alerts by orienting toward the sound, makes an effort to locate its direction and runs to investigate it. Picking up, pawing, or nudging the timer are excellent responses. Since the timer is a faint sound, any response at all is good, even a simple orienting response. In noisy places, the test can be repeated by holding the timer close behind the dog and ringing it. See Fail/Pass above.

Squeaky Toys

Goal: Dog orients and approaches squeak sound.

Method: Tester holds the toy out of sight and squeaks it. If the dog investigates the sound, the tester then throws the toy a few feet away from the dog, not towards it, which might be frightening. The only reason to throw the toy is to determine whether the dog is reacting more to the sound out of sound reactivity or is accustomed to playing with squeaky toys. This is not a retrieve test, although information may be gained about the dog's predatory instincts and familiarity with toys and fetch games.

Reactions: I don't place a great deal of weight on this test. A good response may only show that the dog has been imprinted on squeaky toy sounds. Dogs that have experience hunting small animals will also respond intensely to a squeak toy. There is nothing wrong with a dog that likes squeak toys; it's just that this may be the only sound it is really interested in. There are many toys available with unusual animal noises that would be better test items. See Fail/Pass above.

Door Knock

Goal: Dog shows orientation response to door knock.

Method: Tester knocks on any object while dog is looking away.

Reactions: These are affected by the dog's previous experiences, but the test can still indicate sound reactivity. See Fail/Pass above.

Toy Motivation and Retrieving

Goal: The dog shows that it is motivated by the opportunity to play with toys, which can be used in training.

Method: The tester teases the dog with some standard toys (tennis ball, squeaky toy, etc.), then tosses toy a few feet away from the dog.

Reactions: Any interest is encouraging, particularly if the dog is lacking in food motivation. Dogs that are fanatical about toys but not suitable for Hearing Dog roles might be potential drug or bomb detection dogs, and the tester can contact law enforcement agencies or detection training businesses to inform them that this dog is in the shelter. Truly toy-fanatical dogs are not always suitable as pets and this might be their only chance.

However, if the dog's partner desires retrieving as a practical exercise—picking up dropped items or bringing a portable phone to the partner—then the dog's natural retrieving ability is important.

Fail if dog:
- Is fearful of the toy and interprets a throwing motion as a threat from the tester.

Questionable if dog:
- Ignores toy completely. No big deal; perhaps it could learn.

Pass if dog:
- Chases, bites, paws at the toy, and might carry it around. This dog might be able to learn to retrieve.
- Retrieves toy to tester, or at least picks it up and moves in the tester's direction teasingly.

Overall Final Evaluation: Hard-to-Quantify Traits

The tester now evaluates the dog on its behavior throughout the tests as it applies to visual responsiveness, activity level, reactivity level, resiliency, initiative, and interactivity.

Visual Responsiveness

Goal: The dog looks upward at the tester often, notices body language and facial expressions, is neither fearful nor aggressive if tester makes any eye contact.

A short training session can reveal potential compatibility with ASL users. Using small treats, lure the dog's gaze upwards towards tester's face, using teasing hand motions, friendly body language and/or voice, and bring the treat back down to the dog's mouth when it looks up. Praise. After about ten rewards, note whether the dog responds by looking upwards more frequently when talked to or shown a hand pretending to hold a treat.

Activity Level

Fail if dog:
- Prefers to sit or lie down and can only be briefly motivated to get up and walk. If not severely ill, this dog is very inactive!
- Has slow, deliberate movements, and does not noticeably change speed even when encouraged by the tester. It may approach test objects casually and lazily. Typically, in keeping with its other movements, its tail movements are slow and relaxed.
- Maintains activity for a few minutes, then calms and is hard to motivate to get up and again be active.
- Is extremely active, does not match its activity to the tester's movements, cannot be focused towards any of the testing procedures for more than a second, and constantly resists efforts to calm it down or restrain it. This dog may be hyperactive, with a neurological problem. Further testing such as an attempt at a short training session to sit for treats may reveal clues about the dog's attention span and ability to inhibit its actions.

Pass if dog:
- Is active without stimulation from the tester.
- Remains active for at least fifteen minutes.
- Trots or gallops, rarely walking.
- Shows effortless activity, not forcing itself.
- Remains active when environmental stimuli cease.
- Makes an attempt to run or play even if ill.

Reactivity Levels

As discussed elsewhere, a dog is unsuitable to be a Hearing Dog if it is non-reactive or has a low overall reactivity level. When it comes to sound reactivity, the non-reactive dogs have very slow reactions to unusual or relevant sounds, while the dog with low reactivity reacts to sounds it has learned are relevant, but habituates very quickly to irrelevant ones.

An acceptable dog is one with medium reactivity that shows quick reactions to most stimuli, although it may habituate quickly. The equivalent reaction speed for a human would be similar to that of a vigilant person. A dog like this shows behavior that most people associate with small dogs. In terms of sound reactivity, it reacts to most sounds. It wakes up easily from sleep for unusual or relevant sounds.

The desirable dog is one with high reactivity that reacts to almost all stimuli with reactions so fast that the change cannot be seen by the observer. The dog appears to have instantly changed direction, posture, or expression as if a film had skipped forward a few frames. Reaction speed is similar to that seen in squirrels or small birds. If sound reactivity is equally high, response to sounds overshadows input from other senses, and the dog often orients even to familiar sounds. This dog wakes up quickly upon hearing any sound and often gives the impression of hardly sleeping at all. If the tester imagines that they cannot hear, observing such a dog provides a huge amount of information about the location and nature of everything happening in the environment around them.

Resiliency

The non-resilient dog shows negative effects from anything it doesn't like and cannot be "jollied" out of its anxiety by the tester. Such a dog is not suited to be a Hearing Dog.

A resilient dog recovers within a few seconds from negative experiences. Whether or not the tester can cheer it up, it resumes confident participation in the testing. Social resilience is especially important. The dog recovers quickly from anything the tester does that induces any fear or discomfort in the dog. Hearing Dogs, obviously, must be resilient.

A dog that is too highly resilient, however, shows few negative effects from any stimuli, and therefore learns little from negative experiences. Definitely "bomb-proof," it displays confident behavior that sometimes endangers itself. Because it perceives few consequences as negative, it learns to follow all of its impulses with great determination. Since negative experiences are rarely enough to permanently affect the behavior of these dogs, and "positive" methods often do not provide enough motivation to compete with the fulfillment of natural instincts, such a dog is difficult to influence. I greatly admire dogs that are "too resilient" and they have a valuable place in many roles, such as police work, but I must admit that for the companion and public roles of a Hearing Dog, they are unsuitable unless paired with an equally resilient and determined partner.

Initiative

A dog with good initiative is constantly attempting to make things happen. It is making contact with the tester, investigating the contents of a test kit, or trying to approach dogs or people, and does not need constant encouragement and stimulation.

A dog with low initiative may be active, but does not start new activities often. It responds to social cues, but rarely initiates social interactions. Tester feels as if he or she is "doing all the work." Low levels of exploration and investigation of unusual stimuli are typical of this dog.

The dog with average initiative shows a balance, sometimes reacting to social cues and sometimes initiating activity. It shows investigation and exploration, but also responds to initiative by other dogs or people.

A dog with high initiative will initiate most social interactions, and may sometimes ignore attempts to interact by other dogs or people.

Interactivity

While it is important to be objective in all one's testing, this is one area where decisions are based on feelings. After all, relationships between humans are based on feelings rather than commonsense. I have often selected dogs that just gave me a feeling that I would enjoy having them as a pet, even though they had not tested well on some other aspect. On the other hand, if I feel some hesitation about their personality, I often later regret accepting dogs that tested very well. They might not bite or avoid me, but there is something minimal about the relationship they establish. This lack of intensity is more often a part of the dog's temperament rather than a conflict between my personality and the dog's. If a dog does not feel some form of love towards you, it has no reason not to bite at some point, and it certainly will not want to participate in a training relationship. If it takes a long time to get used to me, then I know that it may have a tendency to trust only me, and have problems with other people. To clarify your feelings about a dog, temporarily ignore what the dog is actually doing, and try to think about the things it is not doing. For instance, the dog is constantly exploring, but comes every time you call. That's good, but why does it leave so quickly? Why do I need to redirect its focus on me? Or, it doesn't bite when handled and accepts control easily, but why doesn't it actually *solicit* handling?

Unacceptable dogs have very low to low interactivity. These dogs do not seem to need social interaction to be content nor do they seek it out. Instead, they find other activities more rewarding. Some dogs do not want any human contact, others enjoy some human contact but show a "take it or leave it" attitude, while still others are content to be near people without much interaction.

A dog with moderate interactivity could be considered acceptable. The dog interacts well, but can be distracted to activities of its own. Most people consider this a good pet; a dog that is playful and interactive when desired, but is not intrusively demanding.

A dog with high interactivity seeks interaction and responds to all attempts by the tester to interact. It is briefly distractible but keeps its focus on the tester. This dog is very eager to interact, even if the interaction is not what most dogs would consider positive.

Dogs that are overly interactive (or clinging) appear insecure and desperately needs constant social interaction. It may have severe separation anxiety if left alone.

Final Evaluation

The tester now envisions the dog in each of the three roles, predicting its reactions to situations encountered in each. Since training provides no miraculous changes in a dog's basic temperament, the tester should picture the dog as it is at present, not after it has somehow learned to be different.

Companion Role. Would the dog cooperate with cues and handling in the normal course of a day's events? Does the dog feel like a companion already? Would the tester personally want the dog? How would the dog react *now* on leash if the tester walked with it and stopped to relax somewhere? If the dog were a person, would it be like an old friend, perhaps a happy child? Imagine the dog's interactions with a bossy, dominant person, a submissive person, and a child. If the tester feels honestly that this dog is wonderful just the way it is (but perhaps just needs a little training to make other people also able to see its wonderfulness!), then perhaps this really is a good companion dog. When testing dogs, I get a definite feeling of love from the really good dogs, as well as a feeling of trust—or if not completely trusting, at least a desperate desire to trust me if only they could. The dogs that act as if they've known you forever will love people unconditionally, cooperate in a partnership, and always have more to give.

Public access. Could this dog enjoy public places, not just get used to them? Does it enjoy exploring with the tester? Does its relationship with the tester give it confidence when scary things happen? Will it approach everything strange, investigate it, then ignore it and go on to the next thing? Dogs that get scared of something are okay, but when fear accumulates and contaminates the dog's attitude to both the new environment and a relationship, the dog simply is not going to be able to adapt easily to new experiences. Dogs that are fearful of things in the environment yet want to be with you anyway and show signs of cheerfully and confidently following your lead may prove to be adaptable. Dogs that make you feel that they would comfort *your* fears are the best ones for public access.

Sound alerting. The tester only need ask one question: "If *I* adopted this dog, would I know about many sounds without ever training it?" Evaluate whether the dog would be suitable or not just by observing its general behavior around sounds. The Deaf or hard-of-hearing tester should get an impression of tapping into the dog's mind and sensations after a short acquaintance. This impression is not derived solely from the dog's ear positions and expressions, but also from its intense interactivity and desire to bond.

Chapter Nine
Training Basics

Dog training is complex and the multitude of canine personalities, all requiring different techniques, keeps training challenging even for professional trainers. It is therefore assumed that the reader has some understanding of the basic concepts of dog training, since discussing learning theory and training philosophies is beyond the scope of this book. There are no simple "cookbook" recipes for teaching dogs anything. The simplistic methods that are sometimes offered are similar to a phrase book for a foreign language, which the tourist uses to convey meaning without real understanding. There are, however, several good books on the subject. I recommend *Teamwork*, by Stewart Nordensson, any book by John Rogerson, *Don't Shoot the Dog* by Karen Pryor, *Excel-erated Learning* by Pamela Reid, *Smart Trainers, Brilliant Dogs*, by Janet Lewis, and *Good Owners, Great Dogs* by Brian Kilcommons.

If training is beyond your ability, then these two chapters can be shown to a professional trainer. Because each trainer has different philosophies about training, my goals are only to explain the tasks that a Hearing Dog can perform and to present a systematic approach to sound alerting training, which I find works for me. Each individual dog needs custom tailoring of this basic plan to suit its temperament, and every trainer will inevitably create a system that works even better for them.

Sound alerting is far more complicated than simply teaching a dog to sit reliably on cue. Since many people want to try training a Hearing Dog themselves, I can only say that if the training is not going well, please seek professional advice. If the dog seems scared, inhibited or reluctant to alert, the trainer must accept the fact that either they are making serious mistakes in training, or perhaps the dog is not suitable for the work.

Creating the Right Attitude in Dog and Partner

It has been previously stressed that dogs with natural ability are easily trained, compared with dogs that lack it. This is true, but sound alerting is a partnership. The partner, even if they're not an experienced trainer, also needs some natural ability or experience in understanding dogs in order to work with the dog's talent. Training mistakes can still ruin a talented dog. In particular, frustration and anger when the dog is not doing well are very damaging. Equally damaging are constant coddling and providing the dog with everything it wants, which lowers the dog's motivation.

The key to good sound alerting training is to remember that the dog should view sound alerting as the high point of its day, the most fun activity possible. The dog (and partner!) should be thrilled at each opportunity to alert. The high contrast between sound alerting and usual daily activities is achieved by positive emotional intensity coming from the partner in addition to other reinforcement that the dog craves. This means that the partner must respond to the dog in a positive way no matter how they are feeling. Every sound that happens is really a training session, an opportunity for the partner to strengthen (or weaken!) the dog's alerting behavior. The worst thing to do is to continue training the same way when a dog is not responding; bad training builds a dislike of the training situation, and may cause permanent damage to the dog's attitude. The quickest way to ruin a dog's alerting is to scold poor alerts either verbally or with angry body language or signs. This causes the dog to believe that its alerting is being punished.

Training has four main aspects:

1. Inhibiting undesirable instinctive behaviors. (Don't kill the hamster.)

Carmen Lee shows the right level of positive emotional intensity to make training fun for her buddy, Hearing Dog Mack.

2. Eliciting of desirable instinctive behaviors. (Herding sheep or orienting towards all sounds.)

3. Learning of new behaviors. (Climbing a ladder or touching for sound alerting.)

4. Inhibiting performance of desired behaviors when necessary. (Stop herding the sheep, now!)

These aspects of training are all totally different in both philosophy and method, yet are grouped together under the term, "training." Another confusing term is "trainable." It actually refers to the lack of training needed for a dog to perform a function. The more a dog's temperament lends itself to the task, the less training is required. Paradoxically, high trainability for many original functions is often antithetical to companion functions. Therefore, dogs that are easily inhibited or lack unwanted instincts are ideal for companionship and are labeled "trainable." Dogs that are dominant, uninhibited, independent, and possess strong instinctive behaviors are much more difficult to control, and are often rated lower in trainability. In actual fact, for certain functions, such as police work, a dog like this might be far more trainable than the first one.

Motivation

The term "motivation" has a lot of different meanings to different people. It is a broad term that refers to the inner state of an animal that cause purposeful behavior, such as satisfying instinctive drives or avoiding pain. All dogs differ in what motivates them and in how strongly it motivates them.

There are several motivations that are "built-in" to the ideal Hearing Dog, which are sounds, social interaction, and food. The more motivations a dog has, the more options the partner has to influence it. A dog with multiple motivations does not depend only on any one of them, and is easily kept sharp in its alerting responses. An unskilled partner with more good will than expertise would have a hard time *not* to succeed with this type of dog. Its real-life performance is safeguarded by appreciation for its efforts, the thrilling feeling of running to sounds, and an occasional food treat. Even if the partner is only able to offer one of these rewards, this dog has a good chance of staying motivated.

Sound Reactivity as a Motivation

Obviously, the most vital motivation for a Hearing Dog is reactivity to sounds. Even if all other trained behavior falls by the wayside, the dog will still retain its orientation reflex and at least turn its head toward sounds. Many Hearing Dogs revert to pet behavior when their partners are unable to keep up with constant maintenance training, but a dog with some natural ability can still be helpful even if its trained behaviors degenerate. There is a huge difference between encouraging behaviors that already occur naturally, and maintaining learned, artificial behaviors. Maintaining the learned behavior asks that the partner understand proper timing and reinforcement theory, and make a determined effort to find time to train the dog regularly. However, even a dog that finds investigating sounds intrinsically rewarding will need some kind of motivation to train it to alert reliably, or it will become sensitized to the exciting sounds of squirrels on the roof, and habituated to the boring sound of the telephone. Therefore, other motivations, such as social and food rewards, are crucial both to focus the dog to the required sounds and to maintain the alerting response in the face of the negative influences of daily life.

Social Interaction as a Motivation

The next most important motivation is social interaction. Interacting with the partner is a natural part of the sound alerting response, and making contact, getting praised, or the fun of running back and forth, can keep the dog motivated to alert. If good partnership exists, true communication can make standard training issues irrelevant.

Take the case of Jellybean, a Border Collie mix. Jellybean was five months old at the start of training, and about nine months when placed. Her sound alerting was great, but her obedience training was at about puppy level: intelligent but a short attention span. Like many herding function dogs, she needed more socialization than we could provide, preferably in a family

Trevor, a Golden Retriever, alerts partner David Mehler to the smoke alarm. Getting on the bed for a hug and some sincere appreciation is a great motivation for this alert. (Photo by Dennard)

environment, so it was essential to either let her graduate early with someone who would continue her obedience training, or release her to become a pet.

Luckily, Bobby Pelz applied for a Hearing Dog. Bobby was fifteen and had the summer off, so he agreed to take the puppy and train her over the summer. He had kept several goldfish and a tortoise healthy for seven years, helped care for the family's old Golden Retriever, and had a small petsitting business, so he was obviously responsible and well qualified. Jellybean was quite destructive at first but much loved by the family. Bobby came and volunteered often at the SPCA, and at one point commented that Jellybean didn't do her sound alerting as well as the dogs in training did. "She doesn't go back and forth or come all the way to me. She starts dancing around and staring at me, and if the doors are shut she jumps around and tries to get me to open them so she can go to the phone." I asked if she got treats from him or at the phone as rewards. "Yes, but sometimes I forget." I explained that Jellybean was actually doing far better than the dogs in training. At this early stage in their training, they only knew how to run back and forth mechanically to alert, not how to best get their partner's attention, not how to solve a problem like a closed door, and certainly not how to continue working without regular reinforcement. In fact, she and Bobby communicated so well that formal training no longer had any relevance; they had gone beyond that and worked out their own system.

Toys as Motivation

Some dogs are more motivated by toys than food. However, one should train with food if possible, because the alerting behavior stops when a toy is given, whereas food is gobbled up and the dog continues working for more. Toys can be used to provide a jump-start to show that sound alerting can be fun, and once the dog has a positive attitude, the trainer can switch over to food rewards. For maintenance training, surprise appearances by beloved toys can keep even a food-trained dog's excitement up.

Niji was not easily motivated in obedience training except by herding beach balls back to me. Concealing this ball under my jacket until time to reward him made the transfer of training to the obedience ring difficult, since it was pretty obvious to him when I didn't have it!

Food as Motivation

Food motivation is useful for all three Hearing Dog roles, but most importantly in sound alerting, since for this training, a motivator is needed that is easy to use. Without high food motivation, the dog needs very high levels of some other useful motivation in order to be trainable in sound alerting. Unfortunately, food motivation disappears when a dog is stressed and feeling endangered. The body prepares for the necessity of instant responses of attack or escape to save its life, and hunger becomes irrelevant. Strange places are stressful to many dogs, so food is not always a useful training aid in public access situations. It's important to try to get the stressed dog to eat, because food treats can help relieve stress. Dogs with true Hearing Dog temperament, however, are not stressed in strange places, and are usually eager to eat anywhere.

On the other hand, there are some drawbacks to dogs that are too highly food-motivated. They are more likely to beg and pester until obese, steal food, accidentally pinch fingers, mug toddlers for cookies, and make their owners feel cruel for denying them free-feeding. High food motivation does not necessarily imply

All of these dogs have been selected for high food motivation. Ren leaps for a treat from Hearing Dog Program trainer, Kathy O'Brien.

high food guarding and even with a hand in the food bowl grabbing for the kibble, such a dog only gobbles more desperately, and does not threaten, growl, or bite.

The trainer must manipulate the dog's food motivation. Dogs with high food motivation are ideal, but dogs with lower food motivation can still have their feeding schedules organized to make the best use of what food motivation they have. There is certainly no need to keep animals underweight to train them, but they do need to be hungry. This means they should have training sessions before meals, not after. Keep in mind that the concept of "meals" is a wholly human invention. Dogs evolved as scavengers, grabbing whatever scraps they could find.

Zoos, in fact, have recently realized that feeding their animals in large portions is actually detrimental to their mental and physical well being. Like dogs, most animals evolved to search out or hunt their food, and this activity takes hours every day, keeping them alert and healthy. Now, many zoos hide the food to make life more interesting for the animals. Only creatures such as ant lions and bottom-dwelling anglerfish lounge about waiting for food to come to them. Dogs evolved to hunt and scavenge, and they enjoy these activities. Many people feel that it is "cruel" to make them work for their food, preferring to let them gorge at a full bowl whenever they are hungry. These people are letting their maternal instincts influence them. Human babies need food on demand, and cannot search for it by themselves, but dogs should be fed differently. A Hearing Dog with constant opportunities to be active and "hunt" food, toys, and social rewards is in many ways fulfilling its nature.

Dogs can be fed their total day's food supply in small handfuls as rewards for obedience or sound alerting. The daily lifestyle of a Hearing Dog presents a random pattern of sounds that can be alerted to, and being fed a portion of its meal whenever it alerts can keep it motivated throughout the day and night. It should still receive the same amount of food as it would if fed in a bowl. If a dog is sleeping off a big meal, it is often "off duty" for a few hours, so many people who prefer to feed once a day feed their Hearing Dog at night, when the dog is needed less.

Hearing Dogs should not have their food left out all day. First, it is hard to keep track of how much the dog is actually eating. Secondly, the dog is never hungry. Thirdly, this free-feeding can destroy food motivation. The dog learns that to eat, it needs only to trot over to its bowl. Instead, it should have the attitude that all good things, like food, come directly from its partner or are associated with alertable sounds.

Types of Food Treats

For sound alerting, treats need to be small, about the size of a pea, both so they are eaten quickly, and so that many of them can be given in one training session without upsetting the dog's digestion or adding too many calories. They need to be soft and able to be eaten without leaving crumbs on the ground, which distract dogs from their alerting. When the partner desires to use portions of the dog's crumbly kibble for training, the best plan is to use other types of treats during the first part of the training session, and end the session with the kibble portion as a reward for the last alert. During daily life, a single alert could be rewarded with a portion of kibble. The most practical training treats I have found are the "Rollover" type of products (several brand names exist). These dog foods are intended to be used as a complete food, but I find them more useful for treats. They are shaped in a large sausage-type roll, can be easily cut into quarter-inch or smaller squares, and are soft and easily eaten. The roll is kept refrigerated after opening, but if cut into treats and kept in containers around the house, out of the sun or heat, can last about two days before they begin to get moldy or smell bad. Another product, "Moist and Meaty" is a soft moist dog food that comes in small squiggles that are a good size for a reward, whole or broken in half. This product does not mold or spoil, just becomes dry and less tasty if kept out too long.

"Phasing out" Food or Other Reinforcement

In an ideal world, it would be possible to reduce the frequency of food reinforcements for sound alerting to a very low level. In the real world, things happen every day that damage the dog's motivation and learned behavior patterns, and the constant effort to maintain alerting behavior at an acceptable level means that the dog needs some form of reinforcement whenever it alerts. Sound alerting is difficult and requires that the dog interrupt its normal, rewarding activities (sleeping, playing, eating) every time a sound happens. The reinforcement for doing so must be more desirable than whatever the dog was doing at that moment.

In other training situations, aversive training could complete the training and the dog would not feel that it had the option to alert or not alert, but this is difficult to achieve in sound alerting, so the partner is faced with a constant goal of maintaining motivation. Talented dogs with several motivators do not develop such a great dependence on food reinforcement as do dogs whose only motivation is food. Good trainers use play, toys, praise, and food interchangeably, so that the dog does not become totally dependent upon the presence of food as a signal to alert, and they are able to use these reinforcements less frequently as training progresses and good alerting habits are built in the dog. Individual dogs vary in how much reinforcement is needed to maintain sound alerting behaviors; some of them never work in real life, only in training situations with constant food treats, and some alert forever with only the faintest encouragement from their partner.

Learning

The simplest way to understand how dogs learn is to realize that all animals, ourselves included, are genetically programmed to learn about our world by reacting to a constant stream of experiences that we classify as positive, negative, or irrelevant, and adjust our behavior accordingly. Because our survival and that of our genes depends on eating, social interaction, sexual reproduction, and social, territorial and predatory aggression, these activities are wired to feel the most rewarding and positive to us. Positive and negative feedback about the consequences of their actions influence the social behavior of both dogs and people. Most successful training systems (for people or dogs) work because they harness these feedback channels. Training systems that attempt to give out information only about positive or only about negative consequences of behavior are inadequate for complete learning.

Having said this, the following sound alerting training, as a system, mostly presents information to the dog about the positive consequences of its behavior. The main aversive consequence is withholding of reinforcement unless the desired behavior is shown. Because we intend to encourage and teach behaviors, not inhibit them, positive reinforcement is the system of choice. When training sound alerting, attempts to build motivation are always more productive than attempts to limit behavior.

The main problem with this type of positive training system is that if the dog has a competing motivation that delivers a far more desirable reinforcement—as in the case of a dog who prefers chasing a cat to getting a treat while doing a sit-stay—the system breaks down. Aversive training to inhibit the chasing then becomes another possible system of choice. For this reason, dogs must be selected that have the temperament and motivation to perform the desired activity anyway.

Corrections

Dogs with the perfect temperament for sound alerting are so easily motivated that they never need any type of aversive training other than withholding of reinforcement to become reliable in training or in real life. It should be remembered that the more a dog wants something, the greater the negative emotional impact when it does not receive it. On the other end of the spectrum are dogs that never alert reliably unless corrected in some way. These dogs are unsuitable for sound alerting, because there are too many opportunities in daily life for the dog to discover that no aversive consequences result from ignoring sounds. The partner may have poor timing of corrections, not hear the sounds the dog is ignoring, have no training equipment on the dog at the time, be unwilling to correct, or be unable to set up realistic training situations.

If corrections are used, they should not be associated with the partner or the sound, and the dog should instantly be positively reinforced when it performs the desired behavior. In this way, the dog is not being forced to alert, but becomes more reliable after its intensely motivational foundation training is completed. The most useful correction is a very light tug on a lightweight long line when the dog, once trained, ignores a "Touch" or "Where" cue or a timer beep. Its function is not to inhibit the dog, but to redirect its attention in the proper direction so that the alerting behavior can then be immediately reinforced with a very desirable motivator.

Corrections in sound alerting training need to be far less strong than would be used for a refusal to come on cue, for example, because the dog is often expected to return to the location where it was corrected a few seconds ago. If corrected too forcefully for lingering by the phone, it may not want to return to that location. Associating the correction with the sound is another undesirable possibility, as is being temporarily too inhibited to leave its partner to approach other sounds. Therefore, using corrections in the context of sound alerting is far more complex than in obedience training. Timing mistakes can result in lengthy re-training that takes longer than the original training.

If a dog is too inhibited or submissive to respond freely and confidently during sound alerting training even with lots of positive reinforcement, any aversive training in sound alerting will be counter-productive. If a dog is bold and uninhibited, and does not respond after a session of light tugs, then either the trainer is not building enough positive motivation or the dog is the wrong one for the job.

Most importantly, when working with a special dog with Hearing Dog temperament, one is trying to produce a relationship that is more than the sum of its parts. Because a Hearing Dog is a connecting link between a person and their world, the partnership between the human and the animal becomes central. If this partnership does not happen, the relationship simply becomes a human manipulating an animal's behavior. If the partnership does happen, positive or aversive experiences stop being the only source of learning, and the relationship itself becomes a reinforcer. Both the dog and the human then start to evolve towards levels of communication that can be astonishing.

Timing

Good timing is essential for fast, efficient sound alerting training. However, if it doesn't matter how long training takes, then even training with bad timing can eventually be successful. If the dog has a good relationship with the partner, is easily motivated by food, toy, or social reinforcement, and has some sound reactivity, a lot of training mistakes can be made and overcome.

Realistic Expectations

One hundred percent reliability in alerting to sounds is an impossible goal. Making the dog and its training the number one priority in the partner's life can result in an acceptable percentage of alerts. The dog's companionship and ability to alert to unusual sounds is, for most people, enough compensation for its lack of reliability when compared to electronic alerting systems. Every dog alerts to some sounds better than other sounds, and every dog is susceptible to some distractions. Additionally, every partner has limitations that prevent their dog from reaching its full potential, and every living situation presents challenges to reliable alerting. When we excuse our own faults simply to "being human," perhaps we should lower our expectations so that we aren't expecting even more of an animal than we expect of ourselves.

Helpers

Some of the same training principles used for dogs also apply to helpers. They need a lot of praise and reinforcement to stay motivated, unless the partner is somehow lucky enough to find a self-motivated helper. Often friends and family are at first interested in helping with sound alerting training, but after a few weeks lose interest in knocking on doors and making phone calls just to train the dog. Children are the best bet, since they often have more interest and can be paid a small "fee" for helping. If a partner's young children are jealous of the attention a new Hearing Dog gets (some previously unhelpful children suddenly start trying to race the dog to the phone), enlisting them as training helpers can make them feel included.

It's actually very common for family members to become jealous when the dog receives a lot of attention and takes over the alerting role they used to fill. Family members are often accustomed to answering sounds, so the arrival of a Hearing Dog requires that everyone will need to change their behavior, from being careful when opening the door to ignoring sounds in order to let the dog alert its partner. This means that they may miss phone calls until the dog is alerting quickly. Because the dog's primary relationship must be with its partner, other people may need to restrain their affection for the dog so that it does not bond too much with them instead. Of course, the dog can have a friendly relationship with everyone, but if it actually prefers another person to its partner, it will either not alert or will alert to that person instead.

Even if the dog prefers its partner, it may still alert to hearing family members. This behavior is fine and should never be corrected or the dog may feel that has been punished for alerting. It's especially important for the partner not to become upset or jealous during this transition stage. Instead, the partner needs to act more rewarding and interesting than the other people during sound alerting training, and the family should gently praise the dog's alerts to them, but not overly encourage them.

Developing Communication

The formal alerting behavior taught during training often changes as the dog and partner develop a closer working relationship. The partner begins to understand subtle body language from the dog that would not have been noticed before, and the dog becomes strongly tuned in to its partner. Where very clear alerting was needed before, now perhaps a glance is enough to indicate the location of a sound. This is different from the behavior of a dog whose alerting is disintegrating due to lack of motivation. Some dogs develop unusual behaviors quite different from what they were taught. Deke, a Rhodesian Ridgeback mix, was a large dog who stopped running back and forth, and changed his alert to staying in one place and leaping and spinning in mid-air. Margaret Taylor, his partner, could hardly fail to notice a sixty-pound dog pogoing at eye level! How a dog alerts is really not relevant. What is important is whether its partner understands its alerts and is able to communicate appreciation back to the dog.

Deaf and Hard-of-Hearing Trainers

In order to reinforce dogs at the right time, the partner must know when sounds are happening. Various strategies and gadgets for this are useful in beginning training, but are no longer needed after the dog is alerting well and the partner can read its body language. Some people feel that these gadgets are too expensive and think that a dog will be cheaper; not true, since proper care of a dog can range from several hundred to a thousand dollars a year even without medical emergencies.

Knowing about sounds is sometimes only accomplished by buying gadgets. Spending all that money for something needed temporarily seems silly, but flashing light devices provide the information necessary to train. The question arises: if a person has the device then why train the dog? Because investing this money and time in the dog's training should result in a dog that can alert in many unusual situations where a gadget might be useless—especially if there's a blackout! Some people have a strong dislike of alerting gadgets because they are in denial of their hearing loss, and the flashing lights are a constant annoying reminder of it.

Other ways to know about sounds include having hearing helpers signal, setting up a mirror to check the signals of a helper in another room, using a vibrating pager device to get signals from a hearing helper, or feeling vibrations in the environment. Nancy Herkimer taught her Hearing Dog, Hugo, to "sing" by putting her hand on his throat and reinforcing his efforts at "Happy Birthday."

Hearing aids can be painful if worn all day or night, so many people wear them intermittently. Whenever wearing them, the partner must resist the temptation to run to the sounds he or she can hear instead of waiting for or encouraging the dog. Otherwise, the dog will not alert when the partner is not wearing aids.

Types of Gadgets

Flashing lights have limited value for alerting people to sounds; they are only useful when close enough to see, and many are hooked up to dim sixty-watt lamps in sunny rooms. Unless a person is watching for them, they are easily missed. Flashers that use strobe lights are much better, but need to be installed in several rooms or hallways for good visibility. Many people don't like bothering with light systems, but they are very useful in training Hearing Dogs. The dog is not trained to respond to the light; the light just alerts the partner that a sound is happening, giving them an opportunity to encourage or cue the dog to alert, or reinforce a tentative alert that otherwise would not be noticed. It also enables the partner to know when the dog is failing to alert, so that extra training situations can be set up to help the dog. Trainers, even if they do not have any hearing impairments and do not need the lights, should use flashing lights during training in order to get the dog used to them, since some dogs are startled or afraid of them when they first see them in a new partner's home.

Special vibrating pagers worn on the belt are available to alert the wearer that their phone is ringing. There are also many good systems available that utilize both light and vibration. They range from thirty-dollar gadgets to expensive full-house systems with multiple microphones and a vibrating pager with coded signals indicating what sounds are happening.

Gadgets that Are Helpful in Training:

I have not comparison tested any of the name brand products; these are simply ones I happen to be familiar with. Harris Communications' catalog sells some of those listed below as well as many other similar products. They can be reached at 1-800-825-6758 (voice) or 1-800-825-9187 (TTY). The web site, hearingdog.com, also has links to sources for training equipment.

Refrigerator magnet telephone

Available from Lechter's (1-800-605-4825) and other housewares stores in most of the U.S. About $5.00, this small novelty item has a loud ring when pressed, and the replaceable battery lasts a long time. It is helpful for training the telephone alert.

Radio Shack Super Loud LED Alarm Clock

About $15.00, this clock is easily set to ring, and because the sound is like a smoke alarm, it can be used to maintain training for both alarm clock and smoke alarm alerts.

Radio Shack Fone Flasher 2

This flashing light device hooks up to a telephone. It has a bright strobe light and a loud ringer. It alerts the partner that the phone is ringing, and some dogs alert better to its louder ringer.

Sonic Alert: Wake Up Alarm WA 300

A book-sized box with a microphone inside that connects to any lamp. Any noisy object placed on top of it (such as a timer or phone, not just an alarm clock) will trigger the lamp to flash. Several other similar products are available.

Vibrating phone ring pager

Not a real pager, but vibrates when the telephone rings.

Radio Shack Bell Ringer

A loud ringer that connects onto any phone; some dogs alert better to a louder ring. This can also be used to cue the dog to one phone line and ignore other phone lines with different ringing sounds.

Remote portable doorbell ringer

These gadgets have a portable button that can be mounted outside the door, and the small ringer itself can be worn on the belt of the partner inside the house or carried from room to room. Its main use is for partners who can hear the bell when close, but cannot hear the knock or bell at a distance. Having the helper knock and ring can clue the partner that the knock is happening, which will help with their timing for rewarding or cueing the dog. The bell itself can be used as a one-way alert if desired.

Door knock flasher

Attaches to a door and flashes a light when someone knocks.

First Alert smoke alarm with flashing light

When pushing a test button on a smoke alarm, there is often a small delay, or the alarm does not go off. The flashing light cues hearing-impaired partners that the sound is happening. This is important when trying to reinforce the dog exactly *after* the alarm starts ringing, not before.

Toy telephones and pagers for children

These have various sounds, such as a cell phone, and are useful if their sound is similar to the partner's real phone.

How Daily Life Affects the Training and Performance of a Hearing Dog

Factors that inhibit the dog from alerting

- Other people answering sounds.
- Overfeeding lowers the dog's food motivation.
- Over-petting and constant attention, which lowers the dog's motivation for inter-action.
- Other food sources, such as crumbs from messy kids.
- Bonding with people other than the partner, which lowers the dog's motivation to interact with its partner.
- Playing with kids becomes more interesting than alerting to sounds.
- Territoriality – dog is distracted by people or sounds outside house.
- Predatory instinct – dog is distracted by hunting other animals such as squirrels or cats.
- Excessively high air temperatures.
- Associating any negative events—whether physical or emotional, such as acci-dentally dropping a phone or family quarrels—with sounds.
- Being scolded or inappropriately corrected for "not alerting" to sounds.
- Lack of maintenance training.
- Changes in normal alert sounds, such as a new telephone.
- Changes in location of sounds.
- Changes in environment such as moving to new apartment or staying in a hotel room.
- Parties and holiday situations (the dog should not be expected to alert).

Factors that can promote alerting

- Family cooperation.
- Positive attitude and encouragement from partner.
- Making sounds easy to alert to.
- Keeping sounds consistent.
- Encouraging alerts to unusual sounds.
- Maintaining practice on difficult sounds.
- Foresight in noticing developing problems.

Chapter Ten
Training Sound Alerting

Definitions of Terms Used

One-way alert: The dog touches the partner to alert to a sound, but remains and does not run back to the sound. An example is the smoke alarm alert, in which it would be dangerous to train the dog to approach the smoke alarm and a possible fire.

Two-way alert: The dog runs back and forth between sound and partner, making it possible to follow the dog to discover which sound is happening. Two-way alerts are more informative, but more complicated to teach.

Partner: Either the dog's real partner or a trainer playing that role temporarily for training. In this book, the terms "trainer" and "partner" are used interchangeably to define the person whom the dog alerts to sounds.

Trainer: Either the partner during a training session or a trainer training the dog for a future partner.

Helper: The role of anyone who assists the partner or trainer. Usually the helper makes the sounds happen, places treats at the sound target areas, and plays the part of a visitor at the door or a family member sending the dog on a "Where?" command. The term "helper" always means a person who assists in training, but is never the one whom the dog alerts.

Cue: A cue is a signal or command that the dog performs a behavior in response to. In sound alerting, the dog must work independently and the few cues that are used by the partner, such as "touch," or luring with body language, need to be phased out for the dog to alert in real life. The actual cues to alert are the sounds themselves; the smoke alarm ring, for instance, has the same meaning to the dog as the cue "Come."

Target area: any place the dog must go when alerting. For instance, in smoke alarm alerting, the target area is the bed or face of a sleeping person. For the door, it is the floor area by the door, and for "touch," the partner's hand or leg is the target area.

Treat: any food used for motivation. Each piece should be tiny, (about the size of a pea is best if the dog will be getting many reinforcements) but big enough that the dog can see it from a few feet away.

Sound Alerting Skills

Sound alerting can be broken down into four separate skills, which can be taught individually. After being taught individually, skills need to be linked into alerting sequences quickly. The partner must be sensitive to the balance between the different parts of the alerting behavior and avoid overemphasizing any one part. In general, linking behaviors into complete alerting routines can start as soon as the dog shows a minimal understanding of the basic skills. These basic skills are: going to the sounds, searching for the partner, touching, and running back and forth.

Going to the sounds – The dog is taught first to associate the sounds with food and other reinforcement at a target area near the sound, then taught to approach the target area when the sound happens. It needs to approach the sounds with great intensity and speed.

Searching for the partner – This skill is similar to a recall, but the dog needs to show initiative and high motivation in searching when its partner is out of sight. It needs to approach very quickly, before callers hang up or visitors leave the door. An obedient but unwilling approach is undesirable.

Touching – The dog alerts the partner physically with a nose-nudge, paw, or by jumping up. A physical alert is useful in case the partner is occupied and not looking at the dog. "Touch" is taught either as a separate exercise or in conjunction with others.

Running back and forth – This response is not necessary for all sounds, but is useful because it indicates the location of the sound. In the dog's mind, the behavior seems to be thought of as "Turn away after each treat or touch to look for the other target" (the partner or the sound). It need not consciously understand the concept of running back and forth. This back-and-forth behavior is taught in the "Where?" exercise.

The basic skills are then linked together, with each skill learned becoming the foundation for a new alert. The one-way timer alert is the foundation for the smoke alarm alert and alarm clock alert. The two-way timer alert is the training for the telephone and door alerts, and the "Where?" exercise (back-and-forth alerting) combined with going to sounds results in the completed door and telephone alert. The "Where?" exercise is also the foundation for the Name Call alert.

Real-Life Situations

Beginning training – Frequent reinforcement, luring with food to produce reinforceable behaviors, and verbal and physical cues all are used to build associations between sounds and reinforcement. Basic skills such as "touch" are taught. Training situations are simple, with no distractions.

Advanced training – Reinforcement becomes less frequent, luring stops, and verbal and physical cues are diminished while the dog is reinforced for showing initiative and spontaneity in its alerts. The sounds themselves are now the cues, and the partner attempts to set up training situations that mimic the distracting and variable conditions of real life.

Real-life training and alerting – Short maintenance practice sessions are set up to keep the dog motivated and to counteract the negative effects of daily life. The household environment is set up so that alerting is reinforced, not discouraged. (For instance, good family cooperation, strategically placed treat containers, phone extensions turned off, and so on.) The dog is reinforced for showing initiative in its alerts, but helped by cueing from the partner whenever needed.

TRAINING SESSIONS

Dogs can be started in sound alerting very early. Many dogs are adopted by the Hearing Dog Program at five or six months old, and progress very rapidly. At six weeks puppies can be imprinted with the sounds they will later alert to by calling them for food while the sounds happen. Baby puppies need very short lessons and cannot be expected to alert reliably for many months, but foundation training with easy versions of the alerting exercises will pay off later. The early "Where?", "touch" and timer exercises are easy and fun for pups.

Influence of Obedience Training on Sound Alerting

Obedience training consists of two primary types of training; inhibiting undesirable behaviors and teaching new behaviors. Both of these may have negative effects on sound alerting training. Inhibitory training may inhibit the dog's overall behavior temporarily. For instance, dogs strongly corrected for ignoring recalls may be temporarily reluctant to leave their trainer. Positive reinforcement training to teach new behaviors can also inhibit behavior, but in a different way. For instance, dogs reinforced intensely for recalls may be more interested in staying with their trainer than investigating sounds on their own. Too much reinforcement for sitting may interfere with "touch" training. Whether positive or aversive, any type of training can cause a dog to focus too much on cues from the trainer and not enough on the independent thought and initiative needed for sound alerting.

One solution is to reduce the amount of all other training during the sound alerting training period, but this is not always an option—especially with newly adopted shelter dogs. Some behavior problems need to be addressed immediately, before they become imprinted into the dog's new lifestyle. This can be done if the trainer understands that dogs seem to classify their experiences according to the locations they happen in, sometimes down to a few square feet. By keeping the sound training location "uncontaminated" by other types of training, the inhibitory effects are minimized. If behavior must be inhibited in the sound training location (the house), then it should be dealt with at other times than during alerting training. The alerting session must be designed so as not to trigger the unwanted behavior until the problem is solved. For instance, many shelter dogs are already "carpet-trained" by previous owners who let them toilet in the house unsupervised. Correcting for urinating during a sound training session may temporarily inhibit the dog from alerting for a short time, thus wasting a training session, yet ignoring the behavior perpetuates it. The solution is to make every effort during sound training to ensure that the dog has already toileted outside, is kept away from tempting areas, and is kept so busy and excited during training that it does not relax and begin sniffing around the carpet. If enough unwanted behavior can be prevented during sound training, yet dealt with at other times or in other locations, eventually everything will come together correctly.

Obedience Training for Hearing Dogs

For good manners when enjoying public access, a dog needs to know basic obedience commands, with particular emphasis on heeling and down-stays, but the basic obedience commands of "sit," "down," "stay," "heel," and "no." are all very useful when training Hearing Dogs. At home, house manners and a good recall are important. The main barrier to people trying to train their own Hearing Dog is that group classes, the most inexpensive way to train a pet, are frustrating for hearing-impaired people. I myself spent several years of classes copying the rest of the students, (always a few beats behind), until finally I was motivated to get a hearing aid. I had always resisted this step and managed without one, but for the first time in my life, I found myself involved in an activity that required better hearing. Expensive private lessons from a trainer are easier for the hard-of-hearing, but if interpreters are needed, can also be impractical. Dog training is complex, and videos and books are not as helpful as a real trainer who can quickly evaluate the best method to train an individual dog. It is best to search for a really good trainer who is willing to make an effort to communicate. The two *Teamwork* books by Stewart Nordensson and Lydia Kelley, published by Top Dog Publications, are valuable resources to anyone training a Hearing Dog or a pet. They are specifically designed for people with any disability who wish to train their own dog. They emphasize building a good working relationship and basic obedience with the dog through very positive techniques and a lot of creativity.

Attention

The first step in communicating with a dog is to teach it to pay attention to visual cues. Even if only voice cues are going to be used, the dog should still be encouraged to frequently make visual contact with its partner. This prevents the dog from getting too distracted and teaches it to be aware of all the body language of its partner. However, the constant attentiveness desired in obedience competitions is undesirable for sound training, since it inhibits the dog from reacting to environmental stimuli that its partner needs to know about. The following method motivates the dog to "keep an eye" on its partner both on cue and on its own.

Goal: Dog looks up to the person's face when waved at or when its name is signed or spoken. In the first steps of this exercise, waving and voice are the signals that attract the dog's attention. The name sign can be used instead of the wave; whichever is easiest. Instead of saying the name, any sound at all can be selected. Later, the dog will be more visually focused and will notice its name sign but for now, a voice cue helps to get attention started.

1. Allow the dog to relax on leash, in a quiet, non-distracting place. The leash just keeps the dog close, and is not going to be used to physically move the dog. Conceal a motivator (small treat or toy) in one hand. Say the name and wave the hand in front of the dog's nose at the same time so that it can smell the motivator. If the dog notices it, give it the food. Repeat from several to about twenty times, depending on attention span and motivation of the dog.

2. When the dog starts to notice the hand movements and voice cue, draw the hand and food away, up towards the partner's face, making the American Sign Language "look" sign. If the dog watches the hand, instantly bring it back to the dog and reward it. Use the ASL sign for "good" on the way down to the dog's face, thus teaching this sign as well. Repeat until the dog watches the hand go all the way to the partner's face. If the dog jumps up to get to the hand, make sure it does not get the reward until the dog is back on the ground.

3. The partner says or signs the dog's name, holds the hand still for a few seconds up at face level, then rewards if the dog watches the whole time.

4. The partner increases the length of time the dog looks, the distraction levels of the environment, and the number of repetitions between reinforcements. The hand is gradually hidden and the dog rewarded for looking up at the face. Either the voice cue or the signed cue can be eliminated if desired. The dog should look up happily whenever it hears or sees its name, and should also look up more frequently on its own. It should be praised whenever it looks up on its own.

5. When the dog looks up reliably, it is mentally and visually focused on the partner,

① WAVE FOR ATTENTION   ② "LOOK" SIGN   ③ REINFORCE FOR LOOKING UP

and is ready to concentrate if a different cue is then given. It has learned that looking up and paying attention starts communication.

Recalls

Most shelter dogs are wary of any grabbing or chasing behavior from people. Even if otherwise trusting, most associate having their collar grabbed with consequences ranging from punishment to being placed somewhere they would rather not be. At best, they playfully evade being grabbed with a "keep away" game. They need to be taught to come when called, but part of their recall training should be to desensitize this avoidance response. The dog needs to become motivated to demand that its collar be grabbed. Ian Dunbar, founder of Sirius Puppy training, points out the important fact that training a dog to enjoy having its collar grabbed does not just give it a more reliable recall, but will save its life if it is ever lost and strangers are trying to capture it. The dog that approaches people rather than running away can be saved from being run over.

1. Goal: Dog approaches a grabbing hand and enjoys having its collar held and being restrained.

2. The dog is on leash. The leash is not used for corrections at this stage, but simply keeps the dog close enough for easy training. The partner calls the dog from a few inches away, reaches toward the collar and scratches and massages the dog's ears and neck. Immediately after the collar is handled, the other hand gives the dog a treat (or toy). The treat is *never* given first. Giving the treat first teaches the dog to grab the treat and then run off to avoid the hand reaching for its collar.

3. At first, the motion towards the collar is slow and gentle, and the collar is not tugged. The neck and ears are scratched while the collar is held and the treat given. As the dog becomes more trusting, the hand motion towards the collar becomes more forceful and fast, and the collar lightly tugged before the petting and massaging. Eventually, the dog should respond positively when the partner mimics a person who is forcefully grabbing at the dog in the same way a stranger might when trying to catch a lost dog. Friends can repeat these training steps under the partner's supervision so that the dog will approach other people as well.

The "Schutzhund" Recall

This recall creates a fast, intensely motivated recall to the partner. It is designed to look flashy and impress Schutzhund judges, who score high when dogs show great intensity and teamwork with their partner. It is a foundation exercise for good sound alerting. It requires a helper whom the dog trusts. The dog can be trained off-leash if in a safe area. Ideally, a fanatical desire to come to the partner is built up.

1. The helper gently but securely restrains the dog while the partner motivates it by showing toys, excited body, sign, and verbal language, food, or whatever it takes to excite the dog.

2. The partner runs away, still exciting the dog but not giving a recall cue, nor does the helper release the dog.

3. The helper instantly releases the dog when the partner calls it. The partner either crouches down or keeps running; whatever motivates the dog to continue its speedy approach all the way. The dog is cued to sit, then reinforced intensely with its favorite motivator. Be sure to tailor the motivation level so that the dog does not jump on or knock down the partner! In competition, the dog would be taught to do a sit-stay while waiting to hurtle forward on the recall cue, but this stage is not needed for the related sound alerting exercises.

Dogs that show no interest in this exercise need to have their motivations developed if possible, or their relationship with their partner improved. This recall training will not put into a dog what is not there; an unsuitable dog might only show intensity when revved up for this specific exercise, and this intensity might never be apparent in everyday life or sound alerting.

Once the dog understands the exercise, the partner can hide in order to build motivation even higher.

This training is more easily begun outside, but should later be transferred to sound-alerting training inside the house. When the partner runs away, then beeps a smoke alarm, timer, or magnet phone while calling the dog, the dog learns to associate the sound with the sudden burst of freedom and happy reunion with its partner. It also learns to search the house intensely for its partner when doing sound alerting. Completing the "Schutzhund recall" first allows the similar exercises in sound alerting training to proceed quickly.

Get Dressed

Putting training gear on a happy, reactive dog is not easy! At the Hearing Dog Program, many new partners of Hearing Dogs have arthritis or are just not accustomed to dealing with reactive dogs. The point of this simple exercise is to make the dog easier to handle and get equipped to go out. It is appropriate for slip collars, head halters, vests with a chest strap, backpacks, or martingales, but a collar is used as an example. (Note: the partner needs to learn how to correctly and humanely use any type of training equipment.)

Goal: the dog pushes its head through the collar.

The collar is held in a loop in front of the dog's face and a treat is poked through the loop towards the dog. The treat is pulled back to lure the dog to poke its nose toward the loop. If the dog makes a slight movement towards the loop, the treat is given. Each time, the cue "get dressed" is given. The dog is gradually reinforced for pushing its head farther and farther into the loop. Because it is concentrating on getting the treat, it will focus on this rather than scattering its energy on leaping and thrashing with excitement about the coming walk. The dog will eventually make an effort to push its nose into any training gear held near it. The treat is gradually discontinued and calming petting is substituted as the collar is put on and the walk or training session that comes after the collar is put on becomes the reinforcement for cooperating.

Putting a Leash on a Submissive Urinator

Avoid leaning over or using intense voice and body language. The best method I know is to show the dog a treat, and while it is sniffing it, gently hold its collar while tossing the treat to the ground a few feet away out of reach. While the dog is eagerly straining towards the treat, it usually does not urinate when handled or leaned over.

Designing Length and Complexity of Training Sessions

Several sounds can be trained in the same session, if the dog has enough motivation to stay interested. Each individual dog's ideal lesson length needs to be determined. For some dogs this might be several minutes, but other dogs can go longer. Controlling the length of a session is more important than how many different sounds or behaviors are practiced in one session. Because intensity in sound alerting training is more important than repetitions, a five-second training session in which the dog feels highly rewarded will be more effective than a five-minute session in which the dog feels mildly interested.

Teaching foundation skills is important, but time should also be made for brief introductions to all the different sounds the dog will later be expected to alert to. For instance, a session might be mostly spent teaching "where?" but thirty seconds spent on a positive introduction to the sound of the smoke alarm will also serve as foundation training for later work on this sound.

Luring Versus Reinforcement

Young children are sometimes lured (bribed) with money to do a chore, but after they understand this connection, are then rewarded with an allowance only after a week's worth of chores. It's the same for dogs. Luring is bribery for a behavior not yet performed, and is useful when beginning to train a behavior, whereas the final goal is for the dog to work for a possible payoff given after the behavior. For instance, when teaching "touch," the partner's hand wiggles a treat backwards exactly as if trolling for a fish. The dog follows it, then is reinforced when it accidentally touches the hand. This is only a first step, and the dog is not considered trained until it touches on cue without luring by the moving hand. The distinction is important because luring helps in beginning sound alerting, but must not be continued if the dog is to alert in real life, in which the sounds themselves become the cues. For instance, the dog must be able to "touch" with no movement from the partner or smell of treats nearby. A conditioned reinforcer effect must be built by using a specific praise word, sign, or sound (such as a clicker) every time the dog is reinforced, which can then be used to mark desired behavior when food cannot be given instantly.

Cheerleading Versus Initiative

Enthusiasm from the partner is an important part of motivating a Hearing Dog. However, the goal of this motivation is to create initiative in the dog so that it works independently and incorporates this enthusiasm into its alerts, not to build dependency on all this help from the partner. Cheerleading can be used as reinforcement after alerting behavior or as conditioning to associate sounds and fun.

Reinforcement: When a dog attempts to alert to sounds, its alert can be intensified if the owner responds by cheerleading. All this emotional excitement and reward should only happen *after* the dog makes some kind of effort to alert or else the dog will learn that the cheerleading is a cue to work and will not alert without it.

Conditioning: If a dog does not show sufficient interest in certain sounds, one way to condition a positive association is for the partner to act happy and excited every time a sound happens. This method appears good in theory, but in reality, most dogs view the cheerleading as a cue to start alerting, and do not alert without this help. Once this type of cheerleading produces a positive attitude change in the dog, the partner must only cheer-lead *after* the dog becomes excited by the sound. All of this help must be phased out in order for the dog to alert in real life.

Cheerleading examples to help motivate a dog:

- Run to the phone clapping and dancing as if it's that call telling you that you won the lottery.
- Approach the door in a party mood ready to welcome a long-lost friend.
- Pretend the practice smoke alarm ring is the real thing and your dog just saved the family. After all, this might really happen one dayæwhy not thank the dog now?
- When the little kitchen timer rings, pretend the dog just saved the Thanksgiving turkey.

BASIC SKILLS FOR SOUND ALERTING

Teaching the Dog to Eat from a Hand

Feed the dog treats or its dinner by hand. Many shelter dogs do not know that food could come from a hand, and some are too hesitant, fumbling and dropping the treat, or too rough, painfully pinching fingers. Hesitant dogs should be encouraged to eat more confidently, and rough ones corrected either by bumping their noses with the hand or by gently but firmly pushing fingers into their mouths until they try to spit them out and learn to grab the treat rather than the fingers. Any corrections must be tailored to the dog's temperament; the dog should not become too inhibited to try to eat the treats.

If you drop a treat during training, which will inevitably happen at one point or another, the dog will attempt to get them. The dog should be allowed to eat the dropped treats. The dog will become badly stressed and confused if sometimes allowed to eat treats on the floor (for the door alert training, for instance) and sometimes corrected. If I drop people food, I either let my dogs eat it or I tell them "Wait" while I pick it up. Outside, they understand that the rules are different, and do not pick up any people food off the ground. Dogs can learn to ignore food and bones on the street or on the floor in restaurants reasonably reliably. Partners who intend to totally "poison-proof" their dog will have to alter these sound training instructions and never allow their dog to pick up treats on the floor at home, and never reward the dog by dropping treats on the floor in any exercise.

Learning Target Areas

Each target area is different, and is taught in the context of a specific exercise. Some

Chihuahua mix Brando (a.k.a. "Commando Brando") is forceful and determined in his sound alerting. Having checked the phone for a treat, he prepares to hurtle back to his partner. (Photo by Dennard)

partners may instead prefer to use a movable target, such as a carpet square, that the dog is reinforced for touching on cue. This target is then placed wherever it is needed, for instance by the door, telephone, partner's body, or on the bed for the smoke alarm. As soon as the dog goes to the square when the sound or cue happens, the square can easily be phased out, after the dog learns that location. This is done by gradually cutting it smaller, pushing it under a piece of furniture, or transferring the dog's focus on the square to a treat container placed at the target area.

The training instructions below train each target area as a separate exercise.

"Touch"

"Touch" is a verbal cue that is only used in training or when the partner notices that the dog needs help while working in real life. The sounds themselves should eventually become the "touch" cue. Before teaching this cue, the partner must first decide whether the dog should be taught to touch with a nose-nudge or by jumping up. If the partner has balance or visual impairment, or if the dog is big enough to knock someone down by jumping up unexpectedly, then it should nudge. One applicant for a Hearing Dog had a dangerous combination of balance impairment and unsteady knees. We matched her with a tiny Chihuahua mix that we trained not to touch at all, but to twirl about on its hind legs from several feet away to alert to sounds.

Goal: On hearing "touch" or seeing the hand movement (patting thigh) or hearing the sound caused by the patting, the dog either nudges the partner's hand or jumps up and touches front paws on the partner's leg. This artificial "patting" sign for "touch" is practical because it can be done while holding a treat and because it makes a sound the dog can hear. When I write about the "touch" cue, I am referring to this strong patting motion, not an ASL sign, although the partner can use an ASL sign if desired.

Like all sound training, "touch" is a happy motivational exercise, but the partner needs to be extra happy because many things can inhibit the dog. If we are sitting in an unusual position the dog may not understand how to touch. If we have been speaking angrily to a family member, the dog may want to avoid us. If our hands are not visible, the dog may be confused until taught to alert by touching the body. Every possible situation should be used for "touch" training; keep some treat containers around the house and be creative in deciding when to cue "touch."

Progression to Nose-Nudge

The cue is a verbal "touch" or a strong pat on the partner's leg. Training will proceed faster if a marker signal, such as "good" or a clicker, is used to mark the exact moment that the dog's nose touches the hand.

One confusing issue is that once a dog is trained to touch on cue, it also tries touching when not being cued, in the hope of getting praise or food. In obedience or other training, non-cued behavior is never rewarded or else stimulus control (in which the dog only performs the behavior when cued) will never be achieved. However, since the goal is for the sounds themselves to become the cues to touch, the partner should only ignore a touch if he or she is one hundred percent sure that there is no sound occurring that the dog might be responding to. Even hearing people cannot always know about faint or distant sounds that a dog's amazing hearing picks up. Therefore, the dog should be reinforced for offering touches. After all, many alerting problems in real life are caused by partners ignoring attempts by the dog to alert, or even scolding it for bothering them. However, rewarding the dog for all touches will create a pest that constantly touches for attention and food, not just for sounds.

An unmistakable alert from Gizmo, a Terrier-Poodle mix. Partner Jean Peters is deliberately ignoring him here in this training session to encourage Gizmo to alert intensely for a reward. In real life, she might be preoccupied and fail to notice a weak alert. (Photo by Dennard)

Confusing? Absolutely, but even more so for the poor dog! Until the dog is fully trained in sound alerting, the partner must react to all touches by praising the dog and checking for sounds in case the dog is trying to alert, but not by mindlessly petting the dog every time it nudges. Eventually, the partner will be able to read the dog's body language and distinguish between touching for attention and the more excited touching given during a sound alert. Just one more reason why building up excitement at hearing sounds is so important.

Starting the "Touch" Cue

1. The partner focuses the dog's attention on training by letting it sniff a treat concealed in an unmoving hand. To lure the dog into touching, the partner cues "touch" verbally while suddenly wiggling the hand, which then opens to hold the treat in view while wiggling the hand like an escaping fish away from the dog, letting the dog catch up to eat it after a few inches. As soon as the dog catches up to the hand it can eat the treat. Repeat

until the dog approaches the hand eagerly to find the treat. If the partner does not use his or her voice, the wiggle alone is okay.

2. The wiggle mimics the motion of a prey escaping and is much more exciting to follow and eat than a motionless or steadily moving treat. This excitation becomes associated with the verbal touch cue and eventually with the sounds of the timer, magnet phone, and smoke alarm. The dog will follow the partner's hand more eagerly if the treat is wiggled. If done correctly, the dog's head will also wiggle slightly as it attempts to keep the treat in focus. The wiggle eventually is transitioned into a visual and auditory "touch" cue of patting the hand against the leg. The wiggle also makes a very clear and dramatic difference between the motionless hand concealing an unattainable treat and the sudden wiggle that becomes associated with the available treat.

3. Once the dog is performing reliably, the partner can increase the distance. The partner moves backwards or moves the hand away from dog after giving the verbal "touch" cue. Trainers who cannot easily walk backwards can sit in a wheeled office chair and roll backwards. When the dog follows confidently even when the hand is not wiggled, it is ready for the next step.

4. The hand is wiggled away, still closed. If the dog just barely touches the hand, the hand opens to give the treat. Each time, the dog must nudge harder and harder to make the hand open. This step teaches the dog to nudge firmly to get the treat.

5. The dog should now be ready to associate the patting motion with the treat. The partner continues to move back from the dog, but reduces the amount of wiggling the hand, and the hand movement now changes to the patting cue against the leg. The dog needs to learn that touching the hand is the only way to get the food reward.

6. Now the luring should be faded out and the backward body motion should stop. The partner stands still, cues "touch," and pats his or her leg, helping the dog if needed. Without the partner's backwards hand movement or walking, dogs are confused and sometimes sit, staring upwards, so extra hand movement and verbal encouragement may be needed.

7. Touching on cue. The dog now needs to learn to touch a hand that does not conceal a treat. The "touch" cue is given, the dog discovers the hand is empty, but the other hand appears from behind the partner's back and either immediately gives a treat, or drops the treat into the empty hand. Treats can also be taken from a high shelf. The dog can be asked to touch two or three times in a row before it gets one treat, until the dog shows a consis-

tent response even if it can smell that the hand is empty. Encouraging the skeptical dog to touch when it is sure there are no treats, then surprising it with an unexpected treat, convinces the dog to "have faith" in the partner's cues.

8. The partner should then vary the distance that the dog comes from and gets the dog used to different partner body positions such as sitting or lying down, or facing away from the dog.

9. The partner puts their hand halfway into a pocket or hides it behind some clothing, and reinforces for touching. The partner

BODY LANGUAGE FOR TOUCH TRAINING:

LEANING FORWARD LOOKS THREATENING.

LEANING BACK LOOKS FRIENDLY.

WALKING FORWARD LOOKS THREATENING.

WALKING BACKWARDS LOOKS FRIENDLY.

then hides hands completely and reinforces for any attempt to touch the partner's body.

10. Dog out of sight of partner. The dog is cued from around corners and other rooms (with verbal cue or loud patting on leg) until it responds when out of sight of the partner.

11. Verbal or visual cue alone. The dog is reinforced for touching on either only a verbal or only a visual cue.

12. In real life, the dog should be able to obey the touch cue, verbal or signed, in various real-life situations (see list). As the other sound alerting training progresses, the partner tries to use the "touch" cue less and less, reinforcing the dog for touching on its own initiative. The dog should begin to touch without any cueing from the partner during sound alerts. The touch cue is then only used to help the dog when it is confused, or when training a new sound.

Jumping up in Response to the "Touch" Cue

The dog should already have learned to touch a hand by following the first seven steps of the "touch" exercise.

1. Some dogs are very submissive or have already been trained not to jump up. The partner needs to appear less intimidating by sitting down or leaning backwards. The dog is first shown a treat, given the verbal "touch" cue, and the hand is wiggled away upwards to lure the dog up. Any effort to jump up even a few inches is reinforced. The partner gradually uses normal body positions as the dog learns to jump.

2. Teaching the dog to put its paws on the partner's leg. The partner is close to the dog, gives the "touch" cue, and lures it upward with a treat. Then the hand is moved close to the leg so that the dog's paws accidentally touch the leg. Any paw touching is instantly reinforced with the treat. It is essential that the treat is only given *after* the dog makes contact with its paws. If the treat is given before then the dog is being reinforced for standing on its hind legs or approaching the hand, not for touching the partner with its paws.

3. The partner fades out the luring by replacing wiggling the hand upward with the patting motion and/or a verbal "touch" cue.

4. Follow steps 8 to 12 of the previous touch progressions.

Name Call Alert

This alert is taught in two stages, the "Where?" exercise and the formal "Name Call" exercise. "Where?" teaches the dog the basic skills of running back and forth between two people, and "Name Call" teaches the actual real-life alert to a specific person.

The ultimate goal is for the dog to be sent to contact a person and lead them back to the person calling. The verbal cue of using the name of the desired person or the ASL "where?" sign or a name sign are used. When completed, the exercise can be used either by a deaf person who doesn't use their voice to send the dog to contact a deaf or hearing person, or it can be used by a hearing person to send the dog to contact a deaf or hard-of-hearing person.

In the early stages of training this alert, the dog learns that the "Where?" sign means "do a recall to the other person in the room." When it can be reliably sent back and forth between two people, it is ready to learn the "Name Call" alert for real-life use. Even if this alert will never be needed, the foundation training provided by the "Where?" exercise strengthens the dog's response to "touch," allowing many repetitions in one session while keeping the dog's interest and motivation high. The cue "where?" is also really the same as the telephone ring, since both are sound cues which start a two-way alert. Even though the cue might be verbal or signed and not similar to a mechanical sound, it provides a foundation for the dog to later generalize to other two-way alerts.

By going back and forth between two different people, the dog becomes more flexible in its work than if it only learns to touch one person. If it is being trained for later placement with a partner, it will be easier to transfer its response to "touch" to a new person. The name call alert teaches the dog the behavior of running back and forth. Even though the dog is running between two people, this behavior later can be adapted to running back and forth between its partner and a sound. Many repetitions are possible because this exercise is fun and motivational for the dog, so training is accomplished faster. There is also no control or complexity in this exercise, and the dog is building a positive relationship with both partner and helper. It needs only to run and get food from each one, so there is not much chance that a partner will make a mistake that affects the dog's motivation.

There are other benefits as well. If the training area (as in the case of a dog that is not used to being inside a house) inhibits the dog, doing this exercise both distracts it from its fears and builds a positive association with the area. If the dog trusts only one of the people, this exercise can build trust. Balancing the availability of treats, so that the dog gets more treats from the less-liked person, can motivate it to work for both people.

Training will progress more rapidly if the dog is already familiar with the "touch" command. If it is not, partner and helper will need to spend more time during the beginning steps until the dog touches confidently. However, the dog must not be expected to perform a perfect touch, even if it knows it in another context. The goal here is for the dog to turn away from one person to get a treat from another person, so it is far more important to reinforce the turning behavior than wait for a touch.

Foundation Training for "Where?"

This exercise teaches the dog to run back and forth. Note: both people in this exercise are referred to as "trainer" because both are playing the same role as targets for the dog to ricochet between. For this exercise, the sign "where?" is used, although a voiced "where?" is optional. Since the dog is only learning to run back and forth between two people at this stage, using only one trainer's name would be confusing, and using both names would be more confusing. By using the "where?" sign, the dog learns a cue for the exercise, and later, in the name call exercise, the partner's name is added to the cue.

Trainers begin by standing or sitting side by side, almost touching, moving their hands only a few inches to lure the dog to touch, so that the dog only needs to move its head or front paws back and forth to touch. "Where?" is similar to a fun, fast game of tennis, but with the dog as the ball. Once the "ball" is served by signing "where?" then it is the other player's job to intercept it and send it back. Usually, even though the other trainer is trying to attract its attention, the dog remains looking at the trainer who is cueing "where?" because the moving hand is interesting or it has just gotten a treat and is hoping for another. If the dog does not leave, this trainer will be tempted to repeat the "where?" cue. This does not work! Additional movement and voice only attract the dog even more. Once a cue has been given, it is always the other trainer's job to attract the dog.

1. To teach that "where?" means to turn towards the other trainer, the first trainer gives the "where?" sign, then ignores the dog. Immediately, the second trainer holds a treat in front of the dog's nose and lures it away by wiggling the treat backwards and cueing "touch." The dog does not need to do a perfect nudge or jump up; just touching the hand as it eats the treat is sufficient. It is more important at this stage that it gets a treat quickly as soon as it turns around. As soon as it eats the treat, this second trainer signs and/or says "where?"

2. To keep the dog moving back and forth, it is now the first trainer's turn to attract the dog to "touch" by luring with a treat. This sequence is repeated up to thirty times if the dog maintains interest. This is a fast-paced exercise, and the dog must be drawn back and forth rapidly in order to build its back-and-forth response. If it is done too slowly, the dog will become distracted by crumbs on the floor or other things and will need constant refocusing on the trainers. The trainers will be tempted to wait briefly to see if the dog responds to the other trainer's "where?" cue before calling the dog back with a touch cue.

This is a big mistake and results in a loss of focus. At this point, the dog does not connect the "where?" cue with anything, and will not for several hundred repetitions. The only reason the cue is being given is so that the dog eventually associates this cue with the "touch" cue that it will immediately hear from the other trainer. Once it makes this connection, the "where?" cue alone will send it to touch the other trainer. The trainers will know the dog is starting to understand when it whips its head around towards the other trainer as soon as the cue is given. Anticipating the cue is desirable; the cue should eventually need only be given once for the dog to continuously run back and forth.

3. In the dog's mind, the back-and-forth movement is the relevant part, not the distance it must run between the trainers. Therefore, the trainers must first build the dog's concentration on moving back and forth many times in a row while the trainers are still within about ten feet of each other. If it can do ten or twenty repetitions in a row at a close distance without losing focus, then the distance can be gradually increased.

4. The trainers then begin to step backwards each time when luring with the treat and calling the dog to touch so that the dog is motivated to follow. As soon as the dog leaves to touch one trainer, the other trainer follows behind the dog in order to be close enough to again lure it to follow him or her for a few steps. This means that each trainer follows the dog each time it leaves.

5. If the dog is not extremely excited and happy during the whole exercise, then the trainers are doing something wrong. This is a fun exercise for dogs. They must examine their behavior and the situation and change accordingly. Common mistakes are to give the cues like stern commands instead of like a fun game, or to stand still and boring, waiting for the dog to approach. Equally mistaken is to give so much praise that the dog becomes distracted and forgets to keep running back and forth. Praise comes only as the dog is approaching, and stops the second it touches. This motivates the dog to then turn for praise to the other trainer. Trainers must move back excitedly each time they call the dog to "touch," cheerleading it to run faster and faster. By building the dog's happy attitude, it will be eager to play this game in real life whenever given the chance.

6. As they move farther apart, the trainers stop following the dog all the way to the other trainer, and now cue it from farther and farther away, still taking a few steps back every time. The trainers should be able to stand at each end of a room. If the dog is not enthusiastic enough, trainers can try giving the "touch" cue and suddenly running away to encourage the dog to chase before sending it to the other trainer.

7. The dog should then be ready to still respond to the "where?" cue even when one trainer is out of sight. To do this, the trainers teach the dog to go around corners by first reducing the distance to a few feet, but standing just out of sight on either side of a corner. The dog will probably have trouble understanding the exercise now that one trainer is out of sight, so the solution is for the trainer to stay visible as the dog is approaching, then quickly pop backwards around the corner. Once the dog follows the trainer around the corner, the other trainer can walk up within the dog's view and then pop back around the corner in the other direction. This makes it clear to the dog that the person is still there and the backward movement motivates the dog to approach faster. The trainers then begin standing in different rooms and sending the dog back and forth. Once the dog understands this, the exercise becomes closer to a game of hide and seek. By gradually learning to find trainers who are out of sight, the dog can apply this skill to more complicated searching situations in later training

8. As soon as the dog can run around corners to find the other trainer, another exercise is helpful. One trainer holds the dog gently as the other shows it a favorite toy or its full food bowl and excites it, then leaves, hurrying to hide, either around the corner or in another room (but always an easy place that ensures the dog's quick success). When the trainer releases the dog with a "where?" cue, it should zoom off excitedly to find the other trainer, who should act totally overjoyed as soon as the dog appears. In this exercise, the dog need not go back and forth, since it will be busy playing with the toy or eating its dinner. This exercise makes the dog much more excited about finding its trainer, but because it distracts the dog from going back and forth, it should not be done too often.

9. During all of this training, the trainers continually vary the reinforcement schedule so that the dog will remain equally motivated to go to both trainers. For instance, the less-liked trainer gives more frequent or better treats than the other does or the trainer in the less-familiar room gives more treats.

10. Decreasing and randomizing the reward schedule: The trainers need to decrease and randomize the reward schedule. They should reinforce the dog for making more trips per treat, but keep up its enthusiasm and consistent response by giving enough treats.

11. The trainers should then also decrease the amount of cueing. They should reinforce the dog for continuing this alert with fewer cues. The "touch" cues are faded out first, then the extra "where?" cues.

12. Transferring the alert to other people: If the dog will later need to work with a different person, other people are recruited to train the dog. Even very intelligent dogs do not generalize this exercise well. In the dog's mind, this exercise applies *only* to the two original people, so it is necessary to go back to the beginning and repeat all of the training steps with every new trainer to help it understand that "where?" can be done with different people.

Progression to Name Call

Once the dog can run between two people in the "where?" exercise, it is much easier to teach it to run between a person and a sound. Once it touches easily and automatically, it quickly learns to touch in other sound-alerting situations. It is now ready for the name call exercise.

Goal: The dog understands that the name call means to do a recall to its partner and run back and forth between partner and helper. The helper sends the dog by signing "where?" and adding a name sign or verbal name call. For these instructions we'll use the name "Mary." The dog finds and touches "Mary," who follows the dog as it returns to the sender. Once together, both people reinforce the dog, especially with social reinforcement, since reuniting the pack is very motivating to the dog. As the dog becomes confident with the "Mary!" cue, the "where?" cue can be gradually phased out if desired.

1. Trainers play different roles now: The two partners separate their roles permanently into a helper (sender) and a partner (either the real partner or a trainer partner playing that role until the dog is placed with the real partner).

2. The helper calls the dog over, giving a treat to focus it on waiting for the cue. It can be asked to sit, but the "sit" cue must not be too forceful, because if the dog becomes inhibited it will not feel free to leave when given the sending cues. The helper then sends the dog by giving the "where?" and "Mary!" cues and then ignores it. If the dog leaves to alert before the cues are given, it is never corrected. Instead, it needs additional motiva-

tion to wait; several treats in a row given for staying with the helper, for instance.

3. If the dog does not approach and touch on its own, the partner cues it. Either way, the touch is reinforced, but the dog is then ignored, and, unlike previous training, no "where?" cue is given to send it back to the helper. As soon as it leaves to go back towards the helper, the partner follows the dog back to the helper.

4. If the dog does not return to the helper on its own, the helper cues it either to "touch" or calls its name, and as it approaches, cues it to sit. Touching the helper is optional; in many situations the partner does not want the dog nudging or jumping on whoever is calling. The touch quickly dies out if not constantly reinforced, and sitting for a treat provides a substitute behavior.

5. Partner, helper, and dog all meet and have a happy "reunion" and praise the dog for bringing the pack together.

6. Increasing distance. Once the distance is more than ten feet or so, the dog will need to run back and forth continuously while the partner is following it back to the helper. It may do this on its own, or the helper might at first need to send it again each time. In real life, the partner might be several rooms away and will not know what sound was being alerted to if the dog disappears and does not continue to run back and forth.

7. As above, the partner and helper should randomize and reduce reward frequency as well as phase out cues for touching and "where?" cues. However, they should reinforce response to the "Mary!" cue and reinforce the dog for sitting on the return without cueing.

8. Body positions: Partner and helper introduce variations in body positions.

9. Real life: Partner and helper introduce variations in other real-life situations (see list).

10. To build motivation to search, the partner hides—at first around corners, then in other hiding places—while the helper gently restrains it, then sends it. The dog will need extra help (calling and treats), if the hiding places are too difficult. Therefore, they should be very easy at first. The goal is to use as little help as possible, so that the dog develops initiative and persistence in searching.

11. When the dog works consistently to find its partner, no matter who sends it, it then can start learning to be sent by the partner to find other family members. The entire training procedure must be briefly repeated, starting again at the beginning, sending it to one family member only until the dog works well finding that person, then retraining with another family member, and so on. If names and name signs are used consistently, the dog can learn to find any family member if given their name.

Name Call for Use in Public or Work Situations

For practical use outside, the dog, on leash, can touch its partner and then indicate the sender's location by going to the end of the leash or looking at the sender. It does not need to run back and forth. To the dog, the name call means "touch." For this version of the exercise, the "where?" part is phased out, because people in public or the workplace either don't know it or will forget to use it, so it is more practical to use the partner's name or name sign alone.

1. To teach the on-leash situation for this exercise, a helper is not needed at first. With the dog on leash, the partner calls out or signs their own name, or the future partner's name, then cues the dog to "touch." (Trust me, it feels really stupid to scream out your

own name over and over.) A tape of the partner calling his or her own name at random intervals can be played so that the partner can act more naturally in various situations while training. To accustom the dog to other voices, a tape recording of calls by other people could also be played. The partner should use a tape only until the dog touches when it hears the name, then real helpers should be used, since the tape's hissing sound cues the dog too much.

2. Once the dog alerts to the partner's voice or the taped calls, a helper stands a few feet away and calls or signs "Mary!" Eventually they will imitate various voice types. The dog is on leash, and is allowed to run back and forth without any corrections if it wants to; unfortunately the leash might tighten when the dog gets to the end of it. This is not supposed to feel like a correction, so the partner must make sure there is no sudden jerk, just a gentle restraint by the leash. If the dog is inhibited and upset by the tightening of the leash when it attempts to run to the helper, it needs lots of praise and cheerleading from the partner so that it keeps a happy attitude and should be encouraged to only touch the partner. It should not be reinforced for going to the helper, who should ignore it. The helper does not reinforce it for approaching because the goal is for the dog to be able to alert while on leash in public to people calling from a distance, and it needs to get used to staying close to its partner. Eventually, the dog will touch the partner, then glance in the direction of the helper or, if it does not, the partner will look around and notice the helper waving.

3. Other helpers are enlisted to call to give the dog a broad range of situations and voices to get used to.

4. The partner should stop cueing "touch" unless the dog needs help, and reinforces touches without cues in real-life situations (see list).

5. Corrections: The dog can be given a light tug on a long line if it ignores a call of "Mary!" It must immediately be praised and reinforced for approaching to touch. If the correction is too strong, the dog will be inhibited from indicating the direction of the call.

Timer: One-Way Alert

Kitchen timers can be used for anything that a person needs reminding about. Many people do not need them in real life, but they are an essential training tool to teach and maintain several skills needed by the dog. They are excellent for teaching Hearing Dogs to touch, to locate their partner, locate sounds, and to reinforce the back-and forth alert to all sounds. The partner can use the timer without needing a helper, making practicing easier. The timer two-way alert is used as foundation training for both the door and the telephone alerts. The timer one-way alert is used as foundation training for both the smoke alarm and for the alarm clock alerts.

The ideal timer should:
- Be an electronic one with a continuous beeping sound, not a wind-up timer with a short buzz or bell.
- Be able to be set for seconds, not just minutes. Training goes too slowly if it can only be set for one minute, especially in the beginning stages when many repetitions are needed.
- Beep for long enough for a dog to make several trips back and forth to its partner. Some timers beep for only fifteen seconds or so.
- Have a clip so it could be attached to clothing.

- Not beep while being set. This beeping unfortunately informs the dog that it's practice time. If the response to the beep while setting the timer is not reinforced, then the dog will habituate to the sound, but if the response *is* reinforced, then the dog is receiving a lot of additional cueing that the timer will soon beep again. In the early stages of training, such cues are helpful, but in real-life stages, they are detrimental. If the timer is one of these, setting it for a few minutes can help. By the time it goes off, the dog may have forgotten about it, so that training will be more realistic.

For some dumb reason, timers have their tiny speaker in the back of the case. This means that fingers or clothing can accidentally muffle their sound. Also, it would be nice if someone invented a timer with a blinking light, but there seems to be no such timer available. If the partner can't hear the timer, it is hard to remember to turn it off, and hard to know if the timer is still sounding or not, unless the dog continues alerting. If the timer were to continue sounding, the dog loses interest instead of continuing its alert. Naturally, this is bad for the dog's training. To solve this problem, the timer can be placed on top of a sound signaler device once training involves a stationary timer at a target area.

The timer is first taught as a one-way alert; the timer is kept on or next to the partner and the dog approaches to touch when it hears the timer. Later, the timer is taught as a two-way alert. This is not practical in real life except at short distances because the timer is not loud, and the dog often can't hear it if there are other noises going on. But it is very practical when trying to teach the dog alerting behaviors.

Training for the one-way timer alert will progress faster if the dog is already familiar with the "touch" cue, but it does not need to do a perfect touch in the beginning phases of timer training. It is much more important that it gets to eat a treat within half a second of the start of the timer ring, whether it touches or not. The timer is held in one hand or clipped to clothing. Setting it for one second is best at this stage. Trainers who can't hear the beep must watch the numbers count down, and must find out at exactly what point their particular timer starts to beep.

1. Introducing the sound. The partner sits or stands within a few feet of the dog, focuses it on the exercise by allowing it to smell a treat concealed in a closed hand, which is held still. The other hand holds the timer. Within half a second after the timer beeps, the treat hand suddenly exposes the treat with a wiggling motion and allows the dog to eat the treat. The dog should feel that the sound caused the concealed treat to suddenly appear, and the wiggling makes it seem alive. The timer is turned off immediately after the dog eats the treat. Turning off the timer is extremely important, but also hard to remember for partners who cannot hear it beeping.

2. The partner focuses it as before, but then lures the dog to touch by drawing the hand back while wiggling it. The dog must now actively follow the treat as if the treat is escaping when the timer rings. This is the foundation for the dog to later burst energetically toward the partner when the timer beeps. The partner praises and acts very excited while luring the dog to follow the treat.

3. To lure the dog to approach the sound and the partner, the partner focuses the dog on the treat, rings the timer, wiggles the treat, and takes a few steps backward.

4. To increase excitement about the timer, the partner rings the timer and runs away, reinforcing the dog for chasing and following.

5. After about three to seven sessions (with about twenty timer beeps and reinforce-

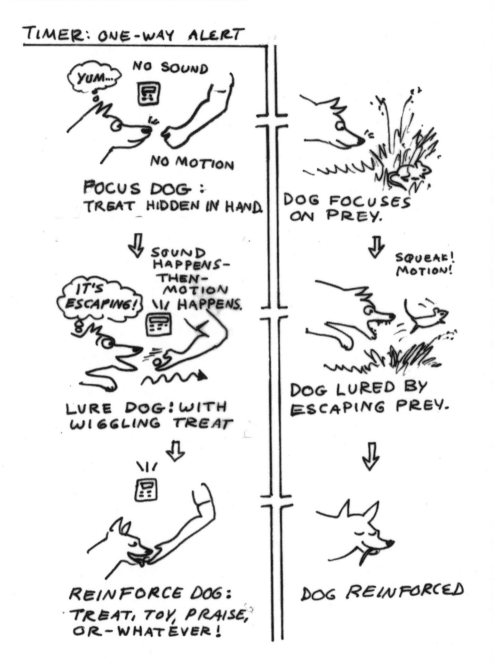

TIMER: ONE-WAY ALERT

YUM... NO SOUND

NO MOTION

FOCUS DOG: TREAT HIDDEN IN HAND

DOG FOCUSES ON PREY.

⇩ SOUND HAPPENS- THEN- MOTION HAPPENS.

IT'S ESCAPING!

⇩ SQUEAK! MOTION!

LURE DOG: WITH WIGGLING TREAT

DOG LURED BY ESCAPING PREY.

⇩

⇩

REINFORCE DOG: TREAT, TOY, PRAISE, OR-WHATEVER!

DOG REINFORCED

ments each), the partner should be watching for an "Ah, ha!" response from the dog when it hears the timer. If tested by ringing the timer when the dog is facing away, the dog should suddenly turn its head toward the sound and partner as if it expects a treat. This indicates that the dog is ready for the next steps.

6. Once a definite "Ah, ha!" response is seen by the dog when the timer rings, the "touch" cue can be introduced within half a second after the timer starts ringing. A verbal

"touch" is given, and the wiggling luring motion begins to change into a patting motion on the partner's leg.

7. The partner can stop moving backwards and just stand or sit. Instead of the partner's stimulating movements, they should use lots of luring and praise for touching.

8. Timer should now become the cue for touching. The partner stops cueing "touch" when the timer rings unless the dog needs help. It is reinforced for all efforts to touch when cued by the timer, not the voice or movements.

9. To increase the dog's motivation to search, a helper holds the dog gently while the partner tempts the dog with a treat and excitedly runs around a corner while holding the timer. The helper lets the dog go when the timer goes off. Another way to do this is for the partner to wait for the dog to be distracted, sneak around the corner, and then ring the timer. When the dog responds well, the partner runs off and hides in increasingly difficult places. The dog learns to locate the partner both by smell and by locating the sound of the timer. For this exercise, reinforcements can be a joyous reunion with the "lost" partner as well as the dog's favorite toy or its dinner.

10. The partner then increases the distance, varies body positions, decreases, randomizes the reward schedule, and sets up real-life situations (see list).

Sleeping Dog and Sleeping Partner

This exercise will help the dog later when it is expected to alert a sleeping partner to a timer or any other sound, such as the smoke alarm and alarm clock alerts. The dog should have completed the previous training for the one-way timer alert. This cuts down on the total number of sessions needed for the deafening smoke alarm.

1. To familiarize the dog with the target area, treats are scattered on the target area of the bed (pillow, body of partner, or flat part of bed) and the dog encouraged to put its paws up and eat the treats or to jump up and eat them, depending on the size of dog and the type of alert desired. Dogs can be encouraged to jump right on top of heavy sleepers, or gently touch only the bed for light sleepers.

2. The partner sits on the bed with the dog on the floor and focuses it with a treat in the closed hand. The timer is rung and within half a second, the hand opens and wiggles up to the bed, luring the dog to put its paws on it or jump on. However, the partner does *not* give food from the hand, but drops it onto the target area, pointing to it if the dog is confused. The dog eats the treat and is praised and hugged. Being allowed to relax on the bed with the partner for a short time is a big part of the motivation to alert to the smoke alarm and alarm clock. To get the dog back into the starting position to repeat the exercise, the partner can lure the dog back to the floor or throw a treat a few feet away on the floor. Alternately, a helper can gently lure or carry the dog away. The dog is never commanded or corrected to get off the bed during a training session lest it be too inhibited to get up next time.

3. To teach the dog to approach the bed from farther away, the partner can throw a treat across the room, wait for the dog to follow and eat it, then ring the timer, cheerleading if needed with a recall or a "touch" cue to motivate the dog to come quickly. Although so much cueing means that the dog is not learning too much about coming to the timer, it is still learning to come to the bed fast from a distance, a necessary skill. This technique works for a session or so until the throwing of the treat becomes a cue that the timer is about to ring; then it becomes non-productive to use. Another method is to not use the

timer at all, but practice the "Where?" alert with the partner in the bed, and the helper moving farther and farther away. The dog is encouraged to make several trips before the partner gets up and follows it to the helper. This also patterns the dog to run towards the bed from long distances.

4. To raise the dog's motivation to alert, the partner can ring the timer and run towards the bed, encouraging the dog to follow and get on the bed.

5. Alerting when the partner is "sleeping." A helper holds the dog while the partner shows the dog a treat, gets into the bed and rings the timer. The dog is released, and reinforced for any attempt to alert. This is then repeated with the partner under the covers, and the dog is encouraged to persistently nudge around the face, pillow, and covers and find treats there. Some cheerleading is often needed to encourage the dog to alert in this new situation.

6. Alerting when the dog is sleeping. The partner waits in the bed until the dog is napping or calm, then rings the timer and reinforces the dog for any attempt to alert, even a sleepy slow response. If the dog is responding well, the partner then waits until the dog is sleeping deeply, then rings the timer and encourages the dog to alert. Very good treats and lots of praise may be needed to motivate a sleepy dog! Remember that waking up to alert is the most difficult part of a Hearing Dog's job, and teach this exercise gradually, using really worthwhile reinforcements.

Once the dog is consistently alerting to the timer in all these situations, it has also learned to locate sounds, locate the partner, learned the layout of its house by heart, and learned to touch in many real-life situations.

Progression to Two-Way Timer Alert

The dog should already be highly motivated to do the one-way alert to the timer. A temporary location for the timer is selected, ideally next to the phone. This will later help the dog with the telephone alert by pre-training the behaviors of going to the phone's target area and the back-and-forth response. Because the phone alert is the most difficult to train and maintain, this timer practice is very important. If the timer is kept in the kitchen, the target area selected should be in a safe place away from the stove. A low stepstool or box makes a good target area. The timer and a treat container are kept permanently here. The dog is taught to go to the timer first, then touch, simply because it makes training consistent. In real life, it does not matter whether the dog goes to the timer first or touches the partner first, and the partner should be happy with either response. If the partner cannot hear the timer, it can be placed on a sound signaling device that will flash a light when the timer rings.

1. To familiarize the dog with the target area, the timer is placed on the selected target area. Without ringing the timer, the partner spends a session taking treats out of the container while the dog watches and placing them *on the target area*—not from the hand—for the dog to eat. If they are given from the hand, then the dog will focus on the hand and never understand that the target area has anything to do with the treats. Dogs that are very hesitant can have treat crumbs sprinkled on the target area to induce them to spend more time there and become comfortable. The treat container remains at the timer's target area permanently, and the dog learns that this container is opened when the partner approaches the timer. Dogs can smell the treats even through a closed container, so it serves as a reminder that this is a feeding location. Small holes can be punched in a plastic treat con-

tainer to make the dog more aware of the food. If the dog tries to chew the container, a glass jar can be used instead. If training with a toy, a favorite small toy can be kept in the container, brought out and played with, then replaced in the container so long as the dog sees the toy being taken out of and being replaced in the container.

2. The dog and partner are within a few feet of the timer. A treat is placed on the target area and the timer is rung. Because of previous training, the dog will probably go to the timer and find the treat. If not, the partner can call the dog over, point to the treat, or roll a treat onto the target area. All of this heavy cueing is then phased out as quickly as possible. The timer should be turned off as soon as the dog is fed the treat. A treat should be waiting at the target area for a majority of the times the dog arrives at the timer.

3. Following the dog to the timer. The training goal for this stage is for the dog to approach the timer from other rooms. The treat is placed and timer set without the dog noticing (dog is in another room, being distracted by a helper, dog is outside, etc.). Alternately, a helper can set the timer while the partner and dog are elsewhere. When the dog goes consistently to the timer from several feet away or farther, the partner starts to follow it every time, opens the container, puts a second treat onto the target area, and praises excitedly while the dog eats. Let the dog lead! Do not get ahead, or the dog will always wait for the partner to take it to the sound source. The timer is turned off immediately and reset.

4. If the dog seems uninterested or slow, the partner can hold the dog gently, at first only a few feet away, while a helper shows it a treat, places it at the target area, then rings the timer. The partner releases the dog when the timer sounds. This exercise can be used to teach the dog to go to the timer from farther and farther away. If no helper is available, the partner can hold a bold dog gently back by the collar at arm's length while showing a treat and placing it at the target area, then letting the dog free when the timer rings.

5. Even though the partner is not yet supposed to be cueing it to touch, the dog may approach the partner to touch before or after it goes to the timer. Either way, it should be reinforced often enough to encourage it, but not so often that it "sticks" to the partner and does not go to the timer.

6. To increase distance, the timer can be set and a treat placed at the target area while the dog is elsewhere or being distracted by a helper.

7. Introducing "touch." Starting a few feet from the timer, the partner now does not follow the dog. Instead, after the dog goes to the timer, the partner calls it back with a "touch" cue. Because the timer is continuing to beep, the dog will want to stay near it, and the partner needs to highly motivate the dog to touch. For instance, the partner can go up to it and actually showing it the treat, then back up and cue "touch." The partner ignores the dog after briefly reinforcing the touch. Because it is now getting no attraction from the partner, the dog should again be drawn back towards the timer. The partner follows the dog back to the timer, takes a treat from the container, and puts it on the target area for the dog to eat. The timer is turned off immediately.

8. Multiple trips back and forth. The partner can sometimes encourage the dog to return two or more times before following it to the timer and rewarding it. At this point, the dog will realize that there is only a treat waiting at the timer the first time, and will stop going back to the timer. To convince the dog that treats can appear at any time, treats can be tossed at random intervals toward the target area *if the dog is facing it and cannot see the partner tossing treats*. A backboard to make thrown treats bounce onto the target area can

be made by standing a plastic file tray on its side and weighting it with a rock or food can taped to the back of it. Letting the dog see the treats being tossed will be disastrous; the dog will then hang around the partner and refuse to go to the timer unless it sees treats tossed. Another way to keep the dog making multiple trips is to have a helper sneak a treat onto the target area at random intervals while the dog is on its way to the partner. The helper must be quick and the dog must not notice the treat being placed.

9. Real-life situations. The partner varies distance, positions, and introduces real-life situations. The partner decreases and randomizes reward schedules for both going to the timer and for touching. The timer and its treat container are moved to different locations around the house until the dog learns to search for it. This will help the dog to generalize its alerts more creatively to unusual sounds or sounds in unfamiliar places. While traveling or in public, training with the timer can develop the dog's skills. For instance, a training session in a strange hotel room helps the dog understand that it can also alert to other sounds in this new place.

Microwave Timers

These beep a few times and then stop. Usually this is not long enough for the dog to start alerting. If the dog already alerts to the regular timer, a target area is set up near the microwave, and a two-way alert (using a timer, not the microwave) practiced to it. Once the dog is responding well, the microwave is set instead using the microwave's own timer. The dog should be reinforced if it shows any response to the beeping while the microwave buttons are being set. The partner remains close in order to make good use of the brief time the microwave beeps, giving very enthusiastic praise and really good treats. (Although giving too much people-food is not supposed to be good for dogs, the best microwave alert dogs I've heard of are those that actually get a little piece of whatever was cooking at the time it beeped!) This intense training can help compensate for the lack of length of the microwave sound. Bread machine alerts can be trained similarly.

Training the Door Alert

Once the dog can perform the beginning "Where?" exercise and a two-way alert to the timer, it has the foundation skills that will make training the door alert go quickly. But there is no need to finish these before training the door alert; steps one through four for the door alert can be done at any time. A dog with natural sound reactivity shows some interest in the knock even with no training or experience, and immediate reinforcement quickly helps this dog orient even more intensely to the knock. Dogs without sound reactivity require many more repetitions before they show any response to the knock. Dogs that are already accustomed to finding a visitor when they hear a knock may be distracted, leap around barking, and need to learn to focus more on the target area. They should not be encouraged to bark excitedly at the door, or they will later be difficult to motivate to return and touch their partner.

Communication between partner and helper for this alert is always difficult. Prearranging the timing of knocking and treat rewards is essential. A gadget can flash a light when the knock happens, and sometimes a mirror can be strategically placed so that if the door is cracked open, the helper can see what is happening inside.

A door must be chosen for training. Training can begin at an interior door, or at the exterior (front) door. There are advantages to each method. Training is easier if started at an interior door, because outside weather doesn't affect training, and the dog cannot escape outside. An interior door can also be altered to make training easier. For example, a pipe for dispensing treats and a window to make the helper's job easier can both be installed. An interior solid door can temporarily be replaced with a screen, glass, windowed, or Dutch door for training; old doors are available at salvage yards for about ten dollars. Although the interior door is easier to train with, it never has actual visitors, so the dog tends to be less interested in going to it. The other drawback is that the dog must later be taught to go to the exterior door; and while this is not a big problem it is something to consider. Also, dogs that already know that visitors arrive at the exterior door are more easily motivated to approach it. If there is more than one exterior door, signs should be placed instructing visitors to use only the chosen door. Later, in advanced training, the dog can learn to alert to other exterior doors.

Controlling the Dog from Escaping

The dog may be allowed to poke its nose near the open door to get a treat from the helper's hand during training, but should never be allowed to go all the way through without-

out a specific release command. For instance, at the Hearing Dog Program, dogs are trained to automatically stop at all doorways and wait for "heel" or "okay" before going through. This command is enforced during obedience training, but during sound alerting training things must be a little different. The dog can be gently corrected for trying to get out the door, but too much correction will make it reluctant to approach the door again.

Controlling the Dog from Jumping on Visitors

When the door is opened, the dog will often be in an excited state. The partner should get control of the dog before opening the door, make the dog sit, and give the visitor a treat as they come in to give the dog while it is sitting. Many dogs need to have their leash kept by the door at all times, and the door never opened until the leash is put on and the dog under control. If the partner needs to concentrate on the visitor, the partner can simply stand on the leash so that the dog gets stopped when it jumps

Scout waits for a cue from his partner, Carrie, instead of rushing out the door or leaping on visitors.

up. This is one way to have both hands free for communicating or accepting packages. The dog should be kept on leash when all visitors come in for as long as it takes to develop good behavior; this could be several months.

Factors that affect alerting to the door:

Dogs can smell a visitor's scent through the cracks of the door. If the visitor is a stranger, the dog stays at the door, perhaps feeling territorial, and does not return to its partner.

If the visitor is a friend, the dog stays at the door to greet the person, feeling friendly and excited, and does not return to its partner.

If the dog is low in territoriality and/or desire for social interaction, it might not be interested in finding out who is at the door.

If the partner rushes too quickly to the door, this does not give the dog enough time or help to alert.

If other family members answer the door, the dog may become confused.

If doors are glass or screen, so that the dog can see the visitor, this makes the dog more excited and might not return to the partner.

If other dogs in the household bark at the door, the Hearing Dog joins in the pack behavior and is almost impossible to motivate to return to the partner.

If the partner has nobody to help train, or rarely gets visitors, the dog gets out of practice.

Progressions for Door Alerting:

The dog should already know "where?" and a two-way alert to the timer. The timer target area should be moved temporarily to the door target area. The timer can be placed on the floor or taped to the wall near the door, and a treat container placed on the floor at the target area. Then, the partner briefly re-trains all the two-way steps for the timer, using this new target area. The timer is set to ring with a treat waiting when the dog is in all parts of the house, doing various activities. The dog needs to be able to run back and forth to the door without thinking from all rooms in the house, until it seems to have routes to the door thoroughly memorized. This pre-training will make door alert training proceed much faster. If desired, the dog can be taught with a clicker or other marker signal to actually touch its nose to the door each time it approaches the timer. Once the dog alerts reliably to the timer in this new target area, the timer and treat container are removed. Because dogs usually become "glued" to the door by the exciting presence of visitors, treats at the door are needed mostly in the beginning stages of training, but actually cause problems in later stages of training by making the dog even more glued to the door.

Even if the house has a doorbell, it is important to train with a knock at first with a new dog, since the bell often rings elsewhere in the house, and the dog needs to go all the way to the door, not be confused by the bell location. Once the dog goes reliably to the door, it will tend to continue this behavior even when the bell is introduced later. The helper's task is also easier if he or she only needs to knock. A sign on the door can tell visitors to knock on the door. If the dog already goes to the door with no problems when it hears the doorbell, then the sign should tell visitors to both knock and ring.

1. To associate the knock with food at the target area, both the partner and the dog stand on the inside of the door. The partner then knocks a few times on the door and within half a second tosses a treat against the door so that it bounces excitingly onto the target area

(the floor by the door). The treat is tossed with a sharp flicking motion of the fingers, so that the whole arm does not move and distract the dog. At first, the dog will be focused on the hand. Gradually, it realizes that although food is in the hand, the treat always falls on the floor, and it makes an effort to watch the floor when the knock is heard. The desired response of turning the head sharply downwards to watch the floor when the knock is heard may take a few sessions of ten to twenty repetitions each. The dog is not corrected if it wants to wander away. Instead, its motivation to stay near the door must be increased by more praise or better food. Keeping it on leash can gently prevent wandering but is no substitute for high motivation.

2. Once the dog orients toward the target area when the knock happens, it needs to learn to move its whole body towards the target area from a distance. From the dog's point of view, it has so far only learned to *look* at the target area, not run toward it. To get the dog to move a short distance away from the door before giving the next knock, the partner throws a treat across the room for the dog to chase and eat, and knocks when the dog finishes eating it. This can be productive for perhaps one session before the throwing becomes a cue that the knock will soon happen.

3. To increase the distance it is necessary to use a helper. A helper now stands where the partner was before (also on the inside of the door), and the partner gently holds the dog back several feet away from the door. The helper focuses the dog by showing it a treat and talking to it. The dog can be restrained gently by the helper's hands—or on leash on a flat buckle collar—but should be pulling eagerly, trying to get to the door. It must not be corrected if it pulls too hard nor even accidentally allowed to get jerked by the leash. Hard pulling means that the restraint is successfully building motivation to go forwards.

TEACH TARGET AREA ALONE... OR USE A HELPER.

≤KNOCK! TARGET AREA HELPER MOVES OUTSIDE.

≤KNOCK! UNSEEN HELPER

HELPER AND PARTNER PRAISE DOG.

This does teach the dog to pull when on a flat collar. If the partner wants to use a flat collar for obedience in public, then the dog could wear a harness in sound training and be allowed to pull only on a harness. The helper knocks and bounces treats off the door, and the dog is released instantly at the knock. The dog must associate the sound with sudden freedom from restraint so that it will later shoot energetically forward when it hears a sound. The distance to the door is then gradually increased.

4. After the dog goes to the door from across the room, it can be encouraged to accompany the partner to another room. The partner runs happily, uses a treat, or pets the dog to lure it away to another room. As soon as the dog is out of sight, the helper at the door knocks. The dog should continue to get treats at the door almost every time. The partner follows the dog to the door, opens the door, and both helper (who is still inside) and partner praise the dog.

5. If the dog "cheats" and goes before the knock, the partner must let it be free to go, and think of a better way to attract the dog away from the door. Cheating always means that the partner has made the training situation too obvious and easy to the dog. In this situation, the dog is ready for surprise knocks. The helper can take a walk, then return to knock in a few minutes. As the partner and dog do the exercise from farther away from the door, the dog may begin on its own to do a two-way alert and touch the partner after it gets to the door. This is excellent and should be reinforced, unless the dog is sticking too much with the partner and not going all the way to the door. Then the partner simply gives treats less often for touching and increases the frequency of treats at the door.

6. Moving the helper outside the door. The distance is reduced to a few feet again. The helper now is positioned outside the cracked-open door, knocks, then puts their hand inside and either holds and wiggles a treat to entice the dog to come all the way to the door or just tosses a treat inside at the target area. The helper's hand can also pet the dog when it approaches. Once the dog shows a good response, the helper can phase out this extra help by drawing the hand back after each knock and gently closing the door before the dog gets close enough to eat a treat that is left on the floor.

7. Once the dog learns to go eagerly to the door even when the helper is outside, the helper then secretly leaves a treat lying on the target area while the dog is not looking, quietly pull the door almost shut (no noises!), and then knocks. (The dog should be playfully distracted by the partner during this sneaky move, and *never corrected* if it tries to go to the door before the knock happens. See "Common Training Mistakes," below.)

8. Adding the doorbell: When the dog has a consistent one-way response to the knock, a sign should be put on the door telling visitors to both knock and ring the bell.

Two-way Training for the Door Knock

The dog should already know the "Touch" command and perform a two-way alert to the timer at the door's target area. When the dog consistently approaches the door for the knock, the partner starts helping the dog return to touch. The ratio of treats at the door is decreased, and is varied depending on whether the dog is returning easily to the partner. These ratios can be tricky to figure out. For instance, if the dog does not find a treat at the door, it is easier to get it away from the door to touch the partner, but it is also less likely to go to the door next time. Constant tinkering with the reinforcement schedules at the door and at the partner is always needed, even in maintenance training. As a new dog gets used to real-life visitors, it may become either friendlier or more territorial. Both of these factors motivate the dog to become "glued" at the door instead of returning to touch. If this is happening, giving too many treats at the door will make the problem worse, so treats should be used mostly to reinforce touching the partner.

1. Touching the partner. After the dog goes to the door, the partner calls the dog back to touch and reinforces it briefly, then ignores it. Ignoring makes it leave the partner and return to the door. The helper knocks again if needed, and the partner follows the dog to the door. If the dog does not go, or goes slowly back to the door the second time, the helper can place a treat through the partially open door when the dog is not watching so that it will be waiting at the target area when they knock the second time. The partner follows the dog, opens the door, and both partner and helper greet and praise the dog excitedly.

2. Multiple trips. The partner occasionally waits and lets the dog make two or more trips back and forth before following it. A really agile and sneaky partner can throw a treat over the dog and towards the door target area while following behind the dog on its way to the door, providing an exciting surprise reinforcement. Again, however, if the dog sees the partner throwing the treat, the opposite result happens and the dog will wait and watch the partner and not approach the door unless a treat is thrown. Still, this technique works so well when done properly that it is worth the risk. It can't be done too often, or the dog figures out what is happening anyway.

3. The partner builds distance and varies body positions for touching while decreasing and randomizing reinforcement schedules. Touch cues are reduced and the dog reinforced for any attempts at touching without any cueing. Real-life situations are introduced (see list).

4. Practicing different knock sounds: Knocks from timid tapping to heavy pounding are used. The dog can easily smell who is outside the door, so using a variety of helpers is important.

5. Every time real-life visitors arrive unexpectedly, the partner must note the dog's behavior and quickly decide how to react to it in a way that will improve its alerts. If the dog does not alert in any way, the partner can excitedly ask the dog to "touch," after which it may feel more excited and go to the door so that the partner can follow it. If no treats for touching are handy because the knock was unexpected, the partner makes up for this by giving extra happy praise. If the dog still does nothing, the partner can rush excitedly to the door and encourage the dog to go along. Dogs that rush to the door by themselves and remain there, barking, can be asked to return to "touch." When the door is opened, cooperative visitors can feed a treat to feed to the dog for sitting. If they are extra-cooperative, they are asked to wait outside for a few minutes, then knock again. This provides an extra training session. Family members should give the dog extra practice in alerting to the door by always knocking instead of letting themselves in with a key.

Apartment Security Buzzer Systems

These systems are difficult to train alerts to. The complicated scenario is as follows: the visitor arrives at the building entrance and rings the buzzer. This causes either the apartment telephone to ring or an intercom system on the wall to buzz. The dog needs to alert to these, not the door. Only after a long while will the visitor knock at the apartment door. At that point, the dog can perform a normal door alert as trained above, but this is useless unless it has already alerted to the building's exterior door buzzer.

If the system is wired into the telephone, then to the dog it is simply another phone alert. If a wall intercom exists, then a target area should be set up near or below the intercom. The treat container and a timer are placed there, and a two-way alert to the timer at this location is trained. Once the dog has a good response to the timer, a helper can ring the buzzer. Communication problems often arise between partner and helper due to the distance from the exterior door. A temporary solution is to attach a microphone device to the buzzer speaker and a lamp to alert Deaf partners that the buzzer is ringing until the dog is alerting well.

Telephone

The telephone alert is the most difficult one in real life, because it is subject to the problem of "learned irrelevance." This means that a sound which happens often without any consequences, good or bad, becomes meaningless and is not only ignored, but not even noticed consciously by the dog. Dogs that have heard phones often prior to training don't just have to learn to alert to the phone, they need to first learn to notice it again. It may be best to buy a different-sounding phone or ringer to begin training.

Additionally, unlike the door knock, nothing exciting happens when the phone rings, unless people get up excitedly to answer it. Even then, their attention is not given to the dog, but soon taken away from it by the phone call, making it a negative experience. Even after the dog is trained, every phone call that it ignores, that is answered by a family member, or that does not result in a reinforcement, is one more nail in the coffin for the phone alert. I am always amazed when Hearing Dogs alert to the phone in real life, no matter how feeble their responses.

The phone alert is also the most difficult to train in the first place unless a system for making the phone ring by remote control is set up. An electrician is needed for this; I know of no remote or wired ringing device available commercially or check hearingdog.com for newly developed product sources. Using other phone lines, cell phones, or a modem to dial the target phone's number is helpful, but the act of dialing makes sounds and move-

ments that cue the dog up for a training session. This is acceptable in early stages, but in real life, the dog may not alert to a phone ring without this additional cueing. This process is slow and frustrating because it may take about one hundred calls (divided up into several sessions) before the dog even *begins* to make the connection between the ring and the reward for the first stages of training. (This amount assumes good timing in delivering reinforcement within half a second to a few seconds after the ringing begins. Training with bad timing takes much longer.) Good

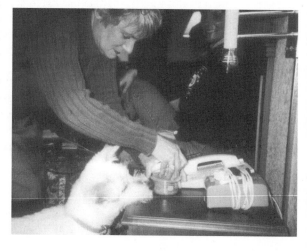

Marilyn Edwards rewards Teri for an alert to the phone. (Photo by Dennard)

timing means that it will be necessary to ask a friend to call with strict guidelines: "Wait one minute then call me, let it ring each time till I pick it up, allow thirty seconds to elapse before dialing, and call fifteen times in a row." This can get complicated and friends can get very bored. Because of all these difficulties, training for the phone often ends up consisting of rather random, badly timed attempts to get the dog alerting, and depends more on the dog's talent and the partner's enthusiasm than anything else.

Factors that affect motivation to alert to the telephone:

- Modern phones have low, "chirpy" rings that are designed not to annoy other people in crowded offices. This means that the sound itself is not exciting to dogs. Phones should be selected for a loud ring or a separate phone ringer (about thirty dollars at Radio Shack) can be plugged in to the existing phone.
- Multiple phones are very confusing for the dog. One main phone should be chosen, a loud ringer added if needed, and the sound on the other phones turned off. The partner should only answer the main phone until the dog is reliable on that phone. Eventually, the dog can be trained to alert to other extensions around the house.
- Answering machines often allow only one to four rings. This is not long enough to get most dogs up and doing a good alert.
- Every time the phone is answered, the partner's attention is then removed from the dog. This may be interpreted as a negative experience by the dog. Extra effort must be made to reinforce alerts.
- Other people often confuse the dog by answering the phone.
- If the dog's alerts are ignored, it loses motivation.
- If the partner rarely gets phone calls or has nobody to help practice by calling, the dog gets out of practice.
- The phone may ring so often that the dog gets overworked and loses interest in the phone.
- Different phone lines need different-sounding ringers if the dog is to be trained to alert to one or both of them. If only one is to be alerted to, the other one should have quiet boring ring.
- If the phone rings when the dog is home alone, the dog becomes habituated and ignores the ring. (Turning off ringers when nobody is home is advisable, at least until the dog is responding well.)

The following is a short summary of the training progressions for the phone alert. Once a remote ringer is marketed (inventors ætake note of the big market for this device!) the following summary can be followed for the easiest way to train the phone alert. Note that the sequences are similar to those of the two-way timer alert.

1. The phone is rung and the dog reinforced at the target area until the dog looks expectantly at the target area when it hears the ring.

2. The dog is reinforced for approaching the target area consistently when the phone rings from several feet away, then from increasing distances such as from other rooms.

3. The partner then waits for the dog to approach the phone, calls the dog back to touch for treats, then the dog returns to the phone and gets reinforced at the target area.

4. The partner builds repetitions of the two-way (back-and forth) response, at the same time reducing and randomizing reinforcement frequency.

5. The partner again builds distance until the dog alerts from other rooms.

6. The partner introduces real-life situations (see list).

Selecting a Target Area

The easiest target area for the dog is for both the phone and treat container to be at the dog's nose level. However, the target area need not actually have the phone right there, as long as the location is kept consistent. For example, if the phone is installed high up on the wall, the target area could be a footstool below it. A container of treats is placed at the target area and kept there permanently.

Training begins by giving the dog treats at the target area without ringing the phone. Several short sessions of giving five or ten "free" treats one at a time, with lots of praise and excited happiness, should teach the dog that this "feeding station" is a darn good place to be. The dog needs to learn that treats are available at this area. Treats for the phone target area should always be removed *from the treat container* and placed *on the target area* for the dog to eat. The goal here is to associate treats with the target area. If treats are given from the hand, then the dog will focus on the hand and never understand that the phone target area has anything to do with the treats. By having the treat container remain at the telephone permanently, the dog learns that this container is opened when the partner approaches the phone.

Training During Unplanned Phone Rings

During the training period, the dog cannot be allowed to habituate to and ignore the normal phone rings that occur in between training sessions. Ideally, the phone ring should be turned off at all other times, but this is not practical for anyone who is training at home. Therefore, something must be done to help the dog maintain a positive association with the phone ring, even if the timing of a reward is not optimal. If the partner can't hear the phone, a flashing light or a hearing helper should signal the ring. The moment the phone rings, the partner excitedly encourages the dog to touch, and if it does not then go to the phone, the partner should entice it over to the phone by making a big deal out of rattling and opening the treat container and placing a treat on the target area. In short, the partner must do whatever it takes to get the dog very excited about this wonderful ringing sound. Depending on the dog's current level of training for the phone alert, its reaction to these real-life rings will vary. *Any reaction at all* should be rewarded and praised even if it is far below what the dog can do during its usual training sessions. Treats can be left secretly on the target area if expecting a call, so that if the dog does go on its own, or is called over to the phone by the partner, a surprise reinforcement will be waiting. If it develops a habit of checking the target area and eating these waiting treats before the phone rings, it must *never* be scolded or prevented from eating them. This behavior of checking the target area for food actually increases the likelihood that the dog will go there when the phone finally does ring. The partner can also feed a portion of the dog's regular food at the target area each time the phone rings, regardless of whether the dog alerted well or needed to be coaxed over to the phone. Rewarding a dog for "not alerting" might seem to go against dog training principles, but the goal here is to condition an association between the target area and food. After being fed for a non-alert, it is more likely to approach the target area the next time the phone rings.

Training the Phone Alert

This method can be successful, but will take longer than if the trainer has access to a remotely controlled phone ringer. The method that will be given here is first to teach the dog to do a two-way alert to the timer when it is placed on the telephone's target area. When the dog is really sharp on this alert, it is ready for the magnet phone alert. After this, it can then learn a two-way alert to a refrigerator magnet "phone" in the same target area, and then the real phone ring can be incorporated, encouraging the dog to generalize its alert to this new sound. To make the real phone ring, helpers can call at specific times, or another phone line or cell phone can be used to ring the phone. Meanwhile, all actual phone calls are used as training opportunities to make the dog excited about this sound, even if its training level is not yet up to a complete alert. Using a tape recording of a phone ring is fine for beginning stages, but does not work well in advanced training; the clicking of the buttons and the hissing sound of the tape provide the dog with many cues that make it start responding early.

A refrigerator magnet phone is available at Lechter's Housewares and other housewares stores. It makes a high-pitched "office" type of phone ring when lightly pressed. It is useful because the partner can easily control it. In initial training this gadget makes it possible to have multiple repetitions to build up the associations between phone ring and food. It is ideal for training the dog to generalize to a similar-sounding real phone. Also available are various children's toy phones and cell phones; try to match the toy's ring to the real phone at home.

1. To develop a one-way alert with magnet phone, follow all of the instructions for the one-way timer alert, but while holding the magnet phone instead of the timer.

2. To develop a two-way alert with magnet phone, follow the instructions for the two-way alert with the timer, but place the magnet phone on the target area. The target area for the real phone is used. Because the magnet phone must be pressed to ring, once the partner more than a few feet away a helper will be needed to ring it.

3.Transferring the magnet phone alert to the real phone. The partner needs to understand that it is very important to consistently reinforce any response (even just a flick of an ear) to the real phone. He or she must set up training situations with the real phone, and use all unexpected phone rings to build a positive attitude in the dog. The more similar-sounding the magnet phone's ring is to the real phone, the easier the transfer will be. To begin, the partner arranges for a phone call, disconnecting any answering machine, so that the phone can ring about ten or twelve times. The partner stands quietly by the target area, with the dog nearby, and within half a second of the start of each ring, tosses a treat on the target area. The treat is tossed with the partner's body blocking the dog's view of the moving hand. If the dog shows no interest, the partner can point to the treat and praise the dog when it approaches the target area. The partner must become still and silent between rings so that the dog will calm down and notice the next ring. When the phone is finally answered (in order to ask the helper to call again) the dog is given a treat from the container onto the target area.

4. Approaching the target area for the real ring. The partner arranges for the real phone to ring, and secretly leaves a treat waiting at the target area without the dog noticing. The partner also has treats ready to reward touching. When the phone rings, the dog's reaction is watched. If it goes to the phone, hopefully it finds and eats the treat. The partner follows the dog to the phone and gives a treat from the container at the target area. If the dog

approaches the partner instead of going to the phone, it is reinforced for touching or cued to touch if it needs help. Either response is equally desirable. The partner can then follow the dog to the phone. Even if the dog showed no interest in the phone and had to be coaxed to the target area, it still gets a treat once there from the container.

5. Multiple trips in training sessions strengthen the dog's alerting response in real life—*if* the dog is gets more excited and happy after several trips, not bored and slowing down. Bored or slow dogs are usually showing that their partner is not making the training fun enough. In real life, the partner should be satisfied with one trip, and can decide whether to encourage more trips or not. A helper is useful to secretly put treats onto the target area at random intervals to keep the dog interested in returning to the target area.

6. Touch cues are reduced and real-life situations are introduced (see list).

7. Incorporating the real phone. Helpers can call on the real phone at specific times, from other phone lines, or from cell phones. When the real phone rings, the partner lets it ring many times; dropping treats on the target area within half a second of every ring and praising the dog as it eats them. This exercise teaches the dog that the real ring is very relevant. Once the dog shows some reaction to the real ring, the partner encourages it to approach the target area and gives treats there every time it rings. Leaving treats there when expecting a call reinforces the dog when it approaches. Once the dog is interested in the real ring, it is encouraged to do a two-way alert to it. "Touch" cues are used until the dog alerts without help, and the partner follows the dog and puts treats from the container onto the target area each and every time—for the dog's lifetime if needed.

8. When the phone rings in real-life, the partner must evaluate the dog's response and decide quickly how to reinforce or improve the dog's alert. Something must be done; either encouraging the dog to touch or to go to the phone. Ideally, the phone ring should be turned off at all times except for training sessions until the dog is fully trained. If this is not practical, then training will take longer and the dog has more opportunities to become habituated to ignore the ring. During the training period, a flashing light helps if the partner can't hear the phone. The partner needs to react intensely and positively to every non-planned ring, no matter how poor the dog's reaction. If the phone rings unexpectedly and the dog does not alert, the partner needs to mask their disappointment and act very excited, encourage the dog to touch, give a treat or praise, and go to the phone to give the dog a treat from the container, no matter how poor its reactions to the ring were. Remember that the only really poor reaction is if the dog continues sleeping without even twitching an ear; anything else can be built upon. The partner must not have poor reactions or show poor leadership. The partner cannot answer the phone and think, "Well, I'll train the dog the next time it rings." Success for this difficult sound depends a lot on how committed the partner is.

9. For portable phones, the phone is first kept on a belt clip, and trained as a one-way alert, even if the partner can hear the ringing. Once the one-way alert is reliable, the phone is left in different places with a treat next to it to teach the dog to find the phone. When the dog can find the phone, a two-way alert is taught.

10. For multiple phone extensions, the dog can learn to alert to the other phones in the house after it alerts well to the first phone in real-life situations. The ring on the first is turned off, and a different phone used until the dog alerts well to that phone. Follow all the steps over again. Training should take less time than the original phone training.

REAL-LIFE PHONE

① TREAT WAITING AT TARGET AREA IN CASE SOUND HAPPENS.

② SILENT — IF DOG FINDS TREAT BEFORE PHONE RINGS — THAT'S OK!

③ PHONE RINGS, DOG GOES TO TARGET AREA...

④ OR TOUCHES FIRST...

⑤ PARTNER FOLLOWS AND REINFORCES AT TARGET AREA.

REAL-LIFE PHONE ALERT: PHASE OUT MOST CUEING AND TREATS, BUT ALWAYS REINFORCE AFTER FOLLOWING DOG TO TARGET AREA!

Smoke Alarm Training

The main challenges with this alert are the difficulty in pushing the test button on an alarm installed high up on a ceiling and the loudness of the alarm. To solve these problems, a second smoke alarm should be installed lower on a wall where a helper *wearing earplugs* can pushing the test button—*not* by holding matches under it! Another option is to use a loose (uninstalled) smoke alarm, which can be muffled with a pillow to avoid damaging the partner or dog's hearing. Muffling and hiding the alarm also helps to avoid frightening the dog, which can quickly be untrained by having the smoke alarm pushed into its face; even though good Hearing Dogs are not afraid of the sound, it is uncomfortably loud and they may begin to avoid it. In addition, the visual cue of seeing the smoke alarm must be avoided so that the dog will alert in real life.

If the alarms already installed in a house are the electrically wired kind, then they have a different sound that cannot be duplicated easily for training. Battery operated smoke alarms need to be installed as well, so that any fire will trigger both alarms and the dog will alert to the sound of the battery operated alarm that it has been trained for.

Standard smoke alarms cost between seven and twenty dollars. One First Alert model has a flashing light when it is ringing. More expensive ones with very bright flashing lights or hookups to bed-shakers can be purchased through Harris Communications.

The smoke alarm alert is a one-way alert, and in the initial stages is trained exactly like the one-way timer alert. Since the timer is more easily used and does not present the problems of potential hearing loss for dog or owner, all of the initial training can be done with the kitchen timer. Once the dog alerts well to the timer, the actual smoke alarm training will require fewer training sessions. To the dog, the smoke alarm is just another high-pitched sound, similar to the timer. Training with an alarm clock that sounds like the smoke alarm is also very helpful.

A dog with no prior smoke alarm training may approach the smoke alarm sound if it is very sound reactive or if it is generalizing from its other alerts to the timer or beeping alarm clock (if trained before the smoke alarm alert). However, because it must not approach a fire, it must be taught not to approach the smoke alarm, but go towards the partner instead. Training done with the partner operating a smoke alarm muffled in a pillow is the easiest way to train this but, unfortunately, also teaches the dog to approach this sound. Therefore, it is best to train from start to finish by only using a wall alarm if a helper is available to ring it.

Advanced smoke alarm training concentrates on teaching the dog to alert a sleeping partner. This means that the dog needs to *alert intensely without any help from the partner*, and it must be taught to wake up instantly when it hears the smoke alarm.

The timer and alarm clock provided the foundation training for this exercise and the dog should already perform a one-way alert to the timer when it is held by the partner lying in bed, as well as in other situations. It can now quickly learn to generalize the same response to the smoke alarm. If the dog ever goes towards the smoke alarm on the wall, not the partner, it is never corrected. It is actually exhibiting a logical curiosity response to the sound, but showing that it needs even higher motivation to go to the partner, who must become more exciting and interesting, using toys, treats, play, or chasing—whatever it takes. If the dog is never rewarded for approaching the wall smoke alarm, it will instead begin consistently approaching the partner. A treat container should be kept permanently by the bed. Another useful aid for foundation training is to use the "Super-Loud LED" alarm clock, because it sounds like a smoke alarm. Other alarm clocks cannot be used this way.

1. Familiarize the dog with the smoke alarm. The ideal dog shows interest, not fearfulness, but not all dogs are ideal. Many show good responses when feeling confident, but fearful responses if they are already feeling inhibited or afraid for any other reason. *The dog must not be allowed to form any negative association with the smoke alarm.* Any sign of fear such as freezing, tucking the tail or even momentary inhibition can potentially build itself into a phobia, and training should be stopped until a better method can be worked out. The key to making a positive association with a potentially scary sound like

this is to only let it ring when the dog is in an excited, happy state, preferably in some instinctive drive such as chasing or play. Merely feeding a dog while making a loud sound is not exciting enough unless the dog is fanatically food motivated. The first introduction to the smoke alarm should be in another room from the wall-mounted alarm, with the door shut, and the dog is first excited by a toy, a chasing game, or an exciting use of treats, such as throwing them to catch. The partner's attitude must be cheerful. When the alarm rings, the dog's reaction is noted, and it is reinforced with food or a toy no matter what it did. If it showed any fear, the partner and dog then move to a farther room so that the sound will be very faint, and repeat. Ideally, the dog shows some orientation response, which can be reinforced, but even no response is far better than any sign of fear. Gradually, the dog is taught to be accustomed to being closer to the alarm sound. The partner must use good judgment in maintaining the dog's good attitude while working towards the goal of a dog that gets excited and happy even when in the same room as the ringing alarm. Trainers without helpers who are holding a smoke alarm must muffle the alarm with a pillow to deaden the sound.

2. Foundation training with the "Super-Loud" alarm clock. The instructions for the alarm clock alert are followed, but when the dog responds well, the alarm clock is moved out of the bedroom. To have a good foundation for the smoke alarm, the dog should alert the partner in bed no matter where the clock is located. Since the dog should never have gotten treats next to the clock, but only on the bed, it may catch on right away. A helper rings the clock in the other room, or the partner sets it and then goes to wait on the bed. When it rings, the partner helps the dog to approach the bed. If the dog goes to the clock, the partner needs to improve the dog's motivation to approach the partner.

3. Alerting to the smoke alarm. Both partner and helpers wear earplugs, even if hard-of-hearing, because remaining hearing could still be damaged. The partner and dog are positioned at least fifteen feet away, preferably a longer distance, from the wall-mounted alarm where the helper is waiting to ring it. The partner shows the dog a treat held in the hand, and when the alarm is rung, gives the "touch" command, wiggles the hand backwards, and rewards the dog for following it. The alarm is only rung until the dog eats the treat.

4. The partner backs away several steps when the alarm rings and rewards the dog. The partner can also run away from the dog when the alarm rings, rewarding the dog for catching up and touching. This works well with dogs who love chasing games.

5. To increase the dog's motivation to touch, another helper gently holds the dog while the partner shows it the treat and excites it, then runs away. As the alarm is rung, the helper lets the dog loose to follow. If the dog responds well, the partner hides while the helper holds the dog, then releases it when the alarm rings. When the dog responds well, it is taught to alert no matter what the partner is doing (see the "real-life situations" section).

6. Familiarize with the bed target area. The partner recaps previous training with the timer and alarm clock by showing treats and encouraging the dog to jump up on the bed when the smoke alarm rings or, in the case of big dogs, to put its front paws or head on the bed. Dogs that are trained to jump all the way onto the bed for the smoke alarm must be also allowed on the bed briefly at other times or they will be too inhibited to get on the bed when the smoke alarm rings. An "off" cue can be used after they have been on the bed for a few seconds. This training must be tailored to the dog's temperament, and adjusted depending on whether it inhibits the dog's alert to the bed. As most partners have noticed,

training a dog to get off furniture on command does not prevent the dog from getting on furniture in the first place. However, it should never be allowed to rest or sleep on the bed, as this will lessen the reinforcement value of being allowed to get on the bed and get lots of attention when the smoke alarm rings. In addition, sleeping on the bed is a well-known cause of behavior problems in dogs.

7. For the bed alert, the partner sits on the bed, shows treats to the dog, and *either* rings the muffled smoke alarm under a pillow or has a helper ring the wall alarm while withdrawing the treat in order to entice the dog to jump up on the bed. Treats can be placed on the bed near the pillow.

8. To increase motivation to approach the bed, the partner shows the treats, the alarm rings, the partner runs to the bed and lies on it, encouraging the dog to follow. It may stay a minute on the bed getting food and petting. If a helper is available, he or she can hold the dog at increasing distances while the partner lies on the bed while showing the dog treats. The dog is then set free when the alarm rings. Treats are left near or under the pillow for the dog to search for.

9. Real-life alerting to bed. Once the dog is confident and reliable about getting on the bed when the alarm rings, the partner gets under the covers and hides treats by his or her face and under the pillow, to encourage the dog to search and get to the partner's face. The timer alert to bed instructions are followed. Teaching the dog to wake up to alert is especially important.

10. Increase the distance. The helper holds the dog while the partner goes to another room and lies on the bed.

Alarm Clock

The alert for the alarm clock is identical to that for the completed one-way alert to the timer. It can be trained before or after the smoke alarm, and follows similar progressions as the smoke alarm.

Successful training to alert to the alarm clock depends on several factors:

- If the clock is set for the same time every day, the dog's natural time sense will take over, and it may wake up by itself every day shortly before the clock rings. If it is motivated to wake its partner, it will often do so *before* the clock rings.
- The sound of the clock is important. Clocks that play radio stations are almost useless, since televisions and radios played in the house habituate the dog to this type of sound. Low buzzing and rattling sounds are fine, but the higher and louder the sounds are, the easier it is to train the dog to alert consistently.
- The clock must be easily set off for training purposes. Any clock that must be set for a certain time while the partner waits is not good. The more fussing over setting it, the more cues are being given to the dog that it is practice time, and the more frustrated and unmotivated the partner gets! Especially in beginning training, multiple repetitions of the sound are essential. Simple wind-up clocks are the most easily triggered to ring, but electronic ones are sometimes difficult. The drawback of wind-up clocks is, of course, the need for frequent winding.

The downside to this is that the partner really must wake up and reinforce the dog and not go back to sleep if training is to be successful!

The best clock for training is the Radio Shack Super Loud LED alarm clock. This clock is only about fifteen dollars and has a sound almost exactly like a smoke alarm, but not quite as loud, which means that the dog that is taught to alert to one of them has an easier time learning to alert to the other one. Either sound's alert can be taught first. This clock can easily be set to make it ring when a lot of repetitions are needed in beginning training. (Note that the partner does not wait for the alarm to ring, but advances the "real" time to catch up to the alarm time.)

1. Set the alarm for any time. Move the alarm buttons to "on" and "loud." Then set the "real" time for one minute before the alarm time.

2. Advance the "real" time one minute and the alarm will ring immediately.

3. For advanced training, set the clock the enough in advance so that the dog has time to relax before the clock rings.

The dog should already perform a one-way alert to the timer when the partner is lying in bed. It is helpful if the dog is also highly motivated and waking up from naps to alert to the timer. A treat container and the clock can be placed on a bedside table next to the bed. However, this treat container does *not* indicate a target area. It is just there for the partner to have treats handy. The target area where the dog will receive treats is the partner's body or the bed itself.

4. To familiarize the dog with the alarm clock, the ring is turned to "low," and the dog happily reinforced at a distance. (for fearful dogs, see the smoke alarm's familiarizing step) The dog should be excited and eager for treats when next to the alarm on the "loud" setting before formal training starts.

5. To start the touch, stand next to the bed. The partner shows the dog a treat, rings the clock alarm (or waits for it to ring), then within half a second wiggles the treat backwards and lets the dog follow and eat it.

6. Approaching the bed. The partner shows the treat, rings the clock alarm, and walks back several steps to sit on the bed, wiggling the treat if needed, and encourages the dog to jump up on the bed or put its paws or head up if it is a large dog.

7. To teach the bed target area, the partner rings the alarm clock, walks backward to the bed, and encourages the dog to come up, but the dog does not get the treat from the hand. Instead, the treat is dropped on the bed. If the dog is confused, the partner can point to the treat, but not pick it up.

8. To increase motivation to approach, the partner gets into the bed after showing the dog a treat, while a helper holds the dog gently. The dog is released when the clock rings. Treats are placed under the pillow or covers for the dog to search for, and the dog gets enthusiastic praise.

9. Increase the distance. The helper lets the dog go from increasing distances or the alarm is rung while the dog is in other rooms.

10. Alerting when the dog is not "cued up." The partner rests on the bed and sets the clock to ring later when the dog has had time to become relaxed. No treats are hidden unless the partner can make sure the dog does not smell them. Since the dog will not relax if it smells treats hidden on the bed, it must be first allowed to check for crumbs. Any treats given for alerting can be taken from the container next to the bed, and placed on the bed for the dog to eat. When the clock goes off, the partner excitedly encourages the dog to alert and reinforces it.

11. Alerting when the dog is sleeping: The partner sets the clock to ring at times when the dog will be asleep. See "Waking Up" in "Advanced Training," below, and the final section in "Timer Alert."

12. Real-life alerting. The partner begins to set the alarm for morning wake-up. Setting it every day will help the dog develop reliability. It is important to be sneaky and creative to make training situations realistic or the dog will only alert when it is cued up and expecting the ring.

Baby Cry

The Hearing Dog Program does not offer this training. Depending on a dog to alert to such an important sound seems like a bad idea, given the unreliability of any trained animal. A good baby monitor and flashing light might be better, even if just used as a back-up system. Additionally, in real life, mothers sometimes wish to ignore certain types of crying and this non-responding to its alerts tends to confuse the dog. Still, many people have trained their dogs to alert to crying. The excited response of parents to their baby probably helps motivate the dog to become interested in alerting to it. Encouraging the dog to touch when the baby cries and establishing a target area with a treat container near the baby's crib to reward it for approaching the crib should get a complete alert accomplished.

Advanced Training

Going from a good response in training sessions to a good response in real-life situations is a big step. As soon as the owner prepares to have a training session, the dog is cued up to respond. It seems psychic, but is actually responding to the sounds of a second phone line being dialed, treat smells, the sound of a treat container being opened, certain body postures used in training, people sneaking out the door quietly, etc. There are hundreds of different cues that can inform the dog that an alertable sound is going to happen and that reinforcement (food) will be soon be available. By contrast, when sounds happen without these cues, it is as if the dog is being informed, "Rewards probably not available!" Since the dog can make a choice to alert or not, it bases its decision on the probability of reinforcement. Therefore, training must be arranged so that the dog discovers that alerting to unexpected sounds also provides reinforcement. Even the sneakiest partner finds it difficult to deceive their dog. Being cued up is okay in the beginning stages of training, since the dog needs lots of help at first. But as quickly as possible, the dog must learn to alert on its own initiative at random times to unexpected sounds, and must be persistent when its partner is busy or sleeping and doesn't notice its alerts.

Setting up more realistic training sessions is one way to accomplish this, but when sounds really happen, the partner needs to make sure the dog feels reinforced for *any* response, even one that is not as good as the dog shows in training sessions. It is normal for dogs to respond well in practice, less so in real situations. The partner also needs to encourage the dog to be flexible and generalize its alerts by encouraging any interest in new or unusual sounds, especially in different places. The overall goal here is to improve communication, so anything that helps the relationship between dog and partner will be useful. This could range from training new sounds, reading training books, or going to seminars about dog behavior.

Waking Up

It seems simple, but this is the most difficult part of sound alerting for most dogs. A dog that alerts rapidly when it is awake may continue to snooze peacefully if the sound occurs while sleeping. Whether a dog wakes up easily is determined more by its reactivity and activity levels than by its training. However, training is still needed to inform the dog that alerting to sounds will be rewarded whether the dog feels sleepy or awake. I once visited the home of a Hearing Dog who alerted when awake, but never woke up for sounds. I described to his partner how she should wake him up and act very enthusiastic when he finally alerted. "Oh, no!" she said. "I couldn't bear to wake him from his nap, the poor thing!" Since dogs "nap" about eighteen hours a day, a Hearing Dog that doesn't wake up to alert is not very useful. Dogs tend to sleep lightly when human or other activity is going on, and waking up is not as hard as it is for us humans. Most sleep when bored, and are happy to wake up if they know something interesting will happen.

Training a dog to wake up to alert involves a gradual progression of waking up when drowsy, napping, and finally when in a deeper sleep such as late at night. The easiest way to encourage this response is to always keep a timer or magnet phone by the bed and other places where you relax, along with a treat container. When the dog is sleeping, or when you wake up in the middle of the night, occasionally ring one of them, and be prepared to reinforce really enthusiastically, no matter how sleepy you are yourself. If you are really dedicated, you could set your alarm clock to ring at various times during the night. Just make sure you have extra-delicious treats in the treat container.

Advanced Real-Life Training Situations

The goal of all the sound-alerting training is, of course, to alert in real life. If the dog won't alert in real life, then the partner has just wasted their time, except that they have a very well educated companion. Therefore, it is critical for the partner and/or trainer to establish some real-life training situations so that the dog will make the transition from learning to practical application. The following are some suggestions for establishing some real-life training.

Treats can be left out on top of high furniture or shelves, then quietly moved to the phone target area while the dog is napping or in another room.

A variety of activities and body positions should be used in training to make training as close to real life as possible.

Continuing to work when knocking on the door stops.

Treats for touching can be left on high shelves and grabbed if the dog alerts or needs help. (Carrying around treats in your pockets not only tells the dog that sounds will happen, but also motivates the dog to stay with you, where treats seem to be a sure bet, rather than leave to go to sounds. If the dog is always trained with treats in pockets, the absence of their smell informs it that no reward is available.)

Individual voice patterns and sign styles of the partner should be used.

Different door knocking sounds, from timid tapping to heavy pounding.

"Waking" heavy sleepers and those under covers.

Alerting people while they are involved in activities such as ironing, holding babies, reading large newspapers, talking, signing, eating dinner, cooking, gardening, etc.

Searching for the partner in various rooms.

Going to the yard in order to alert the partner, then returning into the house.
Going up and down stairs to alert.
Alerting when another pet is in the room.
Alerting while chewing on a toy.
Alerting while being petted.
Alerting while eating or playing with toys.
Alerting in hotel rooms.
Alerting to different sounds such as a different brand of phone.
Alerting when sleepy or sleeping.
Alerting when people are visiting or family is very active.

Common Training Mistakes

Some of the following mistakes are harmless, and some are very damaging, but all of them reflect a lack of understanding of how dogs think, feel, and learn. These mistakes only lead away from the goal of building true communication and partnership. Many people want to believe that dogs have identical motivations and thought processes to humans and are quite stubborn about such a belief. They feel threatened when facing the reality of the dog as a creature with a viewpoint very alien to ours. On the other hand, some aspects of a dog's mentality include those that we as humans deny and dislike in ourselves, so we deny their existence when interpreting our pet's behavior. Only by giving up many sentimental or incorrect notions about dogs can we really discover and benefit from their fascinating lives.

Training under the assumption that the dog "wants to please" the owner. Dogs want to please themselves. For some dogs, pleasing themselves is accomplished by getting social acceptance from people. When people put conditions on getting this, the dog learns to comply, such as coming when called in order for the dog to get the reinforcement *it* wants of being praised and petted.

Training under the assumption that the dog "is trained now and knows it's wrong to disobey," or "is trained and knows he should alert to the phone." The fact is, the dog's poor performance proves that it is not trained to perform at that level. The partner needs to figure out how to complete the training, not blame the dog for the effect of poor training. In some types of training, such as sound alerting, the dog is never completely "trained," because continual maintenance training is needed to counteract deterioration of the alerting behaviors.

Training under the assumption that the dog is mentally capable of "getting even" with the partner for being left behind or punished, by displaying bad behavior later (when left alone, for instance). Remember, dogs never lie about hate! If a dog was "mad" about something, it would show this immediately rather than conceal it by acting affectionate until given a chance for revenge. The behaviors that are blamed on "spite" are all easily explained in other ways. For instance, any bad behavior when left alone is either due to panic attacks (separation anxiety) or to learning that many behaviors are punished when people are present but perfectly okay and fun to do when alone. Expecting a dog not to misbehave when alone is about as realistic as trying to convince humans not to masturbate when alone. Behaviorist John Rogerson points out that dogs that "act guilty" have learned that the presence of feces or spilled garbage in the house means that returning owners will act aggressive, but are not able to make the gigantic mental leap to realize that they therefore should not give in to the feeling of wanting to defecate or eat garbage. This subject has been hammered to death in every dog training book ever published, but needs repeating because so many people, even some professional trainers, punish "spiteful" behavior long after it is done. Undesirable behavior when the dog is alone must either be prevented from happening by changing the situation, or the dog's actions must result in some negative consequence at the exact time of the behavior. From the dog's point of view, being unpredictably corrected by the owner causes confusion and mistrust. Misunderstanding a dog in this way is very damaging to the relationship that must be built in order to form a partnership for sound alerting.

The worst mistake that people make in sound alerting is to make any correction, even a tiny verbal "uh-uh," if the dog tries to "cheat" by going to a target area (for instance, to get a food treat) before the sound happens. The dog will never understand that it is being corrected for "not waiting for the sound to happen." It cannot understand such a complicated concept. It is, however, *guaranteed* to understand that the partner is correcting it for going near the target area. When the sound eventually does happen, the dog will obediently stay away from the target area. Ralph Dennard once visited a partner who complained that her dog ran away and hid whenever the phone rang. Why was this? He found out that every morning, she would place a treat at the phone target area. If the dog tried to get it, he was scolded. When the phone eventually rang, the dog would not go. His partner would then gently coax and drag him to the phone to try to make him get the treat; of course, he thought he was being brought to the phone for more scolding. The dog was being mentally tortured by this well-meaning but totally confusing "training," and chose the solution of hiding when the phone rang. The partner must remember that "cheating," is actually a wonderful thing. It shows that the dog is interested in alerting, as opposed to the dog that does not alert even in easy training situations. Cheating merely shows that the partner is not being creative enough to set up realistic training sessions that will surprise the dog. Scolding the dog for ignoring sounds is absolutely fatal to sound alerting, since there is no way that an animal can comprehend a punishment for "not-doing" a behavior.

Training under the assumption that the dog knows that its partner cannot hear the sounds. Even dogs that seem to have trained themselves and appear to be consciously trying to "help" their partner by alerting to sounds are not at this level of thinking. They may easily understand that alerting to sounds is rewarded, and their relationship with their partner means that they might save their life in the same way they would try to rescue their puppy or a pack member, but they are not able to comprehend a concept like deafness.

If the dog is "sticking" to the partner and will not leave to go to sounds, it might be getting treats too often from the partner, or the partner might have extra treats in their hands or pockets that are "gluing" the dog to the partner. If the dog is sticking to the sound sources and does not return to the partner, the dog might be getting treats too often at the target areas. These treats may be "gluing" the dog to the target areas. Reducing the overall frequency of treats and balancing where the treats are given keeps the dog moving freely back and forth.

Sound training can be viewed as a seesaw that is never in balance. The goal is to keep it moving freely, and accept that constant tinkering with training is necessary.

It is nothing short of miraculous to spot a potential Hearing Dog in the confusion of a shelter, watch as its natural talents unfold, and then see it perfectly paired with a loving human. The dog lends its ear to the human, the human gives their loving trust to the dog, and together they create a new and unique harmony. It is to this incredible partnership, to the dogs and humans who have led the way in pioneering the Hearing Dog movement, and who have helped create the blueprint for this different kind of dog, that I dedicate this book.

Bibliography

Abrantes, Roger. *Dog Language: An Encyclopedia of Canine Behavior.* Naperville, Illinois: Wakan Tanka Publishers, 1997.

Abrantes, Roger, *The Evolution of Canine Social Behavior.* Naperville, Illinois: Wakan Tanka Publishers, 1997.

Baer, Nancy, and Steve Duno. *Choosing the Right Dog.* New York, New York: Berkley Books, 1995.

Benjamin, Carol Lea. *The Chosen Puppy.* New York, New York: MacMillan Pub. Co., 1990.

Campbell, William E.*Better Behavior in Dogs and Cats.* Goleta, California: American Veterinary Press, 1986.

Campbell, William. *Behavior Problems in Dogs.* Santa Barbara, California: American Veterinary Publications, 1975.

Christiansen, Bob. *Choosing and Caring for a Shelter Dog.* Napa, California: Canine Learning Center-Publishing Division, 1996.

Coppinger, Raymond, and Schneider, William. *Evolution of Working Dogs.* Chapter Three in *The Domestic Dog*, ed. by Serpell, James. Cambridge, England: Cambridge University Press, 1995.

Corbett, Laurie. *The Dingo in Australia and Asia.* Ithaca, New York: Cornell University Press, 1995.

Curtis, Patricia. *Cindy: A Hearing Ear Dog* New York, New York: E.P.Dutton, 1981.

Eames, Ed and Toni. *Partners In Independence.* New York, New York:

Howell Book House, 1997.

Fogle, Bruce, DVM, MRCVS. *The Dog's Mind*. New York, New York: Howell Book House, 1990.

Fogle, Bruce, DVM. *Know Your Dog*. London, England: Dorling Kindersley, 1992.

Fox, Michael W. *Behaviour of Wolves Dogs and Related Canids*. Malabar, Florida: Robert E. Krieger Pub. Co., 1971.

Grandin, Temple. *Thinking In Pictures*. New York, New York: Random House, 1995.

Grunow, Steve. *Fearfulness and Failure in Training Working Dogs*. Masters thesis, San Jose State University, 1995.

Johnston, Bruce. *Harnessing Thought: The Guide Dog*. Hertsfordshire, England: Lennard Publishing, 1995.

Kilcommons, Brian. *Mutts: America's Dogs*. New York, New York: Warner Books, 1996.

Kilcommons, Brian. *Good Owners, Great Dogs*. New York, New York: Warner Books, 1994.

Lithgow, Scott. *Training and Working Dogs For Quiet Confident Control of Stock*. Queensland, Australia: University of Queensland Press, 1989.

Locke, Angela, and Harmer, Jenny. *Hearing Dog: The Story of Jennie and Connie*. London, England: Souvenir Press, Ltd. 1997.

Lorenz, Konrad. *Man Meets Dog*. Cambridge, Massachusetts: Riverside Press, 1955.

Lorenz, Konrad. *King Solomon's Ring*. New York, New York: Thomas Y. Crowell Co. 1952.

McFarland, David, ed. *Oxford Companion to Animal Behaviour*. Oxford, England: Oxford University Press, 1982.

Nordensson & Kelley, *Teamwork: A Dog Training Manual for People With Disabilities.* Tucson, Arizona: Top Dog Publications, 1997.

Ogden, Paul. *Chelsea-Story of a Signal Dog*. Boston, Massachusetts: Little, Brown and Co.1992.

Okimoto, Jean Davies. *A Place for Grace*. Seattle, Washington: Sasquatch Books, 1993.

O'Neil, Jacqueline. *Second Start-Creative rehoming for dogs*. New York: Howell Book House, Macmillan Publishing Company, 1997.

Pearsall, Milo D. and Margaret E. *Your Dog: Companion and Helper*. Loveland, Colorado: Alpine Press, 1980.

Pryor, Karen. *Don't Shoot the Dog!*.New York, New York: Bantam Books, 1984.

Pryor, Karen. *On Behavior*. North Bend, Washington: Sunshine Books, 1995.

Reid, Pamela. *Excel-erated Learning*. Oakland, California: James and Kenneth Publishers, 1996.

Rogerson, John. *Understanding Your Dog*. London, England: Popular Dogs, 1991.

Rogerson, John. *Training Your Dog*. London, England: Popular Dogs, 1992.

Rugaas, Turid. *On Talking Terms With Dogs*. Kula, Hawaii: Legacy By Mail, 1997.

Rubenstein, Eliza and Kalina, Shari. *The Adoption Option*. New York, New York: Howell, 1996.

Ryan, Terry. *The Toolbox for Remodeling Problem Dogs*. Pullman, Washington: Legacy, 1994.

Schaffer, Caroline B., DVM. *The Tuskegee Behavior Test for Selecting Therapy Dogs*: Tuskegee, Alabama: Tuskegee University School of Veterinary Medicine, 1993.

Schwartz, Charlotte. *Friend to Friend*. New York, New York: Howell, 1984.

Tortora, Daniel F., Ph.D. *The Right Dog for You*. New York, New York: Simon and Schuster, 1980.

Wilcox, Chris, DVM, and Walkowicz, Bonnie. *Atlas of Dog Breeds of the World*. Neptune City, New Jersey: TFH Publications, Inc., 1989.

Wilkes, Gary. *A Behavior Sampler*. North Bend, Washington: Sunshine Books, 1994.

Yates, Elizabeth. *Sound Friendships*. Woodstock, Vermont: The Countryman Press, 1987.

Appendix

The following figures are based on figured from 1989 through the first half of 1998. In all, 712 dogs were adopted out of which 219 dogs were categorized as "graduated," a 31.5% rate. Although this rate seems low, no time and money was invested in breeding programs or lengthy fostering, and some health, maturation, and temperament problems are just not detectable by temperament testing. Some programs, which breed their own dogs, have similar rates. The high dropout rate is considered an acceptable part of the harsh reality of using shelter dogs, and because the "career change" drop-outs were usually small, friendly, and partially trained, they often found homes easily.

The figures below are a both purebred and mixed breeds that were classified into the various functional groups.

Functional Groups that were Adopted Most Often

Group	Number Adopted	Percentage of All Adopted
Companion/Alarm	163	17.5%
Herding	148	16%
Spaniel	138	15%
Terrier	125	13%
Retriever	67	7%
Hound	55	6%
Guard	7	.07%
Sled	4	.04%
Setter/Pointer	3	.03%
Primeval	1	.01%

Functional Groups with the Most Dogs Graduating

Group	Number Graduated	Percentage of All Graduates
Companion/Alarm:	57	26%
Spaniel	47	21%
Terrier	42	19%
Herding	30	14%
Hounds	20	9%
Retriever	20	9%
Guard	2	.09%
Sled	1	.04%

Total 219 dogs graduated
(No Setter/Pointer or Primeval group dogs graduated.)

Functional Groups' Graduation Percentages

Group	# Adopted	# Graduated	% Graduating Within Each Group
Companion/Alarm	163	57	35%
Terrier	125	42	34%
Hound	55	20	33%
Spaniel	138	47	33%
Retriever	67	20	30%
Guard	8	2	25%
Sled	4	1	25%
Herding	148	30	20%

Graduation Success Rates Comparing Mixed Breed and Purebred

Group	Mixed Percentage Graduating	Purebred Percentage Graduating
Companion/Alarm	34%	36%
Terrier	33%	38%
Hound	37%	33%
Spaniel	39%	17%
Retriever	29%	33%
Herding	20%	19%
Total	31%	29%